# The Definitive Guide to MongoDB

## The NoSQL Database for Cloud and Desktop Computing

Eelco Plugge,
Peter Membrey
and Tim Hawkins

Apress®

**The Definitive Guide to MongoDB: The NoSQL Database for Cloud and Desktop Computing**



ISBN-13 (pbk): 978-1-4302-3051-9

ISBN-13 (electronic): 978-1-4302-3052-6

Printed and bound in the United States of America (POD)



President and Publisher: Paul Manning
Lead Editors: Frank Pohlmann, Michelle Lowman, James Markham
Technical Reviewer: Jonathon Drewett
Editorial Board: Clay Andres, Steve Anglin, Mark Beckner, Ewan Buckingham, Gary Cornell, Jonathan Gennick, Jonathan Hassell, Michelle Lowman, Matthew Moodie, Duncan Parkes, Jeffrey Pepper, Frank Pohlmann, Douglas Pundick, Ben Renow-Clarke, Dominic Shakeshaft, Matt Wade, Tom Welsh
Coordinating Editor: Mary Tobin
Copy Editor: Patrick Meader
Compositor: MacPS, LLC
Indexer: Potomac Indexing, LLC
Artist: April Milne
Cover Designer: Anna Ishchenko

Distributed to the book trade worldwide by Springer-Verlag New York, Inc., 233 Spring Street, 6th Floor, New York, NY 10013. Phone 1-800-SPRINGER, fax 201-348-4505, e-mail `orders-ny@springer-sbm.com`, or visit `www.springeronline.com`.

For information on translations, please e-mail `rights@apress.com`, or visit `www.apress.com`.

Apress and friends of ED books may be purchased in bulk for academic, corporate, or promotional use. eBook versions and licenses are also available for most titles. For more information, reference our Special Bulk Sales–eBook Licensing web page at `www.apress.com/info/bulksales`.



The source code for this book is available to readers at `www.apress.com`. You will need to answer questions pertaining to this book in order to successfully download the code.

*For the love of my life, Marjolein, and my son Jesse—I wouldn't have been able to write this without your everlasting patience and love.*

*—Eelco Plugge*

*For my mother-in-law, Wan Ha Loi. First for actually letting me marry her wonderful daughter and second for coming out of retirement to look after our son Kaydyn. Her selfless generosity made this book possible, as, without her continuous support, there simply wouldn't be enough hours in the day.*

*—Peter Membrey*

*For Ester, for putting up with the long hours I stole from her to produce this book.*

*—Tim Hawkins*

# Contents at a Glance

# Contents

# About the Authors

**Eelco Plugge** was born in 1986 in the Netherlands and quickly developed an interest in computers and everything evolving around it. He enjoyed his study at the ICT Academie in Amersfoort, after which he became a data encryption specialist working at McAfee at the age of 21. He's a young BCS Professional Member and shows a great interest in everything IT security-related as well as in all aspects of the Japanese language and culture. He is currently working upon expanding his field of expertise through study, at the same time as maintaining a young family.

**Peter Membrey** lives in Hong Kong and is actively promoting Open Source in all its various forms and guises, especially in education. He has had the honor of working for Red Hat and received his first RHCE at the tender age of 17. He is now a Chartered IT Professional and one of the world's first professionally registered ICT Technicians. He has recently completed his master's degree and will soon start a PhD program at the Hong Kong Polytechnic University. He lives with his wife Sarah and his son Kaydyn, and is desperately trying (and sadly failing) to come to grips with Mandarin and Cantonese.

**Tim Hawkins** produced one of the world's first online classifieds portals in 1993, `loot.com`, before moving on to run engineering for many of Yahoo EU's non-media-based properties, such as search, local search, mail, messenger, and its social networking products. He is currently managing a large offshore team for a major US eTailer, developing and deploying next-gen eCommerce applications. Loves hats, hates complexity.

# About the Technical Reviewer

**Jonathon Drewett** is an ICT specialist experienced in applying technology within the education sector. He operates his own consultancy and has worked on developing large international e-learning data repositories, as well as managing networks and information systems for educational establishments. Before moving into IT, he worked as an electronic engineer and was contracted to the RAF.

Jonathon graduated with an honors degree in Computer Science and is a member of both the British Computer Society and the Institute of Engineering and Technology. He is an ardent advocate of life-long learning and using technology to improve the world.

In his downtime, he restores classic cars, operates a large on-line social community network and, occasionally, sleeps.

# Acknowledgments

I would like to sincerely thank Peter for giving me the opportunity to work on this book. His constant motivation kept me going and made it possible to enjoy writing every single page I worked on. I would also like to express my gratitude towards all the people at Apress for all the work they have done to get this book out. It goes without saying that this book wouldn't be here without all of you. Finally, I would like to thank Tim and Jon for jumping in at a crucial moment and helping out; the publication of this book would not have been possible without your help.

**Eelco Plugge**

First, I'd like to give special thanks to Eelco Plugge for consistently and constantly going above and beyond the call of duty. He has put an astonishing amount of time and energy into this book and it simply would not have been this good without him. I'd also like to thank Tim Hawkins who brought a tonne of hard-won real-world experience and expertise to the book. He joined the team part way through the project and worked incredibly hard (and fast) not only to write his chapters but also to overhaul them when new features and updates for MongoDB were made available. Both Eelco and Tim were the driving forces for the book and I remain especially grateful for all of their hard work.

Next, I'd like to thank Jon Drewett who provided the vast majority of technical review for the book. Not only did he provide great insights (requiring a not insubstantial amount of work on behalf of us authors), he also contributed greatly to ensuring that the book was both technically accurate and as useful and reader friendly as possible.

Of course, without the support of my dear wife Sarah (who grows wiser and more beautiful every day) and my son Kaydyn (who miraculously knew just how to disrupt the writing process for maximum effect), I would not have been able to start work on the book, much less see it completed.

I'd also like to thank all the guys (and gals) at Apress who as usual showed the patience of saints. Special thanks to Mary Tobin who was tasked with managing us—which is somewhat akin to trying to herd cats.

John Hornbeck and Wouter Thielen both deserve a special mention for helping create the table of contents and the structure for the book. Although unfortunately they weren't able to take part in the actual writing, their effort shaped the way for the rest of us.

Last but certainly not least, special thanks to 10gen for sponsoring the Beijing MongoDB workshop—a great time was had by all.

**Peter Membrey**

I would like to acknowledge the members of the mongodb-user and mongodb-dev maillists for putting up with my endless questions.

**Tim Hawkins**

# A Special "Thanks" to *MongoDB Beijing*

On May the 28th 2010, the first ever official MongoDB event was held in Beijing, China. At Thoughtworks, a group of like-minded people got together to discuss MongoDB and how it could solve the problems that the group were facing. Mars Cheng, who organized the event, arranged for the venue, while 10gen paid for travel and accommodation for Peter Membrey. Apress gave away free copies of the e-book to attendees and this made up a large proportion of the lab work for the session. Special thanks then to Mars, 10gen and Apress who not only put together the first ever MongoDB experience in China but also the first ever collaboratively technical reviewed books!

A presentation was given by Peter to talk about some of the high points of MongoDB and how it had made a difference to him personally. A big part of the presentation looked at how he used MongoDB to save hours of work when developing a project for his master's degree at the University of Liverpool. The presentation also explored the key benefits that MongoDB could offer and the areas where it really shined in comparison to traditional RDBMS such as MySQL.

After the presentation, everyone was invited to go to the Apress website where they could obtain an Alpha version of the e-book. The Alpha version is a collection of chapters written by the authors that haven't yet been through the full editorial process. In other words they can be pretty raw, with typing mistakes and other minor errors. By giving away free Alpha books, Apress was in effect offering a group of people who were very interested in MongoDB the chance to look at what we had so far and to offer suggestions for improvement.

The labs went extremely well with everyone getting involved and offering ideas and insights, many of which were incorporated into the book itself. As a special thank you to the team, we would like to acknowledge those who took part. In no particular order (as provided by Mars):

Mars Cheng
Blade Wang
Sarah Membrey
Yao Wang
Zhen Chen
Jian Han
Fan Pan
Runchao Li
Guozhu Wen
Qiu Huang
Shixin He
Chaoqun Fu
Lin Huang

All in all, everyone had a great day and the presentation and labs were considered to be a big success. It is very likely that this will be the first of many MongoDB activities in China and that there will be a growing demand for related skills in the job market. More details of the event can be found on the MongoDB website at `http://www.mongodb.org/display/community/MongoDB+Beijing+Meetup+2010`.

# Introduction

The seed for *The Definitive Guide to MongoDB* was actually planted some years ago when I walked into a local bookstore, and first spotted a book on databases. I started reading the back-cover copy and a few pages of the front matter, but quickly found the book closed in my hands, as I quietly mumbled to myself: "Humph. Who needs databases, other than a very large enterprise?" I put the book back, and headed home without thinking any more about it.

Nearly two years later, I was toying with the idea of setting up a simple website in plain HTML code, and, while searching for some "funky" ideas that I could use with my limited space and options, I came across the term "databases" again and again. As I was no longer able to ignore the existence of databases, I began to pay more attention to them. But I still wasn't convinced they were my thing, partly because of all the puzzling expressions that were being used, such as "entity-relation models" and "cardinality," and even the more common words, such as "keys," baffled me. That would soon change.

While enrolled at the ICT Academie in the Netherlands for my first proper education in the IT world, I was confronted with databases yet again. This time, I was required to take an actual exam on them, and, knowing just the basic concepts of databases (how they worked, and how to create, manage and delete them), I did what many beginners would do: I panicked.

This was the moment, however, where I finally decided to pull my head out of the sand and learn all I could about databases. Surprisingly, I quickly grew fond of them, and started to use one "just for the fun of it" with my now more sophisticated PHP/MySQL-driven website. I wasn't quite there yet, though. Then came MongoDB...

In early 2010, I was introduced to MongoDB by my close friend and co-author Peter Membrey. I was immediately hooked and intrigued by its concepts, simplicity, and strengths. I found myself reading each section of the MongoDB website over and over again, readily absorbing its capabilities and advantages over the traditional RDBMS applications. I finally felt comfortable with databases.

## Our Approach

And now, in this book, our goal is to present you with the same experiences we had in learning the product: teaching you how you can put MongoDB to use for yourself, while keeping things simple and clear. Each chapter presents an individual sample database, so you can read the book in a modular or linear fashion; it's entirely your choice. This means you can skip a certain chapter if you like, without breaking your example databases.

Throughout the book, you will find that example commands are written in **bold** styled code to distinguish them from the resulting output. In most chapters, you will also come across tips, warnings, and notes that contain useful, and sometimes vital, information.

We trust you will find this book easy to grasp and pleasant to read, and, with that said, we hope you enjoy *The Definitive Guide to MongoDB*.

Eelco Plugge

PART I

# Basics

CHAPTER 1

# Introduction to MongoDB

Imagine a world where using a database is so simple that you soon forget you're even using it. Imagine a world where speed and scalability *just work*, and there's no need for complicated configuration or setup. Imagine being able to focus only on the task at hand, get things done, and then—just for a change—leave work on time. That might sound a bit fanciful, but MongoDB promises to help you accomplish all these things (and many more).

MongoDB (derived from the word *humongous*) is a relatively new breed of database that has no concept of tables, schemas, SQL, or rows. It doesn't have transactions, ACID compliance, joins, foreign keys, or many of the other features that tend to cause headaches in the early hours of the morning. In short, MongoDB is probably a very different database than what you're used to, especially if you've used a relational database management system (RDBMS) in the past. In fact, you might even be shaking your head in wonder at the lack of so-called "standard" features.

Fear not! In a few moments, you will learn about MongoDB's background, guiding principles, and why the MongoDB team made the design decisions that it did. We'll also take a whistle-stop tour of MongoDB's feature list, providing just enough detail to ensure you'll be completely hooked on this topic for the rest of the book.

We'll start things off by looking at the philosophy and ideas behind the creation of MongoDB, as well as some of the interesting and somewhat controversial design decisions. We'll explore the concept of document-orientated databases, how they fit together, and what their strengths and weaknesses are. We'll also explore JSON and examine how it applies to MongoDB. To wrap things up, we'll step through some of the notable features of MongoDB.

## Reviewing the MongoDB Philosophy

Like all projects, MongoDB has a set of design philosophies that help guide its development. In this section, we'll review some of the database's founding principles.

### Using the Right Tool for the Right Job

The most important of the philosophies that underpin MongoDB is the notion that *one size does not fit all*. For many years, traditional SQL databases (MongoDB is a document-orientated database) have been used for storing content of all types. It didn't matter whether the data was a good fit for the relational model (which is used in all RDBMS databases, such as MySQL, PostgresSQL, SQLite, Oracle, MS SQL Server, and so on); the data was stuffed in there, anyway. Part of the reason for this is that, generally speaking, it's much easier (and more secure) to read and write to a database than it is to write to a file system. If you pick up any book that teaches PHP (such as *PHP for Absolute Beginners* (Apress, 2009)) by Jason Lengstorf, you'll probably find that almost right away the database is used to store information, not the file system. It's just so much easier to do things that way. And while using a database as a storage bin works, developers always have to work against the flow. It's usually obvious when we're not using the database the way it was intended; anyone who has ever tried to store information with even slightly complex data, had to set up five tables, and then tried to pull it all together knows what I'm talking about!

The MongoDB team decided that it wasn't going to create another database that tries to do everything for everyone. Instead, the team wanted to create a database that worked with documents rather than rows, was blindingly fast, massively scalable, and easy to use. To do this, the team had to leave some features behind, which means that MongoDB is not an ideal candidate for certain situations. For example, its lack of transaction support means that you wouldn't want to use MongoDB to write an accounting application. That said, MongoDB might be perfect for part of the aforementioned application (such as storing complex data). That's not a problem though because there is no reason why you can't use a traditional RDBMS for the accounting components and MongoDB for the document storage. Such hybrid solutions are quite common, and you can see them in production apps such as Sourceforge.

Once you're comfortable with the idea that MongoDB may not solve all your problems (the coffee-making plug-in is still in development), you will discover that there are certain problems that MongoDB is a perfect fit for resolving, such as analytics (think a realtime Google Analytics for your website) and complex data structures (e.g., as blog posts and comments). If you're still not convinced that MongoDB is a serious database tool, feel free to skip ahead to the "Reviewing the Feature List" section, where you will find an impressive list of features for MongoDB.

---

**Note** The lack of transactions and other traditional database features doesn't mean that MongoDB is unstable or that it cannot be used for managing important data.

---

Another key concept behind MongoDB's design: There should always be more than one copy of the database. If a single database should fail, then it can simply be restored from the other servers. Because MongoDB aims to be as fast as possible, it takes some shortcuts that make it more difficult to recover from a crash. The developers believe that most serious crashes are likely to remove an entire computer from service anyway; this means that, even if the database were perfectly restored, it would still not be usable. Remember: MongoDB does not try to be everything to everyone. But for many things (such as building a web application), MongoDB can be an awesome tool for implementing your solution.

So now you know where MongoDB is coming from. It's not trying to be the best at everything, and it readily acknowledges that it's not for everyone. However, for those who do choose to use it, MongoDB provides a rich document-orientated database that's optimized for speed and scalability. It can also run nearly anywhere you might want to run it. MongoDB's website includes downloads for Linux, the Mac, Windows, and Solaris; it also includes various unofficial versions of the program that enable you to install it on Fedora or CentOS, among other platforms.

MongoDB succeeds at all these goals, and this is why using MongoDB (at least for me) is somewhat dream-like. You don't have to worry about squeezing your data into a table—just put the data together, and then pass it to MongoDB for handling.

Consider this real-world example. A recent application I worked on needed to store a set of eBay search results. There could be any number of results (up to 100 of them), and I needed an easy way to associate the results with the users in my database.

Had I been using MySQL, I would have had to design a table to store the data, write the code to store my results, and then write more code to piece it all back together again. This is a fairly common scenario and one most developers face on a regular basis. Normally, we just get on with it; however, for this project, I was using MongoDB and so things went a bit differently.

Specifically, I added this line of code:

```
request['ebay_results'] = ebay_results_array
collection.save(reqest)
```

In the preceding example, request is my document, ebay_results is the key, and ebay_result_array contains the results from eBay. The second line saves my changes. When I access this document in future, I will have the eBay results in exactly the same format as before. I don't need any SQL; I don't need to perform any conversions; nor do I need to create any new tables or write any special code—MongoDB just worked. It got out of the way, I finished my work early, and I got to go home on time.

## Lacking Innate Support for Transactions

Another important design decision by MongoDB developers: The database does not include transactional semantics (the bit that offers guarantees about data consistency and storage). This is a solid tradeoff based on MongoDB's goal of being simple, fast, and scalable. Once you leave those heavyweight features at the door, it becomes much easier to scale horizontally.

Normally with a traditional RDBMS, you improve performance by buying a bigger, more powerful machine. This is scaling vertically but you can only take this so far. Horizontal scaling is where, rather than having one big machine, you have lots of less powerful small machines. Historically, clusters of servers like this were excellent for load balancing websites, but databases had always been a problem due to internal design limitations.

You might think this missing support constitutes a deal breaker; however, many people forget that one of the most popular table types in MySQL (MYISAM) doesn't support transactions, either. This fact hasn't stopped MySQL from becoming the dominant open-source database for well over a decade. As with most things when developing solutions, using MongoDB is going to be a matter of personal choice and whether the tradeoffs fit your project.

---

■ **Note** MongoDB offers durability when used in tandem with at least two servers, which is the recommended minimum for production deployments. It is possible to make the master server wait for the replica to confirm receipt of the data before the master server itself confirms the data has been accepted.

---

Although single server durability is not guaranteed, this may change in the future and is currently an area of active interest.

## Drilling Down on JSON and How It Relates to MongoDB

JSON is more than a great way to exchange data; it's also a nice way to store data. An RDBMS is highly structured, with multiple files (tables) that store the individual pieces. MongoDB, on the other hand, stores everything together in a single document. MongoDB is like JSON in this way, and this model provides a rich and expressive way of storing data. Moreover, JSON effectively describes all the content in a given document, so there is no need to specify the structure of the document in advance. JSON is effectively schemaless because documents can be updated individually or changed independently of any other documents. As an added bonus, JSON also provides excellent performance by keeping all of the related data in one place.

MongoDB doesn't actually use JSON to store the data; rather, it uses an open data format developed by the MongoDB team called *BSON* (pronounced Bee-Son), which is short for Binary-JSON. For the most part, using BSON instead of JSON doesn't change how you will work with your data. BSON makes

MongoDB even faster by making it much easier for a computer to process and search documents. BSON also adds a couple of features that aren't available in standard JSON, including the ability to add types for handling binary data. We'll look at BSON in more depth later in the chapter when we cover the feature list.

The original specification for JSON can be found in RFC 4627, and it was written by Douglas Crockford. JSON allows complex data structures to be represented in a simple, human-readable text format that is generally considered to be much easier to read and understand than XML. Like XML, JSON was envisaged as a way to exchange data between a web client (such as a browser) and web applications. When combined with the rich way that it can describe objects, its simplicity has made it the exchange format of choice for the majority of developers.

You might wonder what is meant here by *complex data structures*. Historically, data was exchanged using the comma-separated values (CSV) format (indeed, this approach remains very common today). CSV is a simple text format that separates rows with a new line and fields with a comma. For example, a CSV file might look like this:

```
Membrey, Peter, +852 1234 5678
Thielen, Wouter, +81 1234 5678
```

A human can look at this information and see quite quickly what information is being communicated. Or maybe not—is that number in the third column a phone number or a fax number? It might even be the number for a pager. To combat this, CSV files often have a header field, where the first row defines what comes in the file. The following snippet takes the previous example one step further:

```
Surname, Forename, Phone Number
Membrey, Peter, +852 1234 5678
Thielen, Wouter, +81 1234 5678
```

Okay, that's a bit better. But now assume you have more than one phone number. You could add another field for an office phone number, but you face a new set of issues if you want several office phone numbers. And you face yet another set of issues if you also want to incorporate multiple e-mail addresses. Most people have more than one, and these addresses can't usually be neatly defined as either home or work. Suddenly, CSV starts to show its limitations. CSV files are only good for storing data that is flat and doesn't have repeating values. Similarly, it's not uncommon for several CSV files to be provided, each with the separate bits of information. These files are then combined (usually in an RDBMS) to create the whole picture. As an example, a large retail company may receive CSV files from each of its stores at the end of each day. These files must be combined before the company can see how it performed on a given day. This process is not exactly straightforward, and it certainly increases chances of a mistake as the number of required files grows.

XML largely solves this problem, but using XML for most things is a bit like using a sledgehammer to crack a nut: it works, but it feels like overkill. The reason for this: XML is highly extensible. Rather than define a particular data format, XML defines how you define a data format. This can be useful when you need to exchange complex and highly structured data; however, for simple data exchange, this often results in too much work. Indeed, this scenario is the source of the phrase "XML hell."

JSON provides a happy medium. Unlike CSV, it can store structured content; but unlike XML, JSON makes it easy to understand and simple to use. Let's revisit the previous example; however, this time you will use JSON rather than CSV:

```
{
    "forename": "Peter",
    "surname": "Membrey",
    "phone_numbers": [
        "+852 1234 5678",
        "+44 1234 565 555"
    ]
}
```

In the preceding example, each JSON object (or document) contains all the information needed to understand it. If you look at phone_numbers, you can see that you have a list of different numbers. This list can be as large as you want. You could also be more specific about the type of number being recorded, as in this example:

```
{
    "forename": "Peter",
    "surname": "Membrey",
    "numbers": [
        {
            "phone": "+852 1234 5678"
        },
        {
            "fax": "+44 1234 565 555"
        }
    ]
}
```

The preceding example improves on things a bit more. Now you can clearly see what each number is for. JSON is extremely expressive, and, although it's quite easy to write JSON by hand, it is usually generated automatically in software. For example, Python includes a module called `simplejson` that takes existing Python objects and automatically converts them to JSON. Because JSON is supported and used on so many platforms, it is an ideal choice for exchanging data.

When you add items such as the list of phone numbers, you are actually creating what is known as an *embedded document*. This happens whenever you add complex content such as a list (or *array*, to use the term favored in JSON). Generally speaking, there is also a logical distinction too. For example, a `Person` document might have several `Address` documents embedded inside it. Similarly, an `Invoice` document might have numerous `LineItem` documents embedded inside it. Of course, the embedded `Address` document could also have its own embedded document inside it that contains phone numbers, for example.

Whether you choose to embed a particular document is determined when you decide how to store your information. This is usually referred to as *schema design*. It might seem odd to refer to schema design when MongoDB is considered a schemaless database. However, while MongoDB doesn't force you to create a schema or enforce one that you create, you do still need to think about how your data fits together. We'll look at this in more depth in Chapter 3.

# Adopting a Non-Relational Approach

Improving performance with a relational database is usually straightforward: you buy a bigger, faster server. And this works great until you reach the point where there isn't a bigger server available to buy. At that point, the only option is to spread out to two servers. This might sound easy, but it is a stumbling block for most databases. For example, neither MySQL nor PostgresSQL can run a single database on two servers, where both servers can both read and write data (this is often referred to as an *active/active cluster*). And although Oracle can do this with its impressive Real Application Clusters (RAC) architecture, you can expect to take out a mortgage if you want to use that solution—implementing a RAC-based solution requires multiple servers, shared storage, and several software licenses.

You might wonder why having an active/active cluster on two databases is so difficult. When you query your database, the database has to find all the relevant data and link it all together. RDBMS solutions feature many ingenious ways to improve performance, but they all rely on having a complete picture of the data available. And this is where you hit a wall: this approach simply doesn't work when half the data is on another server.

Of course, you might have a small database that simply gets lots of requests, so you just need to share the workload. Unfortunately, here you hit another wall. You need to ensure that data written to the first server is available to the second server. And you face additional issues if updates are made on two separate masters simultaneously. For example, you need to determine which update is the correct one. Another problem you can encounter: someone might query for information on the second server that has just been written to the first server, but that information hasn't been updated yet on the second server. When you consider all these issues, it becomes easy to see why the Oracle solution is so expensive—these problems are extremely hard to address.

MongoDB solves this problem in a very clever way—it avoids it completely. Recall that MongoDB stores data in BSON documents, so the data is self-contained. That is, although similar documents are stored together, individual documents aren't made up of relationships. This means everything you need is all in one place. Because queries in MongoDB look for specific keys and values in a document, this information can be easily spread across as many servers as you have available. Each server checks the content it has and returns the result. This effectively allows almost linear scalability and performance. As an added bonus, it doesn't even require that you take out a new mortgage to pay for this functionality.

Admittedly, MongoDB does not offer *master/master replication*, where two separate servers can both accept write requests. However, it does have sharding, which allows data to split across multiple machines, with each machine responsible for updating different parts of the dataset. The benefit of this design is that, while some solutions allow two master databases, MongoDB can potentially scale to hundreds of machines as easily as it can run on two.

---

■ **Note** We just mentioned that MongoDB doesn't support master-master replication; however, that's not entirely true. It turns out it is possible to use MongoDB in a master-master configuration; however, this approach is not recommended, so we won't discuss it further in this book. If you're curious, you can find additional details on this subject on the MongoDB website at `www.mongodb.org/display/DOCS/Master+Master+Replication`.

---

## Opting for Performance vs. Features

Performance is important, but MongoDB also provides a large feature set. We've already discussed some of the features MongoDB doesn't implement, and you might be somewhat skeptical of the claim that MongoDB achieves its impressive performance partly by judiciously excising certain features common to other databases. However, there are analogous database systems available that are extremely fast, but also extremely limited, such as those that implement a key / value store.

A perfect example is *memcached*. This application was written to provide high-speed data caching, and it is mind-numbingly fast. When used to cache website content, it can speed up an application many times over. This application is used by extremely large websites, such as Facebook and LiveJournal.

The catch is that this application has two significant shortcomings. First, it is a memory-only database. If the power goes out, then all the data is lost. Second, you can't actually search for data using memcached; you can only request specific keys.

These might sound like serious limitations; however, you must remember the problems that memcached is designed to solve. First and foremost, memcached is a data-cache. That is, it's not supposed to be a permanent data store, but only to provide a caching layer for your existing database. When you build a dynamic web page, you generally request very specific data (such as the current top ten articles). This means you can specifically ask memcached for that data—there is no need to perform a search. If the cache is out-of-date or empty, you would query your database as normal, build up the data, and then store it in memcached for future use.

Once you accept these limitations, you can see how memcached offers superb performance by implementing a very limited feature set. This performance, by the way, is unmatched by that of a traditional database. That said, memcached certainly can't replace an RDBMS. The important thing to keep in mind is that it's not supposed to.

Compared to memcached, MongoDB is itself feature rich. To be useful, MongoDB must offer a strong feature set, such as being able to search for specific documents. It must also be able to store those documents on disk, so that they can survive a reboot. Fortunately, MongoDB provides enough features for it to be a strong contender for most web applications and many other types of applications, as well.

Like memcached, MongoDB is not a one-size-fits-all database. As is usually the case in computing, tradeoffs must be made to achieve the intended goals of the application.

## Running the Database Anywhere

MongoDB is written in C++, which makes it relatively easy to port and/or run the application practically anywhere. Currently, binaries can be downloaded from the MongoDB website for Linux, the Mac, Windows, and Solaris. There are also various unofficial versions available for Fedora and CentOS, among other platforms. You can even download the source code and build your own MongoDB, although it is recommended that you use the provided binaries wherever possible. All the binaries are available in both 32-bit and 64-bit versions.

---

**Caution** The 32-bit version of MongoDB is limited to databases of 2GB or less. This is because, internally, MongoDB uses memory-mapped files to achieve high performance. Anything larger than 2GB on a 32 bit system would require some fancy footwork that wouldn't be all that fast and would also complicate the application's code. The official stance on this limitation is that 64-bit environments are easily available; therefore, increasing code complexity is not a good tradeoff. The 64-bit version for all intents and purposes has no such restriction.

---

MongoDB's modest requirements allow it to run on high-powered servers, virtual machines, or even to power cloud-based applications. By keeping things simple and focusing on speed and efficiency, MongoDB provides solid performance wherever you choose to deploy it.

# Fitting Everything Together

Before we look at MongoDB's feature list, we need to review a few basic terms. MongoDB doesn't require much in the way of specialized knowledge to get started, and many of the terms specific to MongoDB can be loosely translated to RDBMS equivalents that you are probably already familiar with. Don't worry, though: we'll explain each term fully. Even if you're not familiar with standard database terminology, you will still be able to follow along easily.

## Generating or Creating a Key

A document represents the unit of storage in MongoDB. In an RDBMS, this would be called a row. However, documents are much more than rows because they can store complex information such as lists, dictionaries, and even lists of dictionaries. In contrast to a traditional database where a row is fixed, a document in MongoDB can be made up of any number of keys and values (you'll learn more about this in the next section). Ultimately, a *key* is nothing more than a label; it is roughly equivalent to the name you might give to a column in an RDBMS. You use a key to reference pieces of data inside your document.

In a relational database, there should always be some way to uniquely identify a given record; otherwise it becomes impossible to refer to a specific row. To that end, you are supposed to include a field that holds a unique value (called a *primary key*) or a collection of fields that can uniquely identify the given row (called a *compound primary key*).

MongoDB requires that each document have a unique identifier for much the same reason; in MongoDB, this identifier is called `_id`. Unless you specify a value for this field, MongoDB will generate a unique value for you. Even in the well-established world of RDBMS databases, opinion is divided as to whether you should use a unique key provided by the database or generate a unique key yourself. Recently, it has become more popular to allow the database to create the key for you.

The reason for this: human-created unique numbers such as car registration numbers have a nasty habit of changing. For example, in 2001, the United Kingdom implemented a new number plate scheme that was completely different from the previous system. It happens that MongoDB can cope with this type of change perfectly well; however, chances are that you would need to do some careful thinking if you used the registration plate as your primary key. A similar scenario may have occurred when ISBN numbers were upgraded from 10 digits to 13.

That said, most developers who use MongoDB seem to prefer creating their own unique keys, taking it upon themselves to ensure that the number will remain unique. However, as is the case when working with RDBMS databases, which approach you take mostly comes down to personal preference. I personally prefer to use a database-provided value because it means I can be sure my key is unique and independent of anything else. Others, as noted, prefer to provide their own keys.

Ultimately, you must decide what works best for you. If you are confident that your key is unique (and likely to remain unchanged), then you should probably feel free to use it. If you're unsure about your key's uniqueness or you don't want to worry about it, then you can simply use the default key provided by MongoDB.

## Using Keys and Values

Documents are made up of keys and values. Let's take another look at the example discussed previously in this chapter:

```
{
    "forename": "Peter",
    "surname": "Membrey",
    "phone_numbers": [
        "+852 1234 5678",
        "+44 1234 565 555"
    ]
}
```

Keys and values always come in pairs. Unlike an RDBMS, where all fields must have a value, even if it's `NULL` (somewhat paradoxically, this means *unknown*), MongoDB doesn't require that a document have a particular value. For example, if you don't know the phone number for a particular document, you simply leave it out. A popular analogy for this sort of thing is a business card. If you have a fax number, you usually put it on your business card; however, if you don't have one, you don't write: "Fax number: none." Instead, you simply leave the information out. If the key value pair isn't included in a MongoDB document, it is assumed that it doesn't exist.

## Implementing Collections

Collections are somewhat analogous to tables, but they are far less rigid. A collection is a lot like a box with a label on it. You might have a box at home labeled "DVDs" into which you put, well, your DVDs. This makes sense, but there is nothing stopping you from putting CDs or even tapes into this box if you wanted to. In an RDBMS, tables are strictly defined, and you can only put designated items into the table. In MongoDB, a collection is simply that: a collection of similar items. The items don't have to be similar (MongoDB is inherently flexible); however, once we start looking at indexing and more advanced queries, you'll soon see the benefits of placing similar items in a collection.

While you could mix various items together in a collection, there's little need to do so. Had the collection been called `media`, then all of the DVDs, CDs, and tapes would be at home there. After all, these items all have things in common, such as an artist name, a release date, and content. In other words, it really does depend on your application whether certain documents should be stored in the same collection. Performance-wise, having multiple collections is no slower than having only one collection. Remember: MongoDB is about making your life easier, so you should do whatever feels right to you.

Last but not least, collections are effectively created on demand. Specifically, a collection is created when you first attempt to save a document that references it. This means that you could create collections on demand (not that you necessarily should). Because MongoDB also lets you create indexes and perform other database-level commands dynamically, you can use leverage this behavior to build some very dynamic applications.

## Understanding Databases

Perhaps the easiest way to think of a database is as a collection of collections. Like collections, databases are created on demand. This means that it's easy to create a database for each customer—your application code can even do it for you. You can do this with databases other than MongoDB, as well; however, creating databases in this manner with MongoDB is a very natural process. That said, just because you can create a database in this manner doesn't mean you have to or even that you should. All the same, you have that power if you want to exercise it.

# Reviewing the Feature List

Now that you understand what MongoDB is and what it offers, it's time to run through its feature list. You can find a complete list of MongoDB's features on the database's website at `www.mongodb.org/`; be sure to visit this site for an up-to-date list of them. The feature list in this chapter covers a fair bit of material that goes on behind the scenes, but you don't need to be familiar with every feature listed to use MongoDB itself. In other words, if you feel your eyes beginning to close as you review this list, feel free to jump to the end of the section!

## Using Document-Orientated Storage (BSON)

We've already discussed MongoDB's document-orientated design. We've also briefly touched on BSON. As you learned, JSON makes it much easier to store and retrieve documents in their real form, effectively removing the need for any sort of mapper or special conversion code. The fact that this feature also makes it much easier for MongoDB to scale up is icing on the cake.

BSON is an open standard; you can find its specification at `http://bsonspec.org/`. When people hear that BSON is a binary form of JSON, they expect it to take up much less room than text-based JSON.

However, this isn't necessarily the case; indeed, there are many cases where the BSON version takes up more space than its JSON equivalent.

You might wonder why you should use BSON at all. After all, CouchDB (another powerful document-orientated database) uses pure JSON, and it's reasonable to wonder whether it's worth the trouble of converting documents back and forth between BSON and JSON.

First, we must remember that MongoDB is designed to be fast, rather than space efficient. This doesn't mean that MongoDB wastes space (it doesn't); however, a small bit of overhead in storing a document is perfectly acceptable if that makes it faster to process the data (which it does). In short, BSON is much easier to *traverse* (i.e., to look through) and index very quickly. Although BSON requires slightly more disk space than JSON, this extra space is unlikely to be a problem because disks are cheap, and MongoDB can scale across machines. The tradeoff in this case is quite reasonable: you exchange a bit of extra disk space for better query and indexing performance.

The second key benefit to using BSON is that it is easy and quick to convert BSON to a programming language's native data format. If the data were stored in pure JSON, a relatively high-level conversion would need to take place. There are MongoDB drivers for a large number of programming languages (such as Python, Ruby, PHP, C, C++ and C#), and each works slightly differently. Using a simple binary format, native data structures can be quickly built for each language, without requiring that you first process JSON. This makes the code simpler and faster, both of which are in keeping with MongoDB's stated goals.

BSON also provides some extensions to JSON. For example, it enables you to store binary data and incorporates a specific date type. Thus, while BSON can store any JSON document, a valid BSON document may not be valid JSON. This doesn't matter because each language has its own driver that converts data to and from BSON without needing to use JSON as an intermediary language.

At the end of the day, BSON is not likely to be a big factor in how you use MongoDB. Like all great tools, MongoDB will quietly sit in the background and do what it needs to do. Apart from possibly using a graphical tool to look at your data, you will generally work in your native language and let the driver worry about persisting to MongoDB.

## Supporting Dynamic Queries

MongoDB's support for dynamic queries means that you can run a query without planning for it in advance. This is similar to being able to run SQL queries against an RDBMS. You might wonder why this is listed as a feature; surely this is something that every database supports—right?

Actually, no. For example, CouchDB (which is generally considered as MongoDB's biggest "competitor") doesn't support dynamic queries. This is because CouchDB has come up with a completely new (and admittedly exciting) way of thinking about data. A traditional RDBMS has static data and dynamic queries. This means that the structure of the data is fixed in advance—tables must be defined, and each row has to fit into that structure. Because the database knows in advance how the data is structured, it can make certain assumptions and optimizations that enable fast dynamic queries.

CouchDB has turned this on its head. As a document-orientated database, CouchDB has no schema (i.e., it is *schemaless*), so the data is dynamic. However, the new idea here is that queries are static. That is, you define them in advance, before you can use them.

This isn't as bad as it might sound because many queries can be easily defined in advance. For example, a system that lets you search for a book will probably let you search by ISBN. In CouchDB, you would create an index that builds a list of all the ISBNs for all the documents. When you punch in an ISBN, the query is very fast because it doesn't actually need to search for any data. Whenever new data is added to the system, CouchDB will automatically update its index.

Technically, you can run a query against CouchDB without generating an index; in this case, however, CouchDB will have to create the index itself before it can process your query. This won't be a problem if you only have a hundred books; however, this will result in poor performance if you're filing hundreds of thousands of books because each query will generate the index again (and again). For this reason, the CouchDB team does not recommend dynamic queries—that is, queries that haven't been predefined—in production.

CouchDB also lets you write your queries as `map` and `reduce` functions. If that sounds like a lot of effort, then you're in good company; CouchDB has a somewhat severe learning curve. In fairness to CouchDB, an experienced programmer can probably pick it up quite quickly; for most people, however, the learning curve is probably severe enough that they won't bother with the tool.

Fortunately for us mere mortals, MongoDB is much easier to use. We'll cover how to use MongoDB in more detail throughout the book, but here's the short version: in MongoDB, you simply provide the parts of the document you want to match against, and MongoDB does the rest. MongoDB can do much more, however. For example, you won't find MongoDB lacking if you want to use `map` or `reduce` functions. At this same time, you can ease into using MongoDB; you don't have to know all the tool's advanced features up front.

## Indexing Your Documents

MongoDB includes extensive support for indexing your documents. All documents are automatically indexed on the `_id` key. This is considered a special case because you cannot delete this index; it is what ensures that each value is unique. One of the benefits of this key is that you can be assured that each document is uniquely identifiable, something that isn't guaranteed by an RDBMS.

When you create your own indexes, you can decide whether you want them to enforce uniqueness. If you do decide to create a unique index, you can tell MongoDB to drop all the duplicates. This may (or may not) be what you want, so you should think carefully before using this option because you might accidentally delete half your data. By default, an error will be returned if you try to create a unique index on a key that has duplicate values.

There are many occasions where you will want to create an index that allows duplicates. For example, if your application searches by surname, it makes sense to build an index on the surname key. Of course, you cannot guarantee that each surname will be unique; and in any database of a reasonable size, duplicates are practically guaranteed.

MongoDB's indexing abilities don't end there, however. MongoDB can also create indexes on embedded documents. For example, if you store numerous addresses in the address key, you can create an index on the zip or post code. This means that you can easily pull back a document based on any post code—and do so very quickly.

MongoDB takes this a step further by allowing *composite indexes*. In a composite index, two or more keys are used to build a given index. For example, you might build an index that combines both the `surname` and `forename` tags. A search for a full name would be very quick because MongoDB can quickly isolate the surname and then, just as quickly, isolate the forename.

We will look at indexing in more depth in Part III of this book, but suffice it to say that MongoDB has you covered as far as indexing is concerned.

## Leveraging Geospatial Indexes

One form of indexing worthy of special mention is *geospatial indexing*. This new, specialized indexing technique was introduced in MongoDB 1.4. You use this feature to index location-based data, enabling you to answer queries such as how many items are within a certain distance from a given set of coordinates.

As an increasing number of web applications start making use of location-based data, this feature will play an increasingly prominent role in everyday development. For now, though, geospatial indexing remains a somewhat niche feature; nevertheless, you will be very glad it's there if you ever find that you need it.

## Profiling Queries

MongoDB comes with a profiling tool that lets you see how MongoDB works out which documents to return. This is useful because, in many cases, a query can be easily improved simply by adding an index. If you have a complicated query, and you're not really sure why it's running so slowly, then the query profiler can provide you with extremely valuable information. Again, you'll learn more about the profiler later in Part III.

## Updating Information In-Place

When a database updates a row (or in the case of MongoDB, a document), it has a couple of choices about how to do it. Many databases choose the multi-version concurrency control (MVCC) approach, which allows multiple users to see different versions of the data. This approach is useful because it ensures that the data won't be changed part way through by another program during a given transaction.

The downside to this approach is that the database needs to track multiple copies of the data. For example, CouchDB provides very strong versioning, but this comes at the cost of writing the data out in its entirety. While this ensures that the data is stored in a robust fashion, it also increases complexity and reduces performance.

MongoDB, on the other hand, updates information *in-place*. This means that (in contrast to CouchDB) MongoDB can update the data wherever it happens to be. This typically means that no extra space needs to be allocated, and the indexes can be left untouched.

Another benefit of this method is that MongoDB performs *lazy writes*. Writing to and from memory is very fast, but writing to disk is thousands of times slower. This means that you want to limit reading and writing from the disk as much as possible. This isn't possible in CouchDB because that program ensures each document is quickly written to disk. While this guarantees that the data is written safely to disk, this also impacts performance significantly.

MongoDB only writes to disk when it has to, which is usually once every second or so. This means that if a value is being updated many times a second—a not uncommon scenario if you're using a value as a page counter or for live statistics—then the value will only be written once, rather than the thousands of times that CouchDB would require.

This approach makes MongoDB much faster, but, again, it comes with a tradeoff. CouchDB may be slower, but it does guarantee that data is stored safely on the disk. MongoDB makes no such guarantee, and this is why a traditional RDBMS is probably a better solution for managing critical data such as billing or accounts receivable.

## Storing Binary Data

*GridFS* is MongoDB's solution to storing binary data in the database. BSON supports saving up to 4MB of binary data in a document, and this could well be enough for your needs. For example, if you want to store a profile picture or a sound clip, then 4MB might be more space than you need. On the other hand, if you want to store movie clips, high-quality audio clips, or even files that are several hundred megabytes in size, then MongoDB has you covered here, too.

GridFS works by storing the information about the file (called *metadata*) in the `files` collection. The data itself is broken down into pieces called *chunks* that are stored in the `chunks` collection. This approach makes storing data both easy and scalable; it also makes range operations (such as retrieving specific parts of a file) much easier to use.

Generally speaking, you would use GridFS through your programming language's MongoDB driver, so it's unlikely you'd ever have to get your hands dirty at such a low level. As with everything else in MongoDB, GridFS is designed for both speed and scalability. This means you can be confident that MongoDB will be up to the task if you want to work with large data files.

## Replicating Data

When we talked about the guiding principles behind MongoDB, we mentioned that RDBMS databases offer certain guarantees for data storage that are not available in MongoDB. These guarantees weren't implemented for a handful of reasons. First, these features would slow the database down. Second, they would greatly increase the complexity of the program. Third, it was felt that the most common failure on a server would be hardware, which would render the data unusable anyway, even if the data were safely saved to disk.

Of course, none of this means that data safety isn't important. MongoDB wouldn't be of much use if you couldn't count on being able to access the data when you need it. MongoDB provides a safety net using a feature called master-slave replication. This means that only one database is active for writing at any given time, an approach that is also fairly common in the RDBMS world.

The theory behind this approach goes something like this: by passing all writes to the first database (the *master database*) to a replica (the *slave database*) of the master database, you have nothing to worry about if the master database fails (for either hardware or software reasons) because the slave database can carry on in its place.

---

**Caution** It is possible that some of the data written by the master database will not yet have made it to the slave database at the point a failure occurs.

---

One powerful feature in MongoDB is the concept of replica pairs. This feature is similar to the master-slave setup, with one exception: the two servers automatically decide which server is the master and which is the slave. If a server fails, the two servers will automatically sort out how to proceed when the failed server comes back online.

## Implementing Auto Sharding

For those involved with large-scale deployments, the auto sharding feature will probably prove one of MongoDB's most significant and oft-used features. Although many people will be perfectly happy with a single server or perhaps a replica pair, sharding enables you to implement much more scalable deployments.

There are a couple different types of sharding: auto and manual. *Manual sharding* is already possible to a certain extent. In that scenario, you set up two MongoDB master servers and store half your data on one and the rest of your data on the other. With manual sharding, you are responsible for keeping track of what data is on which server, as well as for running the queries that pull the data back together. This is doable, but it can get very complex, and you lose one of MongoDB's best features: its simplicity.

In the *auto sharding* scenario, MongoDB takes care of all the data splitting and recombination for you. It makes sure the data goes to the right server and that queries are run and combined in the most efficient manner possible. In fact, from a developer's point of view, there is no difference between talking to a MongoDB database with a hundred shards and talking to a single MongoDB server. This feature is not yet production-ready; when it is, however, it will push MongoDB's scalability through the roof.

In the meantime, if you're just starting out or you're building your first MongoDB-based website, then you'll probably find that a single instance of MongoDB is sufficient for your needs. If you end up building the next Facebook or Amazon, however, you will be glad that you built your site on a technology that can scale so limitlessly.

## Using Map and Reduce Functions

For many people, hearing the phrase *map/reduce* sends shivers down their spines. At the other extreme, many RDBMS advocates scoff at the complexity of map and reduce functions. It's scary for some because these functions require a completely different way of thinking about finding and sorting your data, and many professional programmers have trouble getting their heads around the concepts that underpin map and reduce functions. That said, these functions provide an extremely powerful way to query data. In fact, CouchDB supports only this approach, which is one reason CouchDB has such a high learning curve.

MongoDB doesn't require that you use map and reduce functions. In fact, MongoDB relies on a simple querying syntax that is more akin to what you see in MySQL. However, MongoDB does make these functions available for those who want them. These functions are written in JavaScript and run on the server. The job of the map function is to find all the documents that meet a certain criteria. These results are then passed to the reduce function, which processes the data. The reduce function doesn't usually return a collection of documents; rather, it returns a new document that contains the information derived. As a general rule, if you would normally use GROUP BY in SQL, then the map and reduce functions are probably the right tools for the job in MongoDB.

We won't go into too much depth on the topic of map/reduce here. While these functions are very powerful, you don't need them to get up and running or to accomplish most day-to-day tasks with MongoDB.

---

■ **Note** You should not think of MongoDB's map and reduce functions as poor imitations of the approach adopted by CouchDB. If you so desired, you could use MongoDB's map and reduce functions for everything in lieu of MongoDB's innate query support.

---

# Getting Help

MongoDB has a great community, and the core developers are very active, easily approachable, and typically go to great lengths to help other members of the community. MongoDB is easy to use and comes with great documentation; however, it's still nice to know that you're not alone, and help is available, should you need it.

## Visiting the Website

The first place to look for updated information or help is on the MongoDB website (http://mongodb.org). This site is updated regularly and contains all the latest MongoDB goodness. On this site, you can find drivers, tutorials, examples, frequently asked questions, and much more.

## Chatting with the MongoDB Developers

The MongoDB developers hang out on Internet Relay Chat (IRC) at #MongoDB on the Freenode network (www.freenode.net). MongoDB's developers are based in New York, but they are often found chatting in this channel well into the night. Of course, the developers do need to sleep at some point (coffee only works for so long!); fortunately, there are also many knowledgeable MongoDB users from around the world who are ready to help out. Many people who visit the #MongoDB channel aren't experts; however, the general atmosphere is so friendly that they stick around anyway. Please do feel free to join #MongoDB channel and chat to people there—you may find some great hints and tips. If you're really stuck, you'll probably be able to quickly get back on track.

## Cutting and Pasting MongoDB Code

Pastie (`http://pastie.org`) is not strictly a MongoDB site; however, it is something you will come across if you float about in `#MongoDB` for any length of time. Pastie is a site that basically lets you cut and paste (hence the name) some output or program code, and then put it online for others to view. In IRC, pasting multiple lines of text can be messy or hard to read. If you need to post a fair bit of text (such as three lines or more), then you should visit `http://pastie.org`, paste in your content, and then paste the link to your new page into the channel.

## Finding Solutions on Google Groups

MongoDB also has a Google group called `mongodb-user` (`http://groups.google.com/group/mongodb-user`). This group is a great place to ask questions or search for answers. You can also interact with the group via e-mail. Unlike IRC, which is very transient, the Google group is a great long-term resource. If you really want to get involved with the MongoDB community, joining the group is a great way to start.

## Leveraging the JIRA Tracking System

MongoDB uses the JIRA issue tracking system. You can view this site at `http://jira.mongodb.org/`, and you are actively encouraged to report any bugs or problems that you come across to this site. Reporting such issues is viewed by the community as a genuinely good thing to do. Of course, you can also search through previous issues, and you can even view the roadmap and planned updates for the next release.

If you haven't posted to JIRA before, you might want to visit the IRC room first. You will quickly find out whether you've found something new, and, if so, you will be shown how to go about reporting it.

# Summary

This chapter has provided a whistle-stop tour of the benefits MongoDB brings to the table. We've looked at the philosophies and guiding principles behind MongoDB's creation and development, as well as the tradeoffs MongoDB's developers made when implementing these ideals. We've also looked at some of the key terms used in conjunction with MongoDB, how they fit together, and their rough SQL equivalents.

Next, we looked at some of the features MongoDB offers, including how and where you might want to use them. Finally, we wrapped up the chapter with a quick overview of the community and where you can go to get help, should you need it.

CHAPTER 2

# Installing MongoDB

In Chapter 1, you got a taste of what MongoDB can do for you. In this chapter, you will learn how to install and expand MongoDB even further, enabling you to use it in combination with your favorite programming language.

MongoDB is a cross-platform database, and you can find a significant list of available packages to download from the MongoDB website (`www.mongodb.org`). The wealth of available versions might make it difficult to decide which version is the right one for you. The right choice for you probably depends on the operating system your server uses, the kind of processor in your server, whether you prefer a stable release, and whether you would like to take a dive into a version which is still in development, but offers exciting new features. Perhaps you'd like to install both a stable and a forward-looking version of the database. It's also possible you're not entirely sure which version you should choose yet. In any case, read on!

## Choosing Your Version

When you look at the Download section on the MongoDB website, you will see a rather straightforward overview of the packages available for download. The first thing you need to pay attention to is the actual operating system you are going to run the MongoDB software on. Currently, there are precompiled packages available for Windows, Linux, Mac OS, and Solaris.

---

**Note** An important thing to remember here is the difference between the 32-bit release and the 64-bit release of the product. The 32-bit and 64-bit versions of the database have the same functionality, with one exception: the 32-bit release is limited to a total dataset size of approximately 2.5GB per server. The 64-bit version does not carry this restriction however, so it's generally preferred over the 32-bit version. Also, the differences between these versions are subject to change.

---

You will also need to pay attention to the actual *version* of the MongoDB software itself: there are production releases, previous releases, and development releases. The *production* release indicates that it's the most recent stable version available. When a newer and generally improved or enhanced version is released, the prior most recent stable version will be made available as a *previous release*. This designation means the release is stable and reliable, but it usually has fewer features available in it. Finally, there's the *development release*. This release is generally referred to as the unstable version. This version is still in development, and it will include many changes, including significant new features.

Despite the fact that it has not been fully developed and tested yet, the developers of MongoDB have made it available to the public to test or otherwise try out.

## Understanding the Version Numbers

MongoDB uses the "odd-numbered versions for development releases" approach. In other words, you can tell by looking at the second number of the version number (also called the release number) whether a version is a development version or a stable version. If the second number is even, then it's a *stable* release. If the second number is an odd number, then it's an *unstable*, or *development*, release.

Let's take a closer look at the three digits included in a version number's three parts, A, B, and C:

- A, the first (or left-most) number: Represents the major version and only changes when there is a full version upgrade.
- B, the second (or middle) number: Represents the release number and indicates whether a version is a development version or a stable version. If the number is even, the version is stable; if the number is odd, then the version is unstable and considered a development release.
- C, the third (or right-most) number: Represents the revision number; this is used for bugs and security issues.

For example, at the time of writing, the following versions were available from the MongoDB website:

- 1.6.1 (Production release)
- 1.4.4 (Previous release)
- 1.7.0-pre (Development release)

# Installing MongoDB on Your System

So far, you've learned which versions of are available and—hopefully—were able to select one. Now you're ready to take a closer look at how to install MongoDB on your particular system. The two main operating systems for servers at the moment are based on Linux and Microsoft Windows, so this chapter will walk you through how to install MongoDB on both of these operating systems.

## Installing MongoDB Under Linux

The UNIX-based operating systems are extremely popular choices at the moment for hosting services, including web services, mail services, and, of course, database services. In this chapter, we'll walk you through how to get MongoDB running on a popular Linux distribution: Ubuntu.

To make things simple (or perhaps more complicated, depending on your point of view), you have two ways of installing MongoDB under Ubuntu: you can install the packages automatically through so-called *repositories*, or you can install it manually. The next couple sections will walk you through both options.

## Installing MongoDB Through the Repositories

Repositories are basically online directories filled with software. Every package contains information about the version number, prerequisites, and possible incompatibilities. This information is useful when you need to install a software package that requires another piece of software to be installed first because the prerequisites can be installed at the same time.

The default repositories available in Ubuntu (and other Debian-based distributions) contain MongoDB, but they may be out-of-date versions of the software. Therefore, let's tell *aptitude* (the software you use to install software from repositories) to look at a custom repository. To do this, you need to add the following line to your repository-list (`/etc/apt/sources.list`):

```
deb http://downloads.mongodb.org/distros/ubuntu (version.number) 10gen
```

In the preceding line, `version.number` represents the distribution version. Let's say your Ubuntu is version 10.4 (also called Ubuntu Lucid); in that case, the full line would look like this:

```
deb http://downloads.mongodb.org/distros/ubuntu 10.4 10gen
```

Next, you need to tell aptitude that it contains new repositories; you can do so using aptitude's `update` command:

```
$ sudo aptitude update
```

The preceding line made aptitude aware of your manually added repository. This means you can now tell aptitude to install the software itself. You do this by typing the following command in the shell:

```
$ sudo aptitude install mongodb-stable
```

As you may have guessed, the preceding line installs the current stable (production) version from MongoDB. If you wish to install the unstable (development) version from MongoDB, type in the following command instead:

```
$ sudo aptitude install mongodb-unstable
```

And this command installs the nightly build:

```
$ sudo aptitude install mongodb-snapshot
```

That's all there is to it. At this point, MongoDB has been installed and is (almost) ready to use!

## Installing MongoDB Manually

Next, we'll cover how to install MongoDB manually. Given how easy it is to install MongoDB with aptitude automatically, you might wonder why you would want to install the software manually. For starters, not all Linux distributions use aptitude. Sure, a bunch of them do (including primarily the ones that are based on Debian Linux), but some don't. Also, the packaging remains a *work in progress*, so it might be the case that there are versions not yet available through the repositories. It's also possible that the version of MongoDB you want to use isn't included in the repository (you might want to install an older version automatically). Installing the software manually also gives you the ability to run multiple versions of MongoDB at the same time.

You've decided which version of MongoDB you would like to use, and you've downloaded it to your Home directory. Next, you need to extract the package with the following command:

```
$ tar xzf mongodb-linux-x86_64-latest.tgz
```

The preceding command extracts the entire contents of the package to a new directory called mongodb-linux-x86_64-xxxx-yy-zz; this directory is located under your current directory. This directory will contain a number of subdirectories and files. The directory that contains the executable files is called the bin directory. We will cover which applications perform which tasks shortly.

However, you don't need to do anything further to install the application. Indeed, it doesn't take much more time to install MongoDB manually—depending on what else you need to install, it might even be faster. Manually installing MongoDB does have some downsides, however. For example, the executables that you just extracted and found in the bin directory can't be executed from anywhere except the bin directory by default. Thus, if you want to run the mongod service, you will need to do so directly from the aforementioned bin directory. This downside highlights one of the benefits of installing MongoDB through repositories.

## Installing MongoDB Under Windows

Microsoft's Windows is also a popular choice for server software, including Internet-based services.

Windows doesn't come with a repository application like aptitude, so you'll need to download and extract the software from the MongoDB website to run it. Yes, the preceding information is correct. You do not need to walk through any setup process; installing the software is a simple matter of downloading the package, extracting it, and running the application itself.

Assume you've decided to download the latest stable version of MongoDB for your 64-bits Windows 2008 server. You begin by extracting the package (mongodb-win32-x86_64-x.y.x.zip) to the root of your C:\ drive. At this point, all you need to do is open a command prompt (Start ➤ Run ➤ "cmd" ➤ OK) and browse to the directory you extracted the contents to:

```
> cd C:\mongodb-win32-x86_64-x.y.z\
> cd bin\
```

Doing this brings you to the directory that contains the MongoDB executables. That's all there is to it: as I noted previously, no installation is necessary.

# Running MongoDB

At long last, you're ready to get your hands dirty. You've learned where to get the MongoDB version that best suits your needs and hardware, and you've also seen how to install the software itself. Now it's finally time to look at running and using MongoDB.

## Prerequisites

Before you can start the MongoDB service, you need to create a data directory for MongoDB to store its files in. By default, MongoDB stores the data in the /data/db directory on Unix-based systems (e.g., Linux and OS X) and in the C:\data\db directory on Windows.

---

▒ **Note** MongoDB does not create these data directories for you, so you need to create them manually; otherwise, MongoDB will fail to run and throw an error message. Also, be sure that you set the permissions correctly: MongoDB must have *read*, *write*, and directory *creation* permissions to function properly.

---

If you wish to use a directory other than /data/db or C:\data\db, then you can tell MongoDB to look at the desired directory by using the --dbpath flag when executing the service.

Once you create the required directory and assign the appropriate permissions, you can start the MongoDB core database service by executing the *mongod* application. You can do this from the command prompt or the shell in Windows and Linux, respectively.

## Surveying the Installation Layout

After you install or extract MongoDB successfully, you will have the applications shown in Figure 2–1 available in the bin directory (in both Linux and Windows).

```
|-- bin
|  |-- mongo                    (the database shell)
|  |-- mongod                   (the core database server)
|  |-- mongos                   (auto-sharding process)
|  |-- mongodump                (dump/export utility)
|  `-- mongorestore             (restore/import utility)
```

***Figure 2–1.*** *Drilling down on the included MongoDB applications*

The installed software includes five applications that you will be using in conjunction with your MongoDB databases. The two "most important" applications are the *mongo* and *mongod* applications. The mongo application allows you to use the database shell; this shell enables you to accomplish practically anything you'd want to do with MongoDB.

The mongod application starts the service or *daemon*, as it's also called. There are also many flags you can set when launching the MongoDB applications. For example, the service lets you specify the path where the database is located (--dbpath), show version information (--version), and even print some diagnostic system information (with the --sysinfo flag)! You can view the entire list of options by including the --help flag when you launch the service. For now, you can just use the defaults and start the service by typing mongod in your shell or command prompt.

## Using the MongoDB Shell

Once you create the database directory and start the mongod database application successfully, you're ready to fire up the shell and take a sneak peak at the powers of MongoDB.

Fire up your shell (Unix) or your command prompt in Windows; when you do so, make sure you are in the correct location, so that the mongo executable can be found. You can start the shell by typing mongo at the command prompt and hitting the Return key. You will be immediately presented with a blank window and a blinking cursor (see Figure 2–2). Ladies and gentlemen, welcome to MongoDB!

If you start the MongoDB service with the default parameters, and start the shell with the default settings, then you will be connected to the default test database running on your local host. This database is created automatically the moment you connect to it. This is one of MongoDB's most powerful features: if you attempt to connect to a database that does not exist, MongoDB will automatically create it for you. This can be either good or bad, depending on how well you handle your keyboard.

*Figure 2–2. The MongoDB shell*

Before taking any additional steps, such as implementing any additional drivers that will enable you to work with your favorite programming language, you might find it helpful to take a quick peek at some of the more useful commands available in the MongoDB shell (see Table 2–1).

*Table 2–1. Basic commands within the MongoDB shell*

| Command | Function |
| --- | --- |
| `show dbs` | Shows the names of the available databases. |
| `show collections` | Shows the collections in the current database. |
| `show users` | Shows the users in the current database. |
| `use <db name>` | Sets the current database to `<db name>`. |

**Tip** You can get a full list of commands by typing the `help` command in the MongoDB shell.

# Installing Additional Drivers

You might think that you are ready to take on the world now that you have set up MongoDB and know how to use its shell. That's partially true; however, you probably want to use your preferred programming language rather than the shell when querying or otherwise manipulating the MongoDB database. MongoDB offers several drivers that let you do precisely that.

The MongoDB drivers come in many flavors, and it's relatively easy to install the driver for a particular programming language. Currently, MongoDB includes drivers for the following programming languages:

- C
- C++
- Java
- JavaScript
- Perl
- PHP
- Python
- Ruby

In this section, you will learn how to implement MongoDB support for two of the more popular programming languages in use today: PHP and Python.

# Installing the PHP driver

PHP is easily one of the most popular programming languages in existence today. This language is specifically aimed at web development, and it can be incorporated into HTML easily. This fact makes the language the perfect candidate for designing a web application, such as a blog, a guestbook, or even a business-card database. The next couple sections will cover your options for installing and using the MongoDB PHP driver.

## Getting MongoDB for PHP

Like MongoDB, PHP is a cross-platform development tool, and the steps required to set up MongoDB in PHP vary, depending on the intended platform. Previously, this chapter showed you how to install MongoDB on both Ubuntu and Windows; we'll adopt the same approach here, demonstrating how to install the driver for PHP on both Ubuntu and Windows.

Begin by downloading the PHP driver for your operating system. Do this by firing up your browser and navigating to `www.mongodb.org`. At the time of writing, the website includes a separate menu option called Drivers. Click this menu option to bring up a list of currently available language drivers (see Figure 2–3).

Next, select PHP from the list of languages and follow the links to download the latest (stable) version of the driver. Different operating systems will require different approaches for installing the MongoDB extension for PHP automatically. That's right; just as you were able to install MongoDB on Ubuntu automatically, you can do the same for the PHP driver. And just as when installing MongoDB under Ubuntu, you can also choose to install the PHP language driver manually. Let's look at the two options available to you.

***Figure 2–3.*** *A list of currently available language drivers for MongoDB*

## Installing PHP on Unix-based Platforms Automatically

The developers of PHP came up with a great solution that allows you to expand your PHP installation with other popular extensions: *PECL*. PECL is a repository solely designed for PHP; it provides a directory of all known extensions that you can use to download, install, and even develop PHP extensions. If you are already acquainted with the package-management system called aptitude (which you used previously to install MongoDB), then you will be pleased by how similar PECL's interface is to the one in aptitude.

Assuming that you have PECL installed on your system, open up a console and type the following command to install the MongoDB extension:

```
$ sudo pecl install mongo
```

Entering the preceding command causes PECL to download and install the MongoDB extension for PHP automatically. In other words, PECL will download the extension for your PHP version and place it in the PHP extensions directory. There's just one catch: PECL does not automatically add the extension to the list of loaded extensions; you will need to do this step manually. To do so, open a text editor (e.g., vim, nano, or whichever text editor you prefer) and alter the file called `php.ini`, which is the main configuration file PHP uses to control its behavior, including which extensions it should load.

Next, open the `php.ini` file, scroll down to the *extensions* section, and add the following line to tell PHP to load the MongoDB driver:

```
extension=mongo.so
```

---

■ **Note** The preceding step is mandatory; if you don't do this, then the MongoDB commands in PHP will not function.

---

The "Confirming Your PHP Installation Works" section later in this chapter will cover how to confirm that an extension has been loaded successfully.

That's all, folks! You've just installed the MongoDB extension for your PHP installation, and you are now ready to use it. Next, you will learn how to install the driver manually.

## Installing PHP on Unix-Based Platforms Manually

If you would prefer to compile the driver yourself or for some reason are unable to use the PECL application as described previously (your hosting provider might not support this option, for instance), then you can also choose to download the source driver and compile it manually.

To download the driver, go to the github website (`http://github.com`). This site offers the latest source package for the PHP driver. Once you download it, you will need to extract the package, and *make* the driver by running the following set of commands:

```
$ tar zxvf mongodb-mongdb-php-driver-<commit_id>.tar.gz
$ cd mongodb-mongodb-php-driver-<commit_id>
$ phpize
$ ./configure
$ sudo make install
```

This process can take a while, depending on the speed of your system. Once the process completes, your MongoDB PHP driver is installed and ready to use! After you execute the commands, you will be shown where the driver has been placed; typically, the output looks something like this:

```
Installing '/ usr/lib/php/extensions/no-debug-zts-20060613/mongo.so'
```

You do need to confirm that this directory is the same directory where PHP stores its extensions by default. You can use the following command to confirm where PHP stores its extensions:

```
$ php -i | grep extension_dir
```

The preceding line outputs the directory where all PHP extensions should be placed. If this directory doesn't match the one where the `mongo.so` driver was placed, then you must move the `mongo.so` driver to the proper directory, so PHP knows where to find it.

As before, you will need to tell PHP that the newly created extension has been placed in its extension directory, and that it should load this extension. You can specify this by modifying the `php.ini` file's *extensions* section; add the following line to that section:

```
extension=mongo.so
```

That's it! This process is a little lengthier than using PECL's automated method; however, if you are unable to use PECL, or if you are a driver developer and interested in bug fixes, then you would want to use the manual method instead.

## Installing PHP on Windows

You have seen previously how to install MongoDB on your Windows operating system. Now let's look at how to implement the MongoDB driver for PHP on Windows.

For Windows, there are precompiled binaries available for each release out of the PHP driver for MongoDB. You can get these binaries from the previously mentioned github website (`http://github.com`). The biggest challenge in this case is choosing the correct package to install for your version of PHP (a wide variety of packages is available). If you aren't certain which package version you need, you can use the `<? phpinfo(); ?>` command in a PHP page to learn exactly which one suits your specific environment. We'll take a closer look at the `phpinfo()` command in the next section.

After downloading the correct package and extracting its contents, all you need to do is copy the driver file (called `php_mongo.dll`) to your PHP's extension directory; this enables PHP to pick it up.

Depending on your version of PHP, the extension directory may be called either `Ext` or `Extensions`. If you aren't certain which directory it should be, you can review the PHP documentation that came with the version of PHP installed on your system.

Once you place the driver DLL into the PHP extensions directory, you still need to tell PHP to load the driver. Do this by altering the `php.ini` file and adding the following line in the extensions section:

```
extension=php_mongo.dll
```

You are now ready to use the MongoDB driver in PHP. Before you start leveraging the magic of MongoDB with PHP, however, you need to confirm that the extension is loaded correctly.

# Confirming Your PHP Installation Works

So far you've successfully installed both MongoDB and the MongoDB driver in PHP. Now it's time to do a quick check to confirm whether the driver is being loaded correctly by PHP. PHP gives you a simple and straightforward method to accomplish this: the `phpinfo()` command. This command shows you an extended overview of all the modules loaded, including your version numbers, compilation options, server information, OS information, and so on.

To use the `phpinfo()` command, open a text or HTML editor and type the following:

```
<? phpinfo(); ?>
```

Next, save the document in your webserver's `www` directory and call it whatever you like. For example, you might call it `test.php` or `phpinfo.php`. Now open your browser and go to your localhost or external server (i.e., go to whatever server you are working on) and look at the page you just created. You will see a good overview of all PHP components and all sorts of other relevant information. The thing you need to focus on here is the section that displays your MongoDB information. This section will list the version number, port numbers, hostname, and so on (see Figure 2–4).

Once you confirm that the installation was successful and that the driver loaded successfully, you're ready to write some PHP code and walk through a MongoDB example that leverages PHP.

## mongo

| MongoDB Support | enabled |
| --- | --- |
| Version | 1.0.6 |

| Directive | Local Value | Master Value |
| --- | --- | --- |
| mongo.allow_persistent | On | On |
| mongo.auto_reconnect | On | On |
| mongo.chunk_size | 262144 | 262144 |
| mongo.cmd | $ | $ |
| mongo.default_host | localhost | localhost |
| mongo.default_port | 27017 | 27017 |
| mongo.utf8 | 1 | 1 |

***Figure 2–4.*** *Displaying your MongoDB information in PHP*

## Connecting to and Disconnecting from the PHP Driver

You've confirmed that the MongoDB PHP driver has been loaded correctly, so it's time to start writing some PHP code! Let's take a look at two simple yet fundamental options for working with MongoDB: initiating a connection between MongoDB and PHP, and then severing that connection.

You use the `Mongo` class to initiate a connection between MongoDB and PHP; this same class also lets you use the database server commands. A simple yet typical connection command looks like this:

```
$connection = new Mongo();
```

If you use this command without providing any parameters, then it will connect to the MongoDB service on the default MongoDB port (27017) on your localhost. If your MongoDB service is running somewhere else, then you simply specify the hostname of the remote host you want to connect to:

```
$connection = new Mongo("example.com");
```

The preceding line instantiates a fresh connection for your MongoDB service running on the server and listening to the `example.com` domain name (note that it will still connect to the default port: 27017). If you want to connect to a different port number, however (e.g., you don't want to use the default port, or you're already running another session of the MongoDB service on that port), you can do so by specifying the port number and hostname:

```
$connection = new Mongo("example.com:12345");
```

The preceding examples create a connection to the database service. Next, you will learn how to disconnect from the service. Assuming you used the method just described to connect to your database, you can call `$connection` again to pass the `close()` command to terminate the connection, as in this example:

```
$connection->close();
```

The close doesn't need to be called, except for in unusual circumstances. The reason for this is that the PHP driver closes the connection to the database once the Mongo object goes out of scope. Nevertheless, it is recommended that you call close() at the end of your PHP code; this helps you avoid keeping old connections from hanging around until they eventually time out. It also helps you ensure that any existing connection is closed, thereby enabling a new connection to happen, as in the following example:

```
$connection = new Mongo();
$connection->close();
$connection->connect();
```

The following snippet shows how this would look like in PHP:

```
<?php

// Establish the database connection
$connection = new Mongo()

// Close the database connection
$connection->close();

?>
```

# Installing the Python Driver

Python is a general-purpose and easy-to-read programming language.

These qualities make Python a good language to start with when you are new to programming and scripting. It's also a great language to look into if you are familiar with programming, and you're looking for a multi-paradigm programming language that permits several styles of programming (e.g., object-oriented programming, structured programming, and so on). In the upcoming sections, you'll learn how to install Python and enable MongoDB support for the language.

## Installing PyMongo under Linux

Python offers a specific package for MongoDB support called PyMongo. This package allows you to interact with the MongoDB database, but you will need to get this driver up and running before you can use this powerful combination. As when installing the PHP driver, there are two methods you can use to install PyMongo: an automated approach that relies on setuptools or a manual approach where you download the source code for the project. The following sections show you how to install PyMongo using both approaches.

## Installing PyMongo Automatically

The setuptools that come bundled with a Python module called Easy Install (easy_install) let you automatically download, build, install, and manage Python packages. This is incredibly convenient, enabling you to extend your Python modules installation even as it does all the work for you.

---

**Note** You must have setuptools installed before you can use the Easy Install module.

---

You might have done a quick double-take at the notion that you need to install a module so that you can install a different module that enables you to implement a Python driver for use with MongoDB. But that is exactly how this process works. Fortunately, this process sounds more complicated than it is. To install the setuptools, all you need to do is download the appropriate setuptools-*egg* for your version of Python from the Python Package Index website (`http://pypi.python.org`). Once you do this, you can execute the downloaded egg (e.g., `setuptools-0.6c9-py2.4.egg`) as if it were an actual shell script by typing the following statement in your console:

```
$ sh setuptools-0.6c9-py2.4.egg
```

When the preceding line executes, setuptools will detect the currently running version of Python and installs itself by placing the `easy_install` executable into the default Python scripts location. That's all there is to it. Now you are ready to use the `easy_install` command to download, make, and install the MongoDB module, as in this example:

```
$ easy_install pymongo
```

Again, that's all there is to it! PyMongo is now installed and ready to use.

---

■ **Tip** You can also upgrade your PyMongo module with `easy_install` by using the `easy_install -U pymongo` command. Doing this regularly ensures that you are always running the latest stable version.

---

## Installing PyMongo Manually

You can also choose to install PyMongo manually. Begin by going to the download section of the site with the PyMongo plugin (`http://pypi.python.org/pypi/pymongo`). Next, download the tarball and extract it. A typical download and extract procedure might look like this in your console:

```
$ wget http://pypi.python.org/packages/source/p/pymongo/pymongo-1.7.tar.gz
$ tar xzf pymongo-1.5.2.tar.gz
```

Once you successfully download and extract this file, make your way to the extracted contents directory and invoke the installation of the PyMongo by running the `install.py` command with Python:

```
$ cd pymongo-1.5.2.tar.gz
$ python install.py install
```

The preceding snippet outputs the entire creation and installation process of the PyMongo module. Eventually, this process brings you back to your prompt, at which time you're ready to start using PyMongo.

## Installing PyMongo Under Windows

Installing PyMongo under Windows is a straightforward process. As when installing PyMongo under Linux, Easy Install can simplify installing PyMongo under Windows as well. If you don't have setuptools installed yet (this package includes the `easy_install` command), then go to the Python Package Index website (`http://pypi.python.org`) to locate the setuptools installer.

---

**Caution** The version of setuptools you download must match the version of Python installed on your system.

---

For example, assume you have Python version 2.6.5 installed on your system. You will need to download the setuptools package for v2.6.x. The good news is that you don't need to compile any of this; rather, you can simply download the appropriate package and double-click the executable to install setuptools on your system! It is that simple.

---

**Caution** If you have previously installed an older version of setuptools, then you will need to uninstall that version using your system's Add/Remove Programs feature *before* installing the newer version.

---

Once the installation is complete, you will find the `easy_install.exe` file in Python's Scripts subdirectory. At this point, you're ready to install PyMongo on Windows.

Once you've successfully installed setuptools, you can open a command prompt and `cd` your way to Python's Scripts directory. By default, this is set to `C:\Pythonxy\Scripts\`, where xy represents your version number. Once you navigate to this location, you can use the same syntax shown previously for installing the UNIX variant:

```
C:\Python26\Scripts> easy_install PyMongo
```

Unlike the output that you get when installing this program on a Linux machine, the output here is rather brief, indicating only that the extension has been downloaded and installed (see Figure 2–5). That said, this information is sufficient for your purposes in this case.

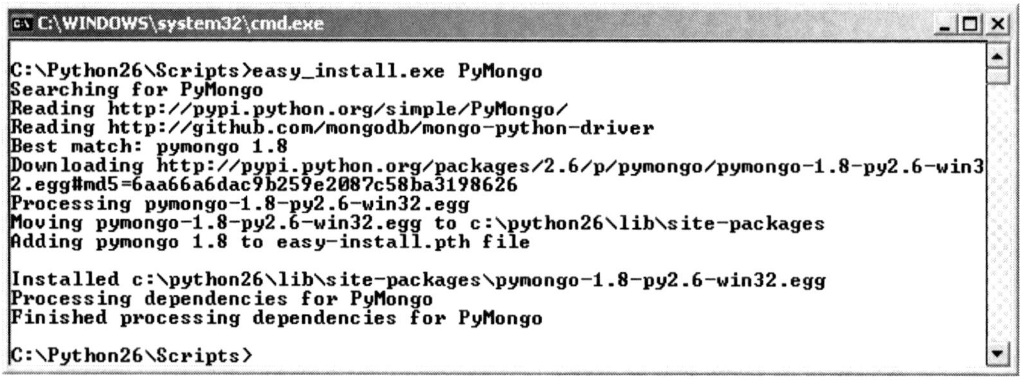


***Figure 2–5.*** *Installing PyMongo under Windows*

## Confirming Your PyMongo Installation Works

To confirm whether the PyMongo installation has completed successfully, you can open up your Python shell. In Linux, you do this by opening a console and typing `python`. In Windows, you do this by clicking Start ➤ Programs ➤ Python xy ➤ Python (commandline). At this point, you will be welcomed to the world of Python (see Figure 2–6).

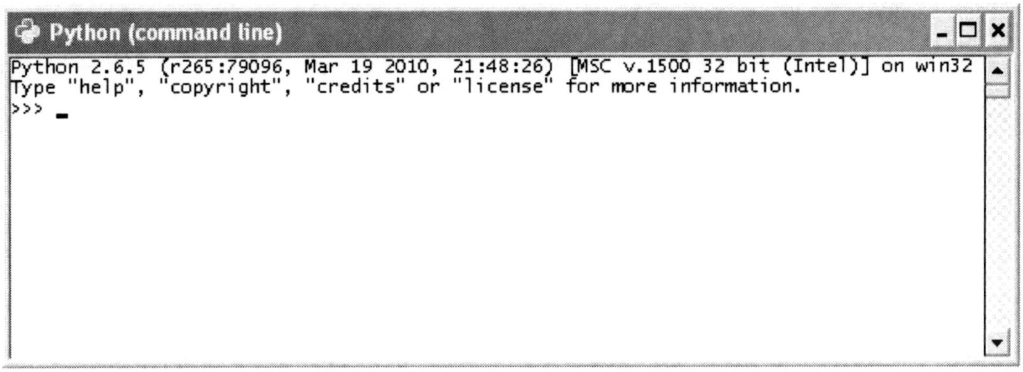


***Figure 2–6.*** *The Python shell*

You can use the `import` command to tell Python to start using the freshly installed extension:

```
>>> import pymongo
>>>
```

---

■ **Note** You must use the `import pymongo` command each time you want to use PyMongo.

---

If all went well, you will not see a thing, and you can start firing off some fancy MongoDB commands. If you received an error message, however, something went wrong, and you might need to review the steps just taken to discover where the error occurred.

# Summary

In this chapter, we examined how to obtain the MongoDB software, including how to select the correct version you need for your environment. We also discussed the version numbers, how to install and run MongoDB, and how to install and run its prerequisites. Next, we covered how to establish a connection to a database through a combination of the shell, PHP, and Python.

We also explored how to expand MongoDB so it will work with your favorite programming languages, as well as how to confirm whether the language-specific drivers installed correctly.

In the next chapter, you will explore how to design and structure MongoDB databases and data properly. Along the way, you'll learn how to index information to speed up queries, how to reference data, and how to leverage a fancy new feature called *geospatial indexing*.

CHAPTER 3

■ ■ ■

# The Data Model

In the previous chapter, you learned how to install MongoDB on two commonly used platforms (Windows and Linux), as well as how to extend the database with some additional drivers. In this chapter, you will shift your attention from the operating system and instead examine the general design of a MongoDB database. Specifically, you'll learn what collections are; what documents look like; how indexes work and what they do; and finally, when and where to reference data instead of embedding data. We touched on some of these concepts briefly in Chapter 1. To refresh your memory though, we'll address some of this material again in this chapter, but this time in more detail. Throughout this chapter, you will see code examples designed to give you get a good feel of what is being discussed. Do not worry too much about the commands you'll be looking at, however, because they will be discussed extensively in Chapter 4.

## Designing the Database

As you learned in the first two chapters, a MongoDB database is non-relational and schemaless. This means that a MongoDB database isn't bound to any predefined columns or datatypes the way that relational databases are (such as MySQL). The biggest benefit of this implementation is that working with data is extremely flexible because there is no actual predefined structure required in your documents.

To put it more simply: you are perfectly capable of having one collection that contains hundreds or even thousands of documents that all carry a different structure—without breaking any of the MongoDB databases rules.

One of the benefits of this flexible schemaless design is that you won't be restricted when programming in a dynamically typed programming language (e.g., Python or PHP). Indeed, it would be a severe limitation if your extremely flexible and dynamically capable programming language couldn't be used to its full potential because of the innate limitations of your database.

Let's take another glance at what the data design of a document in MongoDB looks like, paying particular attention to how flexible data in MongoDB is compared to data in a relational database. In MongoDB, a *document* is an item that contains the actual data, comparable to a row in SQL. In the following example, you will see how two completely different types of documents can co-exist in a single collection called `Media` (note that a *collection* is equivalent to a table in the world of SQL):

```
{
    "Type": "CD",
    "Artist": "Nirvana",
    "Title": "Nevermind",
    "Genre": "Grunge",
    "Releasedate": "1991.09.24",
    "Tracklist": [
        {
```

```
        "Track" : "1",
        "Title" : "Smells like teen spirit",
        "Length" : "5:02"
        },
        {
        "Track" : "2",
        "Title" : "In Bloom",
        "Length" : "4:15"
        }
    ]
}
```

```
{
    "type": "Book",
    "Title": "Definite Guide to MongoDB: The NoSQL
    Database for Cloud and Desktop Computing, the",
    "ISBN": "987-1-4302-3051-9",
    "Publisher": "Apress",
    "Author": [
        "Plugge, Eelco",
        "Membrey, Peter",
        "Hawkins, Tim"
    ]
}
```

As you might have noticed when looking at the pair of preceding documents, most of the fields aren't closely related to one another. Yes, they both have fields called `Title` and `Type`; but apart from that similarity, the documents are completely different. Nevertheless, these two documents are contained in a single collection called `Media`.

MongoDB is called a *schemaless* database, but that doesn't mean MongoDB's data structure is completely devoid of schema. For example, you do define collections and indexes in MongoDB (you will learn more about this later in the chapter). Nevertheless, you do not *need* to predefine a structure for any of the documents you will be adding, as is the case when working with MySQL, for example.

Simply stated, MongoDB is an extraordinarily dynamic database; the preceding example would never work in a relational database, unless you also added each possible field to your table. Doing so would be a waste of both space and performance, not to mention highly disorganized.

## Drilling Down on Collections

As mentioned previously, a collection is a commonly used term in MongoDB. You can think of a collection as a container that stores your documents (i.e., your data), as shown in Figure 3–1.

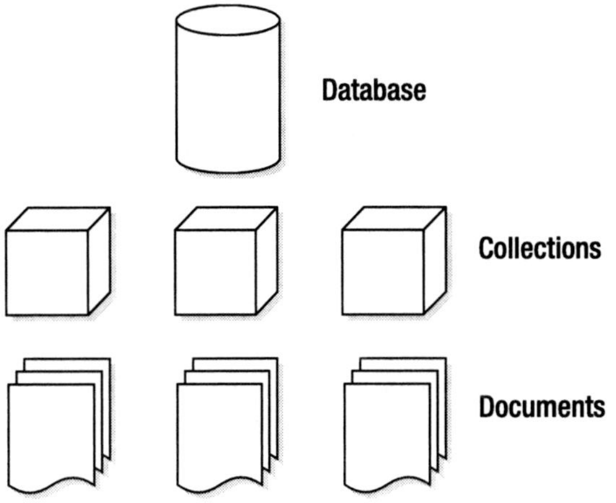


***Figure 3–1.*** *The MongoDB database model*

Now compare the MongoDB database model to a typical model for a relational database (see Figure 3–2).

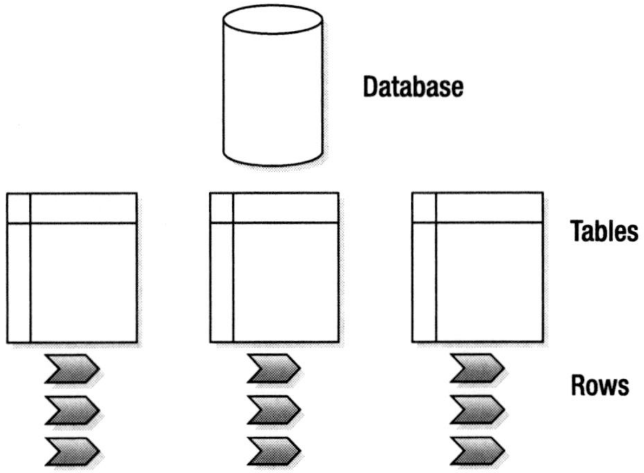


***Figure 3–2.*** *A typical relational database model*

As you can see, the general structure is the same between the two types of databases; nevertheless, you do not use them in even remotely similar manners. There are several types of collections. The default collection type is expandable in size: the more data you add to it, the larger it becomes. There are also collections available that are *capped.* These *capped collections* can only contain a certain amount of data before the oldest document gets replaced by a newer document (you will learn more about these collections in Chapter 4).

Every collection in MongoDB has a unique name. This name should begin with a letter, or optionally, an underscore (_) when created using the `createCollection` function. The name can contain numbers and letters; however, the $ symbol is reserved by MongoDB. Generally, it's recommended that you keep the collection's name simple and short (to around nine characters or so); however, the maximum number of allowed characters in a collection name is 128. Obviously, there isn't much practical reason to create such a long name.

A single database has a default limit of 24,000 namespaces per database. Each collection accounts for at least two namespaces: one for the collection itself and one more for the first index created in the collection. If you were to add more indexes per collection, however, another namespace would be used. In theory, this means that each database can have up to 12,000 collections by default, assuming each collection only carries one index. However, this limit on the number of namespaces can be increased by providing the `nssize` parameter when executing the MongoDB service application (*mongod*).

## Using Documents

Recall that a document consists of key-value pairs. For example, the pair `"type" : "Book"` consists of a key named `type`, and its value, `Book`. Keys are written as *strings*, but the values in them can vary tremendously. Values can be any of a rich set of datatypes, such as arrays or even binary data. Remember: MongoDB stores its data in BSON format (see Chapter 1 for more information on this topic).

Next, let's look at the other possible types of data you can add to a document, and what you use them for:

- *String*: This commonly used datatype contains a string of text (or any other kind of characters). This datatype is used mostly for storing text values (e.g., `"Country" : "Japan"`}.
- *Integer (32b and 64b)*: This type is used to store a numerical value (e.g., `{ "Rank" : 1 }` ). Note that there are no quotes placed before or after the integer.
- *Boolean*: This datatype can be set to either `TRUE` or `FALSE`.
- *Double*: This datatype is used to store floating point values.
- *Min / Max keys*: This datatype is used to compare a value against the lowest and highest BSON elements, respectively.
- *Arrays*: This datatype is used to store arrays (e.g., `["Membrey, Peter","Plugge, Eelco","Hawkins, Tim"]`).
- *Timestamp*: This datatype is used to store a timestamp. This can be handy for recording when a document has been modified or added.
- *Object*: This datatype is used for embedded documents.
- *Null*: This datatype is used for a `Null` value.
- *Symbol*: This datatype is used identically to a string (see above); however, it's generally reserved for languages that use a specific symbol type.
- *Date **: This datatype is used to store the current date or time in UNIX time format (POSIX time).
- *Object ID **: This datatype is used to store the document's ID.
- *Binary data **: This datatype is used to store binary data.

- *Regular expression* *: This datatype is used for regular expressions. All options are represented by specific characters provided in alphabetical order. You will learn more about regular expressions in Chapter 4.
- *JavaScript Code* *: This datatype is used for JavaScript code.

The last five datatypes (date, object id, binary data, regex, and JavaScript code) are non-JSON datatypes; specifically, they are special datatypes that BSON allows you to use. In Chapter 4, you will learn how to identify your datatypes by using the `$type` operator.

In theory, this all probably sounds straightforward. However, you might wonder how you go about actually "designing" the document itself, including what information to put in it. Because a document can contain any type of data, you might think there is no need to reference information from inside another document. In the next section, we'll look at the pros and cons of embedding information in a document vs. referencing that information from another document.

## Embedding vs. Referencing Information in Documents

You can choose either to embed information into a document or reference that information in another document. Embedding information simply means that you place a certain type of data (e.g., an array containing more data) into the document itself. Referencing information simply means that you create a reference to another document that contains that specific data. Typically, you reference information when you use a relational database. For example, assume you wanted to use a relational database to keep track of your CDs, DVDs, and books. In this database, you might have one table for your CD collection and another table that stores the tracklists of your CDs. Thus, you would probably need to query multiple tables to acquire a list of tracks from a specific CD.

With MongoDB (and other non-relational databases), however, it would be much easier to embed such information instead. After all, the documents are natively capable of doing so. Adopting this approach keeps your database nice and tidy, ensures that all related information is kept in one single document, and even works much faster because the data is then co-located on the disk.

Now let's look at the differences between embedding and referencing information by looking at a real-world scenario: storing CD data in a database.

In the relational approach, your data structure might look something like this:

```
|_media
    |_cds
        |_id, artist, title, genre, releasedate
    |_ cd_tracklists
        |_cd_id, songtitle, length
```

In the non-relational approach, your data structure might look something like this:

```
|_media
    |_items
        |_<document>
```

In the non-relational approach, the document might look something like the following:

```
{
    "Type": "CD",
    "Artist": "Nirvana",
```

```
    "Title": "Nevermind",
    "Genre": "Grunge",
    "Releasedate": "1991.09.24",
    "Tracklist": [
        {
        "Track" : "1",
        "Title" : "Smells Like Teen Spirit",
        "Length" : "5:02"
        },
        {
        "Track" : "2",
        "Title" : "In Bloom",
        "Length" : "4:15"
        }
    ]
}
```

In the preceding example, the tracklist information is actually embedded in the document itself. This approach is both incredibly efficient and well organized. All the information that you wish to store regarding this CD is added to a single document. In the relational version of the CD database, this requires at least two tables; in the non-relational database, this requires only one collection and one document.

When retrieving information for a given CD, the information only needs to be loaded from one document into RAM, not from multiple documents. Remember that every reference requires another query in the database.

---

**Tip** The rule of the thumb when using MongoDB is to embed data whenever you can. This approach is far more efficient and almost always viable.

---

At this point, you might be wondering about the use case where an application has multiple users. Generally speaking, a relational database version of the aforementioned CD app would require that you have one table that contains all your users and two tables for the items added. For a non-relational database, it would be good practice to have separate collections for the users and the items added. For these kinds of problems, MongoDB allows you to create references in two ways: manually or automatically. In the latter case, you use the DBRef specification, which provides more flexibility in case a collection changes from one document to the next. You will learn more about these two approaches in Chapter 4.

## Creating the _id Field

Every object within the MongoDB database contains a unique identifier to distinguish that object from every other object. This unique identifier is called the `_id` key, and it is added automatically to every document you create in a collection.

The `_id` key is the first attribute added in each new document you create. This remains true even if you do not tell MongoDB to create this key. For example, none of the code in the preceding examples used the `_id` key. Nevertheless, MongoDB created an `_id` key for you automatically in each document. It did so because `_id` key is a mandatory element for each document in the collection.

If you do not specify the `_id` value manually, then the type will be set to a special BSON datatype that consists of a 12-byte binary value. Due to its design, this value has a reasonably high probability of being unique. The 12-byte value consist of a 4-byte timestamp (seconds since epoch), a 3-byte machine id, a 2-byte process id, and a 3-byte counter. It's good to know that the `counter` and timestamp fields are stored in *Big Endian*. This is because MongoDB wants to ensure that there is an increasing order to these values, and a Big Endian approach suits this requirement best.

---

■ **Note** Big Endian and Little Endian refer to how each individual bytes/bits are stored in a longer data word in the memory. Big Endian simply means that the highest value gets saved first. Similarly, Little Endian means that the smallest value gets saved first.

---

Figure 3–3 shows how the value of the `_id` key is built up and where the values come from.

| | | | | | | | | | | | |
|---|---|---|---|---|---|---|---|---|---|---|---|
| 0 | 1 | 2 | 3 | 4 | 5 | 6 | 7 | 8 | 9 | 10 | 11 |
| Time | | | | machine | | | Pid | | inc | | |

***Figure 3–3.*** *Creating the _id key in MongoDB*

Every additional supported driver that you load when working with MongoDB (such as the PHP driver or the Python driver) supports this special BSON datatype and uses it whenever new data is created. You can also invoke `ObjectId()` from the MongoDB shell to create a value for an `_id` key. Optionally, you can specify your own value by using `ObjectId(string)`, where string represents the specified hex string.

# Building Indexes

As mentioned in Chapter 1, an index is nothing more than a data structure that collects information about the values of specified fields in the documents of a collection. This data structure is used by MongoDB's query optimizer to quickly sort through and order the documents in a collection.

Remember that indexing ensures a quick lookup from data in your documents. Basically, you should view an index as a predefined query that was executed and had its results stored. As you can imagine, this enhances query-performance dramatically. The general rule of the thumb in MongoDB is that you should create an index for the same sort of scenarios where you would want to have an index in MySQL.

The biggest benefit of creating your own indexes is that querying for often-used information will be incredibly fast because your query won't need to go through your entire database to collect this information.

Creating (or deleting) an index is relatively easy—once you get the hang of it, anyway. You will learn how to do so in Chapter 4, which covers how to work with data. You will also learn some more advanced techniques for taking advantage of indexing in Chapter 10, which covers how to maximize performance.

## Impacting Performance with Indexes

You might wonder why you would ever need to delete an index, rebuild your indexes, or even delete all indexes within a collection. The simple answer is that doing so lets you clean up some irregularities. For instance, sometimes the size of a database can increase dramatically for no apparent reason. Other times, the space used by the indexes might strike you as excessive.

Another good thing to keep in mind: you can have a maximum of 40 indexes per collection. Generally speaking, this is way more than you should need, but you could potentially hit this limit someday.

---

▒ **Note** Adding an index increases query speed, but reduces insertion or deletion speed. It's best to consider only adding indexes for collections where the number of reads is higher than the number of writes. When more writes occur than reads, indexes may even prove to be counterproductive.

---

Finally, all index information is stored in the `system.indexes` collection in your database. For example, you can run the `indexes.find()` command to take a quick peek at the indexes that have been stored so far. The following line shows the sample data that has been added by default:

```
db.systems.indexes.find()
```

# Implementing Geospatial Indexing

As was briefly mentioned in Chapter 1, MongoDB has implemented *Geospatial Indexing* since version 1.4. This means that, in addition to normal indexes, MongoDB also supports two-dimensional geospatial indexes that are designed to work in an optimal way with location-based queries. For example, you can use this feature to find a number of closest known items to your current location. Or you might further refine your search to query for a specified number of restaurants near your current location. This type of query can be particularly helpful if you are designing an application where you want to find the closest available branch office to a given customer's zipcode.

A document for which you want to add geospatial information must contain either a subobject or an array where the first two elements contain the x and y coordinates (or `y,x`), as in the following example:

```
{ loc : { lat : 52.033475, long: 5.099222 } }
```

Once the preceding information is added to a document, you can create the index (or even create the index beforehand, of course) and give the `ensureIndex()` function the `2d` parameter:

```
> db.places.ensureIndex( { loc: "2d" } )
```

---

▒ **Note** The ensureIndex() function is used to add a custom index. Don't worry about the syntax of this function at this time—you will learn how to use this function in depth in the next chapter.

---

The 2d parameter tells ensureIndex() that it's indexing a coordinate or some other form of two-dimensional information. By default, ensureindex() assumes that a latitude/longitude key is given, and it uses a range of -180 to 180. However, you can overwrite these values using the min / max parameters:

```
> db.places.ensureIndex( { loc: "2d" }, { min : -500 , max : 500 } )
```

---

■ **Warning** At this time, you cannot insert values at the defined boundaries. For example, you cannot insert values such as (-180 -180) in the default boundaries or (-500 -500) in the example that used the min / max parameters.

---

You can also expand your geospatial indexes by using *secondary key* values (also known as *compound keys*). This can be useful when you intend to query on multiple values, such as a location (geospatial information) and a category (sort ascending):

```
> db.places ensureIndex( { loc: "2d", category: 1 } )
```

---

■ **Note** At this time, the geospatial implementation is based on the idea that the world is perfectly flat. Thus, each degree of latitude and longitude is exactly 111km (69 miles) in length. However, this is only true exactly at the equator; the further you move away from the equator, the smaller the longitude becomes, approaching zero at the poles.

---

## Querying Geospatial Information

In this chapter, we are concerned primarily with two things: how to model the data and how a database works in the background of an application. That said, manipulating geospatial information is increasingly important in a wide variety of applications, so we'll take a few moments to explain how to leverage geospatial information in a MongoDB database.

Once you've added data to your collection, and once the index has been created, you can do a geospatial query. For example, let's look at a few lines of simple yet powerful code that demonstrate how to use geospatial indexing.

Begin by starting up your MongoDB shell and selecting a database with the use function. In this case, the database is named stores:

```
> use stores
```

Once you've selected the database, you can define a few documents that contain geospatial information, and then insert them into the places collection (remember: you do not need to create the collection beforehand):

```
> db.places.insert( { name: "Su Shi's Sushi", loc: [52.12345, 6.749923] } )

> db.places.insert( { name: "Shi Su's Sushi", loc: [51.12345, 6.249923] } )
```

After you add the data, you need to tell the MongoDB shell to create an index based on the location information that was specified in the loc key, as in this example:

```
> db.places.ensureIndex ( { loc: "2d" } )
```

Once the index has been created, you can start searching for your documents. Begin by searching on an exact value (so far this is a "normal" query; it has nothing to do with the geospatial information at this point):

```
> db.places.find( { loc : [52,6] } )
>
```

The preceding search returns no results. This is because the query is *too* specific. A better approach in this case would be to search for documents that contain information *near* a given value. You can accomplish this using the $near operator, as in the following example:

```
> db.places.find( { loc : { $near : [52,6] } } )
{
    "_id" : ObjectId("4bc2de69b2571f7d62ee30a6"),
    "name" : "Su Shi's Sushi",
    "loc" : [ 52.12345, 6.749923 ]
}
{
    "_id" : ObjectId("4bc2de7cb2571f7d62ee30a7"),
    "name" : "Shi Su's Sushi",
    "loc" : [ 51.12345, 6.249923 ]
}
```

This set of results looks better. Using the $near operator causes the find() function to look for anything close to the coordinates of 52 and 6; the results are sorted by their distance from the point specified by the $near operator. The default output will be limited to one hundred results. If you feel this number is too few, then you can append the limit function to your query, as in this example:

```
> db.places.find( { loc : { $near : [52,6] } } ).limit(200)
```

---

**Note** There is a direct correlation between the number of results returned and how long a given query will take to execute.

---

In addition to the $near operator, MongoDB also includes a $within operator. You use this operator to find items in a particular shape. At this time, you can find items located in a $box or $center shape, where $box represents a rectangle and $center represents a circle. Let's look at a couple additional examples that illustrate how to use these shapes.

To use the $box shape, you first need to specify the lower-left and the upper-right corners of the box, and then save these values into a variable. For example, the first line in the following code snippet stores the values in a variable called box, while the second line executes the query:

```
> box = [[40, 60], [4, 8]]
> db.places.find( { loc: { $within : { $box : box } } } )
```

The code to find in items in a $circle shape looks quite similar. In this case, you need to specify the center of the circle and its radius before executing the find() function:

```
> center = [50, 15]
> radius = 10
> db.places.find( { loc: { $within : { $center : [center, radius] } } } )
```

By default, the find() function is ideal for running queries. However, MongoDB also provides the geoNear() function, which functions like the find() function, but also displays the distance from the specified point for each item in the results. The geoNear() function also includes some additional diagnostics. The following example uses the geoNear() function to find the two closest results to the specified position:

```
> db.runCommand( { geoNear : "places", near : [52,6], num : 2 } )
{
    "ns" : "stores.places",
    "near" : "1100100000110000101110101001100000110000101110101001",
    "results" : [
        {
            "dis" : 0.7600121516405387,
            "obj" : {
                "_id" : ObjectId("4bc2de69b2571f7d62ee30a6"),
                "name" : "Su Shi's Sushi",
                "loc" : [
                        52.12345,
                        6.749923
                    ]
            }
        },
        {
            "dis" : 0.911484268395441,
            "obj" : {
                "_id" : ObjectId("4bc2de7cb2571f7d62ee30a7"),
                "name" : "Shi Su's Sushi",
                "loc" : [
                    51.12345,
                    6.249923
                ]
            }
        }
    ],
    "stats" : {
        "time" : 0,
        "btreelocs" : 2,
        "nscanned" : 2,
        "objectsLoaded" : 2,
        "avgDistance" : 0.8357482100179898
    },
    "ok" : 1
}
```

That's all on this topic for now; however, you'll see a few more examples that show you how to leverage geospatial functions in this book's upcoming chapters.

# Using MongoDB in the Real World

Now that you have MongoDB and its associated plug-ins installed, as well as having gained an understanding of the data model, it's time to get to work. In the remainder of the book, you will learn how to build, query, and otherwise manipulate a variety of sample MongoDB databases (see Table 3–1 for a quick view of the topics to come). Each chapter will stick primarily to using a single database that is unique to that chapter; we took this approach to make it easier to read this book in a modular fashion.

***Table 3–1.*** *MongoDB Sample Databases Covered in This Book*

| Chapter | Database Name | Topic |
|---|---|---|
| 4 | `library` | Working with data and indexes |
| 5 | `Test` | GridFS |
| 6 | `contacts` | PHP and MongoDB |
| 7 | `Inventory` | Python and MongoDB |
| 8 | `blog` | Blogs |
| 9 | `blog` | Database administration |
| 10 | `blog` | Optimization |
| 11 | `blog` | Replication |
| 12 | `blog` | Sharding |

# Summary

In this chapter, we looked at what's happening in the background of your database. We also explored the primary concepts of collections and documents in more depth; and we covered the datatypes supported in MongoDB, as well as how to embed data and reference data.

Next, we covered what indexes do, including when and why they should be used (or not).

We also touched on the concepts of geospatial indexing. For example, we covered how geospatial data can be stored; we also explained how you can search for such data using either the regular `find()` function or the more geospatially based `geoNear` database command.

In the next chapter, we'll take a closer look at how the MongoDB shell works, including which functions can be used to insert, find, update, or delete your data. We will also explore how conditional operators can help you with all of these functions.

CHAPTER 4

# Working with Data

In the previous chapter, you learned how the database works on the backend, what indexes are, how to use a database to quickly find the data you are looking for, and what the structure of a document looks like. You also saw a brief example that illustrated how to add data and find it again using the MongoDB shell. In this chapter, we will focus more on working with the data from your shell.

We will use one database (named `library`) throughout this chapter, and we will performactions such as adding data, searching data, modifying data, deleting data, and creating indexes. We'll also look at how to navigate the database using various commands, as well as what DBRef is and what it does. If you have followed the instructions in the previous chapters to set up the MongoDB software, you can follow the examples in this chapter to get used to the interface. Along the way, you will also attain a solid understanding of which commands can be used for what kind of operations.

## Navigating Your Databases

The first thing you need to know is how to navigate your databases and collections. With traditional SQL databases, the first thing you would need to do is to create an actual database; however, as you probably remember from the previous chapters, this is not required with MongoDB because the program creates the database and underlying collection for you automatically the moment you store data in it.

To switch to an existing database or create a new one, you can use the `use` function in the shell, followed by the name of the database you would like to use, whether it exists or not. This snippet shows you how to use the `library` database:

```
> use library
Switched to db library
```

The mere act of invoking the `use` function, followed by the database's name, sets your `db` (database) global variable to `library`. Doing this means that all the commands you pass down into the shell will automatically assume they need to be executed on the `library` database until you reset this variable to another database.

### Viewing Available Databases and Collections

MongoDB automatically assumes a database needs to be created the moment you save data to it. It is also case-sensitive. For these reasons, it can be quite tricky to ensure that you're working in the correct database. Therefore, it's best to view a list of all current databases available to MongoDB prior to switching to one, in case you forgot the database's name or its exact spelling. You can do this using the `show dbs` function:

```
> show dbs
admin
local
```

Note that this function will only show a database that already exists. At this stage, the database does not contain any data yet, so nothing else will be listed. If you want to view all available collections for your current database, you can use the `show collections` function:

```
> show collections
system.indexes
```

Note that the `system.indexes` collection gets created automatically the moment data is saved. This collection contains an index based on the `_id` key value from the document just inserted; it also includes any custom-created indexes that you've defined.

---

**Tip** To view the database you are currently working in, simply type `db` into the MongoDB shell.

---

# Inserting Data into Collections

One of the most frequently used pieces of functionality you will want to learn about is how to insert data into your collection. All data is stored in BSON-format (which is both compact and reasonably fast to scan), so you will need to insert the data in BSON-format as well. You can do this in several ways. For example, you can define it first, and then save it in the collection using the `insert` function, or you can type the document while using the `insert` function on the fly:

```
> document = ( { "Type" : "Book", "Title" : "Definitive Guide to MongoDB,
the", "ISBN" : "987-1-4302-3051-9", "Publisher" : "Apress", "Author": [
"Membrey, Peter", "Plugge, Eelco", "Hawkins, Tim" ] } )

> db.media.insert(document)
```

Linebreaks can also be used while typing in the shell. This can be convenient if you are writing a rather lengthy document, as in this example:

```
> document = ( { "Type" : "Book",
..."Title" : "Definitive Guide to MongoDB, the",
..."ISBN" : "987-1-4302-3051-9",
..."Publisher" : "Apress",
..."Author" : ["Membrey, Peter","Plugge, Eelco","Hawkins, Tim"]
...} )

> db.media.insert(document)
```

As mentioned, the other option is to insert your data directly through the shell, without defining the document first. You can do this by invoking the **insert** function straight away, followed by the document's contents:

```
> db.media.insert( { "Type" : "CD", "Artist" : "Nirvana", "Title" : "Nevermind" })
```

Or you can insert the data while using linebreaks, as before. For example, you can expand the preceding example by adding an array of tracks to it. Pay close attention to how the commas and brackets are used in the following example:

```
> db.media.insert( { "Type" : "CD",
..."Artist" : "Nirvana",
..."Title" : "Nevermind",
... "Tracklist" : [
... {
... "Track" : "1",
... "Title" : "Smells like teen spirit",
... "Length" : "5:02"
... },
... {
... "Track" : "2",
... "Title" : "In Bloom",
... "Length" : "4:15"
... }
... ]
...}
... )
```

As you can see, inserting data through the Mongo shell is straightforward.

The process of inserting data is extremely flexible, but you must adhere to some rules when doing so. For example, the names of the keys while inserting documents have the following limitations:

- The $ character must not be the first character in the key name. Example: $tags
- The period [.] character must not appear anywhere in the key name. Example: ta.gs
- The name `_id` is reserved for use as a primary key ID; although it is not recommended, it can store anything unique as a value, such as a string or an integer.

# Querying for Data

You've seen how to switch to your database and how to insert data; next, you will learn how to query for data in your collection. Let's build on the preceding example and look at all the possible ways to get a good clear view of your data that is in a given collection.

---

**Note** When querying your data, you have an extraordinary amount of options, operators, expressions, filters, and so on available to you. We will spend the next few sections reviewing these options.

---

The `find()` function provides the easiest way to retrieve data from multiple documents within one of your collections. This function is one that you will be using often.

Let's assume that you have inserted the preceding two examples into a collection called `media` in the `library` database. If you were to use a dead-simple `find()` function on this collection, you would get all of the documents you've added so far printed out for you:

```
> db.media.find()
{ "_id" : "ObjectId("4c1a8a56c603000000007ecb"), "Type" : "Book", "Title" :
"Definitive Guide to MongoDB, the", "ISBN" : "987-4302-3051-9", "Publisher" :
"Apress", "Author" : ["Membrey, Peter", "Plugge, Eelco", "Hawkins, Tim"] }

{ "_id" : "ObjectId("4c1a86bb2955000000004076"), "Type" : "CD", "Artist" :
"Nirvana", "Title" : "Nevermind", "Tracklist" : [
    {
        "Track" : "1",
            "Title" : "Smells like teen spirit",
            "Length" : "5:02"
    },
    {
        "Track" : "2",
        "Title" : "In Bloom",
        "Length" : "4:15"
    }
] }
```

This is simple stuff, but typically you would not want to retrieve all the information back from all the documents in your collection. Instead, you probably want to retrieve a certain type of document. For example, you might want to return all the CDs from Nirvana. If so, you can specify that only the desired information is requested and returned:

```
> db.media.find ( { Artist : "Nirvana" } )
{ "_id" : "ObjectId("4c1a86bb2955000000004076"), "Type" : "CD", "Artist" :
 "Nirvana", "Title" : "Nevermind", "Tracklist" : [
    {
        "Track" : "1",
        "Title" : "Smells like teen spirit",
        "Length" : "5:02"
    },
    {
        "Track" : "2",
        "Title" : "In Bloom",
        "Length" : "4:15"
    }
] }
```

Okay, so the preceding looks much better! You don't have to see all the information from all the other items you've added to your collection, but only the information that interests you. However, what if you're still not satisfied with the results returned? For example, assume you want to get a list back that shows only the titles of the CDs you have by Nirvana, ignoring any other information, such as tracklists. You can do this by inserting an additional parameter into your query that specifies the name of the key that you want to return, followed by a `1`:

```
> db.media.find ( {Artist : "Nirvana"}, {Title: 1} )
{ "_id" : ObjectId("4c1a86bb2955000000004076"), "Title" : "Nevermind" }
```

Inserting the `{ Title : 1 }` information specifies that only the information from the title field should be returned. The results are sorted and presented to you in ascending order.

---

■ **Tip** The ascending order is based upon the insertion order of the document.

---

You can also accomplish the opposite: inserting { `Type : 0` } retrieves a list of all items you have stored from Nirvana, showing all information except for the `Type` field.

---

■ **Note** The `_id` field will always remain visible: even when asked to not show itself.

---

Take a moment to run the revised query with the { `Title : 1` } insertion; no unnecessary information is returned at all. This saves you time because you see only the information you want to know. It also spares your database the time required to return unnecessary information.

## Using the Dot Notation

When you start working with more complex document structures such as documents containing arrays or embedded objects, you can begin using other methods for querying information from those objects as well. For example, assume you want to find all CDs that contain a specific song you like. The following code executes a more detailed query:

```
> db.media.find( { "Tracklist.Title" : "In Bloom" } )
{ "_id" : "ObjectId("4c1a86bb2955000000004076"), "Type" : "CD", "Artist" :
"Nirvana", "Title" : "Nevermind", "Tracklist" : [
    {
        "Track" : "1",
        "Title" : "Smells like teen spirit",
        "Length" : "5:02"
    },
    {
        "Track" : "2",
        "Title" : "In Bloom",
        "Length" : "4:15"
    }
] }
```

Using a period [`.`] after the key's name tells your find function to look for information embedded in your documents. Things are a little simpler when working with arrays. For example, you can execute the following query if you want to find a list of books written by Peter Membrey:

```
> db.media.find( { "Author" : "Membrey, Peter" } )
{ "_id" : "ObjectId("4c1a8a56c603000000007ecb"), "Type" : "Book", "Title" :
"Definitive Guide to MongoDB, the", "ISBN" : "987-4302-3051-9", "Publisher" :
"Apress", "Author" : ["Membrey, Peter", "Plugge, Eelco", "Hawkins, Tim"] }
```

However, the following command will not match any documents, even though it might appear identical to the earlier tracklist query:

```
> db.media.find ( { "Tracklist" : {"Track" : "1" }} )
```

Subobjects must match exactly; therefore, the preceding query would only match a document that contains no other information, such as `Track.Title`:

```
{"Type" : "CD",
"Artist" : "Nirvana"
"Title" : "Nevermind",
"Tracklist" : [
    {
        "Track" : "1",
    },
    {
        "Track" : "2",
        "Title" : "In Bloom",
        "Length" : "4:15"
    }
]
}
```

# Using the Sort, Limit, and Skip Functions

MongoDB includes several functions that you can use to give you more precise control over your queries. We'll cover how to use the `sort`, `limit`, and `skip` functions in this section.

You can use the `sort` function to sort the results returned from a query. You can sort the results in ascending or descending order using `1` or `-1`, respectively. The function itself is analogous to the `ORDER BY` statement in SQL, and it uses the key's name and sorting method as criteria, as in this example:

```
> db.media.find().sort( { Title: 1 })
```

The preceding example sorts the results based on the `Title` key's value in ascending order. This is the default sorting order when no parameters are specified. You would add the `-1` flag to sort in descending order.

---

**Note** If you specify a key for sorting that does not exist, the values will be returned in their ascending insertion order.

---

You can use the `limit()` function to specify the maximum number of results returned. This function requires only one parameter: the number of the desired results returned. The following example returns only the first ten items in your media collection:

```
> db.media.find().limit( 10 )
```

Another thing you might want to do is skip the first *n* number of documents in your collection. The following example skips the first twenty documents in your media collection:

```
> db.media.find().skip( 20 )
```

As you probably surmised, the preceding command returns all documents within your collection, except for the first twenty it finds. Remember: it finds documents in the order they were inserted.

MongoDB wouldn't be particularly powerful if it weren't able to combine these commands. However, practically any function can be combined and used in conjunction with any other function. The following example limits the results by skipping a few and then sorts the results in descending order:

```
> db.media.find().sort ( { Title : -1 } ).limit ( 10 ).skip ( 20 )
```

You might use the preceding example if you want to implement paging in your application. As you might have guessed, the preceding example wouldn't return any results in the media collection created so far because it contains fewer documents than were skipped in this example.

---

■ **Note** You can use the following shortcut in the `find()` function to skip and limit your results: `find ( {}, {}, 10, 20 )`. Here, you limit the results to 10 and skip the first 20 documents.

---

## Working with Capped Collections, Natural Order, and $natural

There are some additional concepts and features you should be aware of when sorting queries with MongoDB, including capped collections, natural order, and $natural. We'll explain what all of these terms mean and how you can leverage them in your sorts in this section.

The *natural order* is the database's native ordering method for objects within a (normal) collection. So, when you query for items in a collection, the items are returned by default in the *forward natural order*. This is usually identical to the order items were inserted; however, this is not guaranteed to be the case, as data can move when it doesn't fit on its old location anymore after being modified.

A *capped collection* is a collection in your database where the natural order is guaranteed to be the order the documents were inserted. Guaranteeing that the natural order will always match the insertion order can be particularly useful when you're querying data and need to be absolutely certain that the results returned are already sorted based on the order they were inserted.

Capped collections have another great benefit: they are a fixed size. Once they are full, the oldest data will be purged, and newer data will be added at the end, ensuring that the natural order follows the order the records were inserted. These kinds of collections can be used for logging data, and auto-archiving data.

Unlike with a standard collection, you must create a capped collection explicitly using the `createCollection` function. You must also supply parameters that specify the size (in bytes) of the collection you want to add. For example, imagine you want to create a capped collection named `audit` with a maximum size of 20480 bytes:

```
> db.createCollection("audit", {capped:true, size:20480})
{ "ok" : 1 }
```

Given that a capped collection guarantees that the natural order matches the insertion order, you don't need to include any special parameters or any other special commands or functions when querying the data either, except of course when you want to reverse the default results. This is where the $natural parameter comes in. For example, assume you want to find the ten *most recent* entries from your capped collection that lists failed login attempts. You could use the `$natural` parameter to find this information:

```
> db.audit.find().sort( { $natural: -1 } ).limit ( 10 )
```

---

▒ **Note** Documents already added to a capped collection can be updated, but they must not grow in size. The update will fail if they do. Deleting documents from a capped collection is also not possible; instead, the entire collection must be dropped and re-created if you want to do this. You will learn more about dropping a collection later in this chapter.

---

You can also limit the number of items added into a capped collection using the `max:` parameter when you create the collection. However, you must take care that you ensure that there is enough space in the collection for the number of items you want to add. If the collection becomes full before the number of items has been reached, the oldest item in the collection will be removed. The MongoDB shell includes a utility that lets you see the amount of space used by an existing collection, whether it's capped or uncapped. You invoke this utility using the `validate()` function. This can be particularly useful if you want to estimate how large a collection might become.

As stated previously, you can use the `max:` parameter to cap the number of items that can be inserted into a collection, as in this example:

```
> db.createCollection("audit100", { capped:true, size:20480, max: 100})
{ "ok" : 1 }
```

Next, use the `validate()` function to check the size of the collection:

```
> db.audit100.validate()
{
    "ns" : "media.audit100",
    "result" : "
        validate
        capped:1 max:100
        firstExtent:0:54000 ns:media.audit100
        lastExtent:0:54000 ns:media.audit100
        # extents:1
        datasize?:0 nrecords?:0 lastExtentSize:20736
        padding:1
        first extent:
        loc:0:54000 xnext:null xprev:null
        nsdiag:media.audit100
        size:20736 firstRecord:null lastRecord:null
        capped outOfOrder:0 (OK)
        0 objects found, nobj:0
        0 bytes data w/headers
        0 bytes data wout/headers
        deletedList: 1100000000000000000
        deleted: n: 2 size: 20560
        nIndexes:0
    ",
    "ok" : 1,
    "valid" : true,
    "lastExtentSize" : 20736
}
```

The resulting output shows that the table (named "audit100") is a capped collection with a maximum of 100 items to be added, and currently contains zero items.

## Retrieving a Single Document

So far we've only looked at examples that show you how to retrieve multiple documents. If you want to receive only one result, however, querying for all documents—which is what you generally do when executing a `find()` function—would be a waste of CPU time and memory. For this case, you can use the `findOne()` function to retrieve a single item from your collection. Overall, the result is identical to what occurs when you append the `limit(1)` function, but why make it harder on yourself than you should?

The syntax of the `findOne()` function is identical to the syntax of the find() function:

```
> db.media.findOne()
```

It's generally advised that you use the `findOne()` function if you expect only one result.

## Using the Aggregation Commands

MongoDB comes with a nice set of aggregation commands. You might not see their significance at first, but once you get the hang of them, you will see that the aggregation commands comprise an extremely powerful set of tools. For instance, you might use them to get an overview of some basic statistics about your database. In this section, we will take a closer look at how to use three of the functions from the available aggregate commands: `count`, `distinct`, and `group`.

### Returning the Number of Documents with Count()

The `count()` function returns the number of documents in the specified collection. So far we've added a number of documents in the *media* collection. The `count()` function can tell you exactly how many:

```
> db.media.count()
2
```

You can also perform additional filtering by combining `count()` with conditional operators, as in this example:

```
> db.media.find( { Publisher : "Apress", Type: "Book" } ).count()
1
```

The preceding example returns only the number of documents added in the collection that are published by Apress and of the type Book. Note that the `count()` function ignores a `skip()` or `limit()` parameter by default. To ensure that your query doesn't skip these parameters and that your count results will match the `limit` and/or `skip` parameters, use `count(true)`:

```
> db.media.find( { Publisher: "Apress", Type: "Book" }).skip ( 2 ) .count (true)
0
```

### Retrieving Unique Values with Distinct()

The preceding example shows a great way to retrieve the total number of documents from a specific publisher. However, this approach is definitely not precise. After all, if you own more than one book with the same title (for instance, the hardcopy and the e-Book), then you would technically have just one book. This is where `distinct()` can help you: it will only return unique values.

For the sake of completeness, you can add an additional item to the collection. This item carries the same title, but has a different ISBN number:

```
> document = ( { "Type" : "Book","Title" : "Definitive Guide to MongoDB, the", ISBN:
"1-4302-3051-7", "Publisher" : "Apress", "Author" :
["Membrey, Peter","Plugge, Eelco","Hawkins, Tim"] } )
> db.media.insert (document)
```

At this point, you should have two books in the database with identical titles. When using the `distinct()` function on the titles in this collection, you will get a total of two unique items. However, the titles of the two books are unique, so they will be grouped into one item. The other result will be the title of the album "Nevermind":

```
> db.media.distinct( "Title")
[ "Definitive Guide to MongoDB, the", "Nevermind" ]
```

Similarly, you will get two results if you query for a list of unique ISBN numbers:

```
> db.media.distinct ("ISBN")
[ "1-4302-3051-7", "987-4302-3051-9" ]
```

Distinct also takes nested keys when querying; for instance, this will give you a list of unique titles of your CDs:

```
> db.media.distinct ("Tracklist.Title")
[ "In Bloom", "Smells like teen spirit" ]
```

## Grouping Your Results

Last but not least, you can group your results. MongoDB's `group()` function is similar to the SQL's `GROUP BY` function, although the syntax is a little different. The purpose of the command is to return an array of grouped items. The group function takes three parameters: `key`, `initial`, and `reduce`.

The `key` parameter specifies which results you want to group. For example, assume you want to group results by `Title`. The `initial` parameter lets you provide a base for each grouped result (i.e., the base number of items to start off with). By default, you want to leave this parameter at zero if you want an exact number returned. The `reduce` parameter groups all similar items together. Reduce takes two arguments: the current document being iterated over and the aggregation counter object. These arguments are called `items` and `prev` in the example that follows. Essentially, the `reduce` parameter adds a `1` to the sum of every item it encounters that matches a title it has already found.

The `group()` function is ideal when you're looking for a *`tagcloud`* kind of function. For example, assume you want to obtain a list of all unique titles of *any* type of item in your collection. Additionally, assume you want to group them together if any doubles are found, based on the title:

```
> db.media.group (
{
    key: {Title : true},
    initial: {Total : 0},
    reduce : function (items,prev)
    {
        prev.Total += 1
    }
}
)

[
    {
```

```
        "Title" : "Nevermind",
        "Total" : 1
    },
    {
        "Title" : "Definitive Guide to MongoDB, the",
        "Total" : 2
    }
]
```

In addition to the key, initial, and reduce parameters, you can specify three more optional parameters:

- keyf: You can use this parameter to replace the key parameter if you do not wish to group the results on an existing key in your documents. Instead, you would group them using another function you design that specifies how to do grouping.
- cond: You can use this parameter to specify an additional statement that must be true before a document will be grouped. You can use this much as you use the find() query to search for documents in your collection. If this parameter isn't set (the default), then all documents in the collection will be checked.
- finalize: You can use this parameter to specify a function you want to execute before the final results are returned. For instance, you might calculate an average or perform a count and include this information in the results.

---

▒ **Note** The group() function does not currently work in sharded environments. For these, you should use the mapreduce() function instead. Also, the resulting output cannot contain more than 10,000 keys in all with the group() function, or an exception will be raised. This too, can be bypassed by using mapreduce().

---

# Working with Conditional Operators

MongoDB supports a large set of conditional operators to better filter your results. The following sections provide an overview of these operators, including some basic examples that show you how to use them. Before walking through these examples, however, you should add a few more items to the database; doing so will let you see the effects of these operators more plainly:

```
dvd = ( { "Type" : "DVD",       "Title" : "Matrix, The", "Released" : 1999,
    "Cast" : ["Keanu  Reeves","Carry-Anne Moss","Laurence Fishburne","Hugo
     Weaving","Gloria Foster","Joe Pantoliano"] } )
{
        "Type" : "DVD",
        "Title" : "Matrix, The",
        "Released" : 1999,
        "Cast" : [
                "Keanu Reeves",
                "Carry-Anne Moss",
                "Laurence Fishburne",
                "Hugo Weaving",
                "Gloria Foster",
                "Joe Pantoliano"
        ]
```

```
}
> db.media.insert(dvd)

> dvd = ( { "Type" : "DVD", Title : "Blade Runner", Released : 1982 } )
{ "Type" : "DVD", "Title" : "Blade Runner", "Released" : 1982 }
> db.media.insert(dvd)

> dvd = ( { "Type" : "DVD", Title : "Toy Story 3", Released : 2010 } )
{ "Type" : "DVD", "Title" : "Toy Story 3", "Released" : 2010 }
> db.media.insert(dvd)
```

## Performing Greater and Less Than Comparisons

You can use the following special parameters to perform greater than and less than comparisons in queries: $gt, $lt, $gte, and $lte. In this section, we'll look at how to use each of these parameters.

The first one we'll cover is the $gt (greater than) parameter. You can use this to specify that a certain integer should be greater than a specified value in order to be returned:

```
> db.media.find ( { Released : {$gt : 2000} }, { "Cast" : 0 } )
{ "_id" : ObjectId("4c4369a3c603000000007ed3"), "Type" : "DVD", "Title" :
"Toy Story 3", "Released" : 2010 }
```

Note that the year 2000 itself will not be included in the preceding query. For that, you use the $gte (greater than or equal to) parameter:

```
> db.media.find ( { Released : {$gte : 1999 } }, { "Cast" : 0 } )
{ "_id" : ObjectId("4c43694bc603000000007ed1"), "Type" : "DVD", "Title" :
"Matrix, The", "Released" : 1999 }
{ "_id" : ObjectId("4c4369a3c603000000007ed3"), "Type" : "DVD", "Title" :
"Toy Story 3", "Released" : 2010 }
```

Likewise, you can use the $lt (less than) parameter to find items in your collection that predate the year 1999:

```
> db.media.find ( { Released : {$lt : 1999 } }, { "Cast" : 0 } )
{ "_id" : ObjectId("4c436969c603000000007ed2"), "Type" : "DVD", "Title" : "Blade Runner",
"Released" : 1982 }
```

You can also get a list of items older than or equal to the year 1999 by using the $lte (less than or equal to) parameter:

```
> db.media.find( {Released : {$lte: 1999}}, { "Cast" : 0 })
{ "_id" : ObjectId("4c43694bc603000000007ed1"), "Type" : "DVD", "Title" :
"Matrix, The", "Released" : 1999 }
{ "_id" : ObjectId("4c436969c603000000007ed2"), "Type" : "DVD", "Title" :
"Blade Runner", "Released" : 1982 }
```

You can also combine these parameters together to specify a range:

```
> db.media.find( {Released : {$gte: 1990, $lt : 2010}}, { "Cast" : 0 })
{ "_id" : ObjectId("4c43694bc603000000007ed1"), "Type" : "DVD", "Title" :
"Matrix, The", "Released" : 1999 }
```

These parameters might strike you as relatively simple to use; however, you will be using them a lot when querying for a specific range of data.

## Retrieving All Documents but Those Specified

You can use the $ne (not equals) parameter to retrieve every document in your collection, except for the ones that match certain criteria. For example, you can use this snippet to obtain a list of all books where the author is not Eelco Plugge:

```
> db.media.find( { Type : "Book", Author: {$ne : "Plugge, Eelco"})
```

## Specifying an Array of Matches

You can use the $in operator to specify an array of possible matches. The SQL equivalent is the IN operator.

You can use the following snippet to retrieve data from the media collection using the $in operator:

```
> db.media.find( {Released : {$in : ["1999","2008","2009"] } }, { "Cast" : 0 } )
{ "_id" : ObjectId("4c43694bc603000000007ed1"), "Type" : "DVD", "Title" : "Matrix, The",
"Released" : 1999 }
```

The preceding example returns only one item because only one item matches the release year of 1999, and there are no matches for the years 2008 and 2009.

## Finding a Value Not in an Array

The $nin operator functions similarly to the $in operator, except that it searches for the objects where the specified field does *not* have a value in the specified array:

```
> db.media.find( {Released : {$nin : ["1999","2008","2009"] },Type : "DVD" },
{ "Cast" : 0 } )
{ "_id" : ObjectId("4c436969c603000000007ed2"), "Type" : "DVD", "Title" :
"Blade Runner", "Released" : 1982 }
{ "_id" : ObjectId("4c4369a3c603000000007ed3"), "Type" : "DVD", "Title" :
"Toy Story 3", "Released" : 2010 }
```

## Matching all Attributes in a Document

The $all operator also works similarly to the $in operator. However, the $all operator requires that all attributes match in the documents, whereas only one attribute must match for the $in operator. Let's look at an example that illustrates these differences. First, here's an example that uses the $in operator:

```
> db.media.find ( { Released : {$in : ["2010","2009"] } }, { "Cast" : 0 } )
{ "_id" : ObjectId("4c4369a3c603000000007ed3"), "Type" : "DVD", "Title" :
"Toy Story 3", "Released" : 2010 }
```

One document is returned for the $in operator because there's a match for 2010, but not for 2009. However, the $all parameter doesn't return any results because there are no matching documents with 2009 in the value:

```
> db.media.find ( { Released : {$all : ["2010","2009"] } }, { "Cast" : 0 } )
```

## Searching for Multiple Expressions in a Document

You can use the $or operator to search for multiple expressions in a single query, where only one criterion needs to match to return a given document. Unlike the $in operator, the $or operator allows you to specify both the key and the value, rather than only the value:

```
> db.media.find({ $or : [ { "Title" : "Toy Story 3" }, { "ISBN" :
"987-1-4302-3051-9" } ] } )
{ "_id" : ObjectId("4c5fc7d8db290000000067c5"), "Type" : "Book", "Title" :
"Definitive Guide to MongoDB, the", "ISBN" : "987-1-4302-3051-9",
"Publisher" : "Apress", "Author" : [ "Membrey, Peter", "Plugge, Eelco",
"Hawkins, Tim" ] }
{ "_id" : ObjectId("4c5fc943db290000000067ca"), "Type" : "DVD", "Title" :
"Toy Story 3", "Released" : 2010 }
```

It's also possible to combine the $or operator with another query parameter. This will restrict the returned documents to only those that match the first query (mandatory), and then either of the two key/value pairs specified at the $or operator, as in this example:

```
> db.media.find({ "Type" : "DVD", $or : [ { "Title" : "Toy Story 3" }, {
"ISBN" : "987-1-4302-3051-9" } ] })
{ "_id" : ObjectId("4c5fc943db290000000067ca"), "Type" : "DVD", "Title" :
"Toy Story 3", "Released" : 2010 }
```

You could say that the $or operator allows you to perform two queries at the same time, combining the results of two otherwise unrelated queries.

## Retrieving a Document with $slice

You can use the $slice operator to retrieve a document that includes a specific area from an array in that document. This can be particularly useful if you want to limit a certain set of items added to save bandwidth. The operator also lets you retrieve the results on a *n* items per page basis. This is generally known as *paging.*

In theory, the $slice operator combines the capabilities of the limit() and skip() functions; however, limit() and skip()do not work on an array, whereas the $slice operator does. The operator takes two parameters. The first parameter indicates the total number of items to be returned. The second parameter is optional. If used, however, it ensures that the *first* parameter defines the offset, while the *second* defines the limit. The limit parameter can also indicate a negative condition.

The following example limits the items from the Cast list to only the first three items:

```
> db.media.find({"Title" : "Matrix, The"}, {"Cast" : {$slice: 3}})
{ "_id" : ObjectId("4c5fcd3edb290000000067cb"), "Type" : "DVD", "Title" :
"Matrix, The", "Released" : 1999, "Cast" : [ "Keanu Reeves", "Carry-Anne
Moss", "Laurence Fishburne" ] }
```

You can also get only the last three items by making the integer negative:

```
> db.media.find({"Title" : "Matrix, The"}, {"Cast" : {$slice: -3}})
{ "_id" : ObjectId("4c5fcd3edb290000000067cb"), "Type" : "DVD", "Title" :
"Matrix, The", "Released" : 1999, "Cast" : [ "Hugo Weaving", "Gloria Foster",
"Joe Pantoliano" ] }
```

Or you can skip the first two items and limit the results to three from that particular point (pay careful attention to the brackets):

```
> db.media.find({"Title" : "Matrix, The"}, {"Cast" : {$slice: [2,3] }})
{ "_id" : ObjectId("4c5fcd3edb290000000067cb"), "Type" : "DVD", "Title" :
"Matrix, The", "Released" : 1999, "Cast" : [ "Laurence Fishburne", "Hugo
Weaving", "Gloria Foster" ] }
```

Finally, when specifying a negative integer, you can skip to the last five items and limit the results to four, as in this example:

```
> db.media.find({"Title" : "Matrix, The"}, {"Cast" : {$slice: [-5,4] }})
{ "_id" : ObjectId("4c5fcd3edb290000000067cb"), "Type" : "DVD", "Title" :
"Matrix, The", "Released" : 1999, "Cast" : [ "Carry-Anne Moss","Laurence
Fishburne","Hugo Weaving","Gloria Foster"] }
```

## Searching for Odd/Even Integers

The $mod operator lets you search for specific data that consists of an even or uneven number. This works because the operator takes the modulus of 2 and checks for remainder of 0, thereby providing even-numbered results only.

For example, the following code returns any item in the collection that has an even-numbered integer set to its Released field:

```
> db.media.find ( { Released : { $mod: [2,0] } }, {"Cast" : 0 } )
{ "_id" : ObjectId("4c45b5c18e0f0000000062aa"), "Type" : "DVD", "Title" :
"Blade Runner", "Released" : 1982 }
{ "_id" : ObjectId("4c45b5df8e0f0000000062ab"), "Type" : "DVD", "Title" :
"Toy Story 3", "Released" : 2010 }
```

Likewise, you can find any documents containing an uneven value in the Released field by changing the parameters in $mod, as follows:

```
> db.media.find ( { Released : { $mod: [2,1] } }, { "Cast" : 0 } )
{ "_id" : ObjectId("4c45b5b38e0f0000000062a9"), "Type" : "DVD", "Title" :
"Matrix, the", "Released" : 1999 }
```

---

**Note** The $mod operator only works on integer values, not on strings that contain a numbered value. For example, you can't use the operator on { Released : "2010" } because it's in quotes and therefore a string.

---

## Filtering Results with $size

The $size operator lets you filter your results to match an array with the specified number of elements in it. For example, you might use this operator to do a search for those CDs that have exactly two songs on them:

```
> db.media.find ( { Tracklist : {$size : 2} } )
{ "_id" : ObjectId("4c1a86bb2955000000004076"), "Type" : "CD", "Artist" :
"Nirvana", "Title" : "Nevermind", "Tracklist" : [
        {
                "Track" : "1",
                "Title" : "Smells like teen spirit",
```

```
                "Lenght" : "5:02"
        },
        {
                "Track" : "2",
                "Title" : "In Bloom",
                "Length" : "4:15"
        }
] }
```

■ **Note** You cannot use the `$size` operator to find a range of sizes. For example, you cannot use it to find arrays with more than one element in them.

## Returning a Specific Field Object

The `$exists` operator allows you to return a specific object if a specified field is either missing or found. The following example returns all items in the collection with a key named `Author`:

```
> db.media.find ( { Author : {$exists : true } } )
```

Similarly, if you invoke this operator with a value of `false`, then all documents that don't have a key named `Author` will be returned:

```
> db.media.find ( { Author : {$exists : false } } )
```

■ **Warning** Currently, the `$exists` operator is unable to use an index; therefore, using it requires a full table scan.

## Matching Results Based on the BSON Type

The `$type` operator lets you match results based on their BSON type. For instance, the following snippet lets you find all items that have a tracklist of the type `Embedded Object` (i.e., it contains a list of information):

```
> db.media.find ( {  Tracklist: { $type : 3 } } )
{ "_id" : ObjectId("4c1a86bb2955000000004076"), "Type" : "CD", "Artist" :
"Nirvana", "Title" : "Nevermind", "Tracklist" : [
        {
                "Track" : "1",
                "Title" : "Smells like teen spirit",
                "Lenght" : "5:02"
        },
        {
                "Track" : "2",
                "Title" : "In Bloom",
                "Length" : "4:15"
        }

] }
```

The known data types are defined in Table 4–1.

***Table 4–1.** Known BSON Types and Codes*

| # | Data Type | # | Data Type |
|---|---|---|---|
| -1 | MiniKey | 11 | Regular Expression |
| 1 | Double | 13 | JavaScript Code |
| 2 | Character string (UTF8) | 14 | Symbol |
| 3 | Embedded object | 15 | JavaScript Code with scope |
| 4 | Embedded array | 16 | 32-bit integer |
| 5 | Binary Data | 17 | Timestamp |
| 7 | Object ID | 18 | 64-bit integer |
| 8 | Boolean type | 127 | MaxKey |
| 9 | Date type | 255 | Min Key |
| 10 | Null type | | |

## Matching an Entire Array

If you want to match an entire array within a document, you can use the `$elemMatch` operator. This is particularly useful if you have multiple documents within your collection, some of which partially have the same information. This can make a default query incapable of finding the exact document you are looking for. This is because the standard query syntax doesn't restrict itself to a single document within an array.

Let's look at an example that illustrates this principle. For this to work, we need to add another document to the collection, one that has an identical item in it, but is otherwise different. Specifically, we'll add another CD from Nirvana that happens to have the same track on it as the aforementioned CD ("Smells like teen spirit"). However, on this version of the CD, the song is track 5, not track 1:

```
{
        "Type" : "CD",
        "Artist" : "Nirvana",
        "Title" : "Nirvana",
        "Tracklist" : [
                {
                        "Track" : "1",
                        "Title" : "You know you're right",
                        "Length" : "3:38"
                },
                {
```

```
                        "Track" : "5",
                        "Title" : "Smells like teen spirit",
                        "Length" : "5:02"
                }
        ]
}
```

```
> nirvana = ( { "Type" : "CD", "Artist" : "Nirvana", "Title" : "Nirvana",
"Tracklist" : [ { "Track" : "1", "Title" : "You know you're right", "Length"
: "3:38"}, {"Track" : "5", "Title" : "Smells like teen spirit", "Length" :
"5:02" } ] } )

> db.media.insert(nirvana)
```

If you want to search for an album from Nirvana that has the song "Smells Like Teen Spirit" as Track 1 on the CD, you might think that the following query would do the job:

```
> db.media.find ( { "Tracklist.Title" : "Smells like teen spirit",
"Tracklist.Track" : "1" } )
```

Unfortunately, the preceding query will return both documents. The reason for this is that both documents have a track with the title called "Smells Like Teen Spirit" and both have a tracknumber 1. If you want to match an entire document within the array, you can use `$elemMatch`, as in this example:

```
> db.media.find ( { Tracklist: { "$elemMatch" : { Title:
"Smells like teen spirit", Track : "1" } } } )

{ "_id" : ObjectId("4c1a86bb2955000000004076"), "Type" : "CD", "Artist" :
"Nirvana", "Title" : "Nevermind", "Tracklist" : [
        {
                "Track" : "1",
                "Title" : "Smells like teen spirit",
                "Lenght" : "5:02"
        },
        {
                "Track" : "2",
                "Title" : "In Bloom",
                "Length" : "4:15"
        }
] }
```

This preceding query will give you the desired result and only return the first document.

## $not (meta-operator)

You can use the `$not` meta-operator to negate any check performed by a standard operator. The following example returns all documents in your collection, except for the one seen in the `$elemMatch` example:

```
> db.media.find ( { Tracklist : { $not : { "$elemMatch" : { Title:
"Smells like teen spirit", "Track" : "1" } } } } )
```

### Specifying Additional Query Expressions

Apart from the structured query syntax you've seen so far, you can also specify additional query expressions in JavaScript. The big advantage of this is that JavaScript is extremely flexible and allows you to do tons of additional things. The downside of using JavaScript is that it's a tad slower than the native operators baked into MongoDB.

For example, assume you want to search for a DVD within your collection that is older than 1995. All of the following code examples would return this information:

```
db.media.find ( { "Type" : "DVD", "Released" : { $lt : "1995" } } )

db.media.find ( { "Type" : "DVD", $where: "this.Released < 1995" } );

db.media.find ("this.Released < 1995");

f = function() { return this.Released < 1995; }
db.media.find(f)
```

And *that's* how flexible MongoDB is! Using these operators should enable you to find just about anything throughout your collections.

## Leveraging Regular Expressions

Regular expressions are another powerful tool you can use to query information. *Regular expressions—regex*, for short—are special text strings that you can use to describe your search pattern. These work similar to wildcards, but they are far more powerful and flexible.

MongoDB allows you to use these regular expressions when searching for data in your collections; however, it will attempt to use an index whenever possible for simple prefix queries.

The following example uses regex in a query to find all items in the media collection that start with the word "Matrix":

```
> db.media.find ( { Title : /Matrix*/i } )
```

Using regular expressions from MongoDB can make your life much simpler, so we'd recommend exploring this feature in greater detail as time permits or your circumstances can benefit from it.

# Updating Data

So far you've learned how to insert and query for data in your database. Next, you'll learn how to update that data. MongoDB supports quite a few update operators that you'll learn how to use in the following sections.

## Updating with update()

MongoDB comes with the `update()` function for performing updates to your data. The `update()` function takes four arguments: `criteria`, `objNew`, `upsert`, and `multi`.

The `criteria` argument lets you specify the query that selects the record you want to update. You use the `objNew` argument to specify the updated information; or you can use an operator to do this for you. The `upsert` argument lets you specify whether the update should be an upsert. An `upsert` argument tells MongoDB to update the record if it exists, and create it if it doesn't. Finally, the `multi` argument lets you specify whether all matching documents should be updated or just the first one (the default action). Note that the `multi` argument only works with $ operators.

The following simple example uses the `update()` function without any fancy operators:

```
> db.media.update( { "Title" : "Matrix, the"}, {"Type" : "DVD", "Title" :
"Matrix, the", "Released" : "1999", "Genre" : "Action"}, true)
```

The preceding example overwrites the document in the collection and saves it with the new values specified. Note that any fields that you leave out are removed (the document is basically being rewritten). Because the `upsert` argument is specified as `true`, any fields that do not exist yet will be added (the `Genre` key/value pair, in this case).

---

■ **Note** An `Upsert` tells the database to "update a record if a document is present or to insert it if it doesn't."

---

# Implementing an Upsert with the save() Command

You can also perform an upsert with the `save()` command. To do this, you need to specify the `_id` value; you can have this value added automatically or can specify it manually yourself. If you do not specify the `_id` value, the save() command will assume it's an insert and simply add the document into your collection.

The main benefit of using the save() command is that you do not need to specify that the `upsert` method should be used in conjunction with the update() command. Thus, the `save()` command gives you a quicker way to upsert data. In practice, the `save()` and `update()` commands look similar:

```
> db.media.update( { "Title" : "Matrix, the"}, {"Type" : "DVD", "Title" :
"Matrix, the", "Released" : "1999", "Genre" : "Action"}, true)

> db.media.save( { "Title" : "Matrix, the"}, {"Type" : "DVD", "Title" :
"Matrix, the", "Released" : "1999", "Genre" : "Action"})
```

Obviously, the preceding example assumes that the `Title` value acts as the `id` field.

# Updating Information Automatically

You can use the modifier operations to quickly and simply update information in your documents, but without needing to type everything in manually. For example, you might use these operations to increase a number or to remove an element from an array.

We'll be exploring these operators next, providing practical examples that show you how to use them.

## Incrementing a Value with $inc

The `$inc` operator enables you to perform an (atomic) update on a key to increase the value by the given increment, assuming that the field exists. If the field doesn't exist, it will be created. To see this in action, begin by adding another document to the collection:

```
> manga = ( { "Type" : "Manga", "Title" : "One Piece", "Volumes" : 612,
"Read" : 520 } )
{
        "Type" : "Manga",
        "Title" : "One Piece",
        "Volumes" : "612",
        "Read" : "520"
}
> db.media.insert(manga)
```

Now you're ready to update the document. For example, assume you've read another four volumes of the One Piece manga, and you want to increment the number of Read volumes in the document. The following example shows you how to do this:

```
> db.media.update ( { "Title" : "One Piece"}, {$inc: {"Read" : 4} } )
> db.media.find ( { "Title" : "One Piece" } )
{
        "Type" : "Manga",
        "Title" : "One Piece",
        "Volumes" : "612",
        "Read" : "524"
}
```

---

■ **Note** When defining a variable in the shell (e.g., `manga = ( { ... } )`), the contents of the variable will be printed out immediately.

---

## Setting a Field's Value

You can use the `$set` operator to set a field's value to one you specify. This goes for any type of datatype, as in the following example:

```
> db.media.update ( { "Title" : "Matrix, the" }, {$set : { Genre :
"Sci-Fi" } } )
```

This snippet would update the genre in the document created earlier, setting it to `Sci-Fi` instead.

## Deleting a Given Field

The `$unset` operator lets you delete a given field, as in this example:

```
> db.media.update ( {"Title": "Matrix, the"}, {$unset : { "Genre" : 1 } } )
```

This snippet would delete the `Genre` key and its value from the document.

## Appending a Value to a Specified Field

The $push operator allows you to append a value to a specified field. If the field is an existing array, then the value will be added. If the field doesn't exist yet, then the field will be set to the array [value]. If the field exists, but it isn't an array, then an error condition will be raised.

Begin by adding another author to your entry in the collection:

```
> db.media.update ( {"ISBN" : "1-4302-3051-7"}, {$push: { Author : "Griffin,
Stewie"} } )
```

The next snippet raises an error message because the Title field is not an array:

```
> db.media.update ( {"ISBN" : "1-4302-3051-7"}, {$push: { Title :
"This isn't an array"} } )
Cannot apply $push/$pushAll modifier to non-array
```

The following example shows how the document looks in the meantime:

```
> db.media.find ( { "ISBN" : "1-4302-3051-7" } )
{
    "Author" :
    [
        "Membrey, Peter",
        "Plugge, Eelco",
        "Hawkins, Tim",
        "Griffin, Stewie",
    ],
    "ISBN" : "1-4302-3051-7",
    "Publisher" : "Apress",
    "Title" : "Definitive Guide to MongoDB, the",
    "Type" : "Book",
    "_id" : ObjectId("4c436231c603000000007ed0")
}
```

## Specifying Multiple Values in an Array

The $pushAll operator works similarly to the $push operator, with one exception: the $pushAll operator lets you specify that multiple values should be added to an array. The same rules discussed previously apply here: if the array already exists, the operator will add the values. If the array doesn't exist, then it will be created. And if the field already exists, but it isn't an array, then an error condition will be raised. The following snippet shows how to use the $pushAll operator:

```
> db.media.update( {"ISBN" : "1-4302-3051-7"},{$pushAll: {Author : ["Griffin,
Louis","Griffin, Peter"] } } )
```

As you probably realized, the preceding example adds a few more authors to the document.

## Adding Data to an Array with $addToSet

The $addToSet operator is another command that lets you add data to an array. However, this operator only adds the data to the array if the data is not already there. In this way, $addToSet is unlike $pushAll and $push. By default, the $addToSet operator takes one argument. However, you can use the $each operator to specify additional arguments when using the $addToSet operator. The following snippet adds the author Griffin, Brian into the authors array because it isn't there yet:

```
> db.media.update( { "ISBN" : "1-4302-3051-7" }, {$addToSet : { Author :
"Griffin, Brian" } } )
```

Executing the snippet again won't change anything because the author is already in the array.

To add more than one value, however, you should take a different approach and use the $each operator, as well:

```
> db.media.update( { "ISBN" : "1-4302-3051-7" }, {$addToSet : { Author :
{ $each : ["Griffin, Brian","Griffin, Meg"] } } } )
```

At this point, our document, which once looked tidy and trustworthy, has been transformed into something like this:

```
{
    "Author" :
    [
        "Membrey, Peter",
        "Plugge, Eelco",
        "Hawkins, Tim",
        "Griffin, Stewie",
        "Griffin, Peter",
        "Griffin, Brian",
        "Griffin, Louis",
        "Griffin, Meg"
    ],
    "ISBN" : "1-4302-3051-7",
    "Publisher" : "Apress",
    "Title" : "Definitive Guide to MongoDB, the",
    "Type" : "Book",
    "_id" : ObjectId("4c436231c603000000007ed0")
}
```

## Removing Elements from an Array

MongoDB also includes several methods that let you remove elements from an array, including $pop, $pull, $pullAll. In the sections that follow, you'll learn how to use each of these methods for removing elements from an array.

The $pop operator lets you remove a single element from an array. This operator lets you remove the first or last value in the array, depending on the parameter you pass down with the operator. For example, the following snippet removes the last element from the array:

```
> db.media.update( { "ISBN" : "1-4302-3051-7" }, {$pop : {Author : 1 } } )
```

In this case, the $pop operator will *pop* Meg's name off the list of authors. Passing down a negative number would remove the first element from the array. The following example removes Peter Membrey's name from the list of authors:

```
> db.media.update( { "ISBN" : "1-4302-3051-7" }, {$pop : {Author : -1 } } )
```

---

■ **Note** Specifying a value of -2 or a 1000 wouldn't change which element gets removed. Any negative number would remove the first element, while any positive number would remove the last element. Using the number 0 removes the last element from the array.

---

### Removing Each Occurrence of a Specified Value

The $pull operator lets you remove each occurrence of a specified value from an array. This can be particularly useful if you have multiple elements with the same value in your array. Let's begin this example by using the $push parameter to add Stewie back to the list of authors:

```
> db.media.update ( {"ISBN" : "1-4302-3051-7"}, {$push: { Author :
"Griffin, Stewie"} } )
```

Stewie will be in and out of the database a couple more times as we walk through this book's examples. You can remove all occurrences of this author in the document with the following code:

```
> db.media.update ( {"ISBN" : "1-4302-3051-7"}, {$pull : { Author : "Griffin,
Stewie" } } )
```

### Removing Multiple Elements from an Array

You can also remove multiple elements with different values from an array. The $pullAll operator enables you to accomplish this. The $pullAll operator takes an array with all the elements you want to remove, as in the following example:

```
> db.media.update( { "ISBN" : "1-4302-3051-7"}, {$pullAll : { Author :
["Griffin, Louis","Griffin, Peter","Griffin, Brian"] } } )
```

The field from which you remove the elements (Author in the preceding example) needs to be an array. If it isn't, you'll receive an error message.

## Specifying the Position of a Matched Array

You can use the $ operator in your queries to specify the position of the matched array item in your query. You can use this operator for data manipulation after finding an array member. For instance, assume you've added another track to your tracklist, but you accidently made a typo when entering the tracknumber:

```
> db.media.update( { "Title" : "Nirvana" }, {$addToSet : { Tracklist :
{"Track" : 2,"Title": "Been a son", "Length":"2:23"} } } )

{
    "Artist" : "Nirvana",
    "Title" : "Nirvana",
    "Tracklist" : [
        {
                "Track" : "1",
                "Title" : "You know you're right",
```

```
                "Length" : "3:38"
        },
        {
                "Track" : "5",
                "Title" : "Smells like teen spirit",
                "Length" : "5:02"
        },
        {
                "Track" : 2,
                "Title" : "Been a son",
                "Length" : "2:23"
        }
    ],
    "Type" : "CD",
    "_id" : ObjectId("4c443ad6c603000000007ed5")
}
```

It so happens you know that the tracknumber of the most recent item should be 3 rather than 2. You can use the $inc method in conjunction with the $ operator to increase the value from 2 to 3, as in this example:

```
> db.media.update( { "Tracklist.Title" : "Been a son"},
{$inc:{"Tracklist.$.Track" : 1} } )
```

Note that only the first item it matches will be updated. Thus, if there are two identical elements in the comments array, only the first element will be increased.

# Atomic Operations

MongoDB supports atomic operations executed against *single documents*. An atomic operation is a set of operations that can be combined in such a way that the set of operations appears to be merely one single operation to the rest of the system. This set of operations will have either a positive outcome or a negative outcome as the final result.

You can call a set of operations an atomic operation if it meets the following pair of conditions:

1. No other process knows about the changes being made until the entire set of operations has completed.
2. If one of the operations fails, the entire set of operations (the entire atomic operation) will fail, resulting in a full roll back, where the data is restored to its state prior to running the atomic operation.

A standard behavior when executing atomic operations is that the data will be *locked* and therefore unable to be reached by other queries. However, MongoDB does not support locking or complex transactions for a number of reasons:

- In sharded environments (see Chapter 12 for more information on such environments), distributed locks can be expensive and slow. MongoDB's goal is to be lightweight and fast, so expensive and slow goes against the principle.
- MongoDB developers don't like the idea of deadlocks. In their view, it's preferable for a system to be simple and predictable instead.

- MongoDB is designed to work well for realtime problems. When an operation is executed that locks large amounts of data, it would also stop some smaller light queries for an extended period of time. Again, this goes against the goal of MongoDB being fast.

MongoDB includes several update operators (as noted previously), all of which can atomically update an element:

- `$set`: Sets a particular value.
- `$unset`: Sets a particular value.
- `$inc`: Increments a particular value by a certain amount.
- `$push`: Appends a value to an array.
- `$pushAll`: Appends several values to an array.
- `$pull`: Removes a value(s) from an existing array.
- `$pullAll`: Removes several values from an existing array.

## Using the Update if Current Method

Another strategy that atomic update uses is the `Update if Current` method. This method takes the following three steps:

1. It fetches the object from the document.
2. It modifies the object locally (with any of the previously mentioned operations, or a combination of them).
3. It sends an update request to update the object to the new value, in case the current value still matches the old value fetched.

You can use the `getlasterror` method to check whether all went well. Note that all of this happens automatically. Let's take a new look at an example shown previously:

```
> db.media.update( { "Tracklist.Title" : "Been a son"},
{$inc:{"Tracklist.$.Track" : 1} } )
```

Now you can use the `getlasterror` command to check whether the update went smoothly:

```
> db.$cmd.findOne({getlasterror:1})
```

If the atomic update executes successfully, you get the following result back:

```
{ "err" : null, "updatedExisting" : true, "n" : 1, "ok" : 1 }
```

In the preceding example, you increment `Tracklist.Track` using the tracklist title as an identifier. But now consider what happens if the tracklist data is changed by another user using the same method while MongoDB was modifying your data. Because `Tracklist.Title` remains the same, you might assume (incorrectly) that you are updating the original data, when in fact you are overwriting the changes.

This is known as *the ABA problem*. This scenario might seem unlikely, but in a multi-user environment, where many applications are working on data at the same time, this can be a significant problem.

To avoid this problem, you can do one of the following:

- Use the entire object in the update's query expression, instead of just the `_id` and `comments.by` field.
- Use `$set` to set the field you care about. If other fields have changed, they won't be affected by this.
- Put a version variable in the object and increment it on each update.
- When possible, use a $ operator instead of an update-if-current sequence of operations.

---

**Note** MongoDB does not support updating multiple documents atomically in a single operation. Instead, you can use nested objects, which effectively make them one document for atomic purposes.

---

## Modifying and Returning a Document Atomically

The findandmodify command also allows you to perform an atomic update on a document. This command modifies the document and returns it. The command takes two main operators: the `<collection>` operator, which you use to specify the collection you're executing it against; and the `<operations>` operator, which you use to specify the query command, the sorting criteria, and what needs to be done.

Now let's look at a handful of examples that illustrate how to use this command. The first example finds the document you're searching for and removes it once it is found:

```
> db.media.findAndModify( { "Title" : "One Piece",sort:{"Title": -1}, remove:
true} )
{
        "_id" : ObjectId("4c445218c603000000007ede"),
        "Type" : "Manga",
        "Title" : "One Piece",
        "Volumes" : 612,
        "Read" : 524
}
```

The preceding code returned the document it found matching the criteria. In this case, it found and removed the first item it found with the title "One Piece." If you execute a `find()` function now, you will see that the document is no longer within the collection.

The next example modifies the document rather than removing it:

```
> db.media.findAndModify( { query: { "ISBN" : "987-1-4302-3051-9" }, sort:
{"Title":-1}, update: {$set: {"Title" : " Different Title"} } } )
```

The preceding example updates the title from "Definitive Guide to MongoDB, the" to "Different Title"—and returns the old document (as it was before the update) to your shell. If you would rather see the results of the update on the document instead, you can add the `new` operator after your query:

```
> db.media.findAndModify( { query: { "ISBN" : "987-1-4302-3051-9" }, sort:
{"Title":-1}, update: {$set: {"Title" : " Different Title"} }, new:true } )
```

Note that you can use any modifier operation with this command, not just $set.

# Renaming a Collection

Obviously, it might happen that you have a collection that you named incorrectly, but you've already inserted some data into it. This might make it troublesome to remove and read the data again from scratch.

Instead, you can use the `renameCollection()` function to rename your existing collection. The following example shows you how to use this simple and straightforward command:

```
> db.media.renameCollection("newname")
{ "ok" : 1 }
```

If the command executes successfully, an `OK` will be returned. If it fails, however (if the collection doesn't exist, for example), then the following message is returned:

```
{ "errmsg" : "assertion: source namespace does not exist", "ok" : 0 }
```

The `renameCollection` command doesn't take many parameters (unlike some commands you've seen so far); however, it can be quite useful in the right circumstances.

# Removing Data

So far we've covered how to add, search for, and modify data. Next, we'll examine how to *remove* documents from your collections, entire collections, and the databases themselves.

Previously, you learned how to remove data from a specific document (using the `$pop` command, for instance). In this section, you will learn how to remove full documents and collections. Just as the `insert()` function is used for inserting and `update()` is used for modifying a document, `remove()` is used to remove a document.

To remove a single document from your collection, you need to specify the criteria you'll use to find the document. A good approach is to perform a `find()` first; this ensures that the criteria used is specific to your document. Once you are sure of the criteria, you can invoke the `remove()` function using that criteria as a parameter:

```
> db.newname.remove( { "Title" : "Different Title" } )
```

The preceding statement removes the book added previously or any other item in your collection that has the same title. The fact this statement removes all books by that title is one reason why it's best to specify the item's `_id` value—it's always unique.

Or you can use the following snippet to remove all documents from the `newname` library (remember: we renamed the `media` collection this previously):

```
> db.newname.remove({})
```

---

■ **Warning** When removing a document, you need to remember that any reference to that document will remain within the database. For this reason, be sure you manually delete or update those references as well; otherwise, these references will return null when evaluated.

---

If you want to remove an entire collection, you can use the `drop()` function. The following snippet removes the entire `newname` collection, including all of its documents:

```
> db.newname.drop()
true
```

The drop() function returns either true or false, depending on whether the operation has completed successfully. Likewise, if you want to remove an entire database from MongoDB, you can use the dropDatabase() function, as in this example:

```
> db.dropDatabase()
{ "dropped" : "library", "ok" : 1 }
```

Note that the preceding snippet will remove the database you are currently working in (again, be sure to check db to see which database is your current database).

# Referencing a Database

At this point, you have an empty database again. You're also familiar with inserting various kinds of data into a collection. Now you're ready to take things a step further and learn about *database referencing*. As you've already seen, there are plenty of scenarios where embedding data into your document will suffice for your application (such as the tracklist or the list of authors in the book entry). However, sometimes you do need to reference information in another document. The following sections will explain how to go about doing so.

Just as with SQL, references between documents in MongoDB are resolved by performing additional queries on the server. MongoDB gives you two ways to accomplish this: referencing them manually or using the DBRef standard, which many drivers also support.

## Referencing Data Manually

The simplest and most straightforward way to reference data is to do so manually. When referencing data manually, you store the value from the _id of the other document in your document, either through the full ID or through a simpler common term. Before proceeding with an example, let's add a new document and specify the publisher's information in it (pay close attention to the _id field:

```
> apress = ( { "_id" : "Apress", "Type" : "Technical Publisher", "Category" :
["IT", "Software","Programming"] } )
{
        "_id" : "Apress",
        "Type" : "Technical Publisher",
        "Category" : [
                "IT",
                "Software",
                "Programming"
        ]
}
> db.publisherscollection.insert(apress)
```

Once you add the publisher's information, you're ready to add an actual document (e.g., a book's information) into the media collection. The following example adds a document, specifying Apress as the name of the publisher:

```
> book = ( { "Type" : "Book", "Title" : "Definitive Guide to MongoDB, the",
"ISBN" : "987-1-4302-3051-9", "Publisher" : "Apress","Author" : ["Membrey,
Peter","Plugge, Eelco","Hawkins, Tim"] } )
{
```

```
        "Type" : "Book",
        "Title" : "Definitive Guide to MongoDB, the",
        "ISBN" : "987-1-4302-3051-9",
        "Publisher": "Apress",
        "Author" : [
                "Membrey, Peter",
                "Plugge, Eelco",
                "Hawkins, Tim"
        ]
}
> db.media.insert(book)
```

All the information you need has been inserted into the publisherscollection and media collections, respectively. You can now start using the database reference. First, specify the document that contains the publisher's information to a variable:

```
> book = db.media.findOne();
{
        "_id" : ObjectId("4c458e848e0f00000000628e"),
        "Type" : "Book",
        "Title" : "Definitive Guide to MongoDB, the",
        "ISBN" : "987-1-4302-3051-9",
        "Publisher" : "Apress",
        "Author" : [
                "Membrey, Peter",
                "Plugge, Eelco",
                "Hawkins, Tim"
        ]
}
```

To obtain the information itself, you combine the findOne function with some dot notation:

```
db.publisherscollection.findOne( { _id : book.Publisher } )
{
        "_id" : "Apress",
        "Type" : "Technical Publisher",
        "Category" : [
                "IT",
                "Software",
                "Programming"
        ]
}
```

As the preceding example illustrates, referencing data manually is straightforward and doesn't require much brainwork. In the preceding example, the _id in the documents placed in the users collection has been manually set and has not been generated by MongoDB (otherwise, the _id would be an object ID).

## Referencing Data with DBRef

DBRef provides a more formal specification for referencing data between documents. The main reason for using DBRef over a manual reference is that the collection can change from one document to the next. So, if your referenced collection will always be the same, the referencing data manually (as just described) is fine.

With DBRef, the database reference is stored as a standard embedded (JSON/BSON) object. Having a standard way to represent references means that drivers and data frameworks can add helper methods that manipulate the references in standard ways.

The syntax for adding a DBRef reference value looks like this:

```
{ $ref : <collectionname>, $id : <id value>[, $db : <database name>] }
```

In the preceding example, `<collectionname>` represents the name of the collection referenced (e.g., `posts`); `<id value>` represents the value of the `_id` field for the object you are referencing; and last but not least, `$db` is optional and allows you to reference documents that are placed in other databases.

Let's look at another example for using DBRef from scratch. Begin by emptying your two collections and adding a new document:

```
> db.publisherscollection.drop()
true
> db.media.drop()
true
> apress = ( { "Type" : "Technical Publisher", "Category" :
["IT","Software","Programming"] } )
{
        "Type" : "Technical Publisher",
        "Category" : [
                "IT",
                "Software",
                "Programming"
        ]
}
> db.publisherscollection.save(apress)
```

So far you've defined the variable `apress` and saved it using the `save()` function. Next, display the updated contents of the variable by typing in its name:

```
> apress
{
"Type" : "Technical Publisher",
"Category" : [
        "IT",
        "Software",
        "Programming"
],
"_id" : ObjectId("4c4597e98e0f000000006290")
}
```

So far you've defined the publisher and saved it to the `publisherscollection` collection. Now you're ready to add an item to the *media* collection that references the data:

```
> book = { "Type" : "Book", "Title" : "Definitive Guide to MongoDB, the",
"ISBN" : "987-1-4302-3051-9", "Author": ["Membrey, Peter","Plugge,
Eelco","Hawkins, Tim"], Publisher : [ new DBRef ('publisherscollection',
apress._id) ] }
```

```
{
        "Type" : "Book",
        "Title" : "Definitive Guide to MongoDB, the",
        "ISBN" : "987-1-4302-3051-9",
        "Author" : [
                "Membrey, Peter",
                "Plugge, Eelco",
                "Hawkins, Tim"
        ],
        "Publisher" : [
                {
                        "$ref" : "publisherscollection",
                        "$id" : ObjectId("4c4597e98e0f000000006290")
                }
        ]
}
> db.media.save(book)
```

And that's it! Granted, the preceding example looks a little less simple than the manual method of referencing data; however, it's a good alternative for cases where collections can change from one document to the next.

# Implementing Index-Related Functions

In the previous chapter, you took a brief look at what indexes can do for your database. Now it's time to briefly learn how to create and use indexes. Indexing will be discussed in greater detail in Chapter 10, but for now let's have a look at the basics. MongoDB includes a fair number of functions available for maintaining your indexes; we'll begin by creating an index with the `ensureIndex()` function.

The `ensureIndex()` function takes at least one parameter, which is the name of a key in one of your documents that you will use to build the index. In the previous example, you added a document to the `media` collection that used the `Title` key. This collection would be well served by an index on this key.

---

■ **Tip** The rule of the thumb in MongoDB is to create an index for the same sort of scenarios where you'd want to create one in MySQL.

---

You can create an index for this collection by invoking the following command:

```
> db.media.ensureIndex( { Title : 1 } )
```

This command ensures that an index will be created for all the `Title` values from all documents in the `media` collection. The `:1` at the end of the line specifies the direction of the index: `1` stores the items in ascending order, whereas `-1` stores them in descending order.

```
// Ensure ascending index
db.media.ensureIndex( { Title :1 } )

// Ensure descending index
db.media.ensureIndex( { Title :-1 } )
```

---

■ **Tip** Searching through indexed information is fast. Searching for non-indexed information is slow as each document needs to be checked to see if it's a match.

---

BSON allows you to store full arrays in a document; however, it would also be beneficial to be able to create an index on an embedded key. Luckily, the developers of MongoDB thought of this, too, and added support for this feature. Let's build on one of the earlier examples in this chapter, adding another document into the database that has embedded information:

```
> db.media.insert( { "Type" : "CD", "Artist" : "Nirvana","Title" :
"Nevermind", "Tracklist" : [ { "Track" : "1", "Title" : "Smells like teen
spirit", "Length" : "5:02" }, {"Track" : "2","Title" : "In Bloom", "Length" :
"4:15" } ] } )
```

```
{ "_id" : ObjectId("4c45aa2f8e0f000000006293"), "Type" : "CD", "Artist" :
"Nirvana", "Title" : "Nevermind", "Tracklist" : [
        {
                "Track" : "1",
                "Title" : "Smells like teen spirit",
                "Length" : "5:02"
        },
        {
                "Track" : "2",
                "Title" : "In Bloom",
                "Length" : "4:15"
        }
] }
```

Next, you can create an index on the `Title` key for all entries in the tracklist:

```
> db.media.ensureIndex( { "Tracklist.Title" : 1 } )
```

The next time you perform a search for any of the titles in the collection—assuming they are nested under `Tracklist`—the titles will show up instantly. Next, you can take this concept one step further and use an entire (sub)document as a key, as in this example:

```
> db.media.ensureIndex( { "Tracklist" : 1 } )
```

The preceding statement indexes each element of the array, which means you can now search for any object in the array. These types of keys are also known as *Multi Keys*. You can also create an index based on multiple keys in a set of documents. This process is known as *compound indexing*. The method you use to create a compound index is mostly the same; the difference is that you specify several keys instead of one, as in this example:

```
> db.media.ensureIndex({"Tracklist.Title": 1, "Tracklist.Length": -1})
```

The benefit of this approach is that you can make an index on multiple keys (as in the previous example, where you indexed an entire subdocument). Unlike the subdocument method, however, compound indexing lets you specify whether you want one of the two fields to be indexed in descending order. If you perform your index with the subdocument method, you are limited to ascending or descending order only. There is more on compound indexes in Chapter 10.

## Surveying Index-Related Commands

So far you've taken a quick glance at one of the index-related commands, ensureIndex(). Without a doubt, this is the command you will primarily use to create your indexes. However, you might also find a pair of additional functions useful: hint() and min()/max(). You use these functions to query for data. We haven't covered them to this point because they won't function without a custom. But now let's take a look at what they can do for you.

## Forcing a Specified Index to Query Data

You can use the hint() function to force the use of a specified index when querying for data. The intended benefit of using this command is to improve the query performance. To see this principle in action, try performing a find with the hint() function without defining an index:

```
> db.media.find( { ISBN: "987-1-4302-3051-9"} ) . hint ( { ISBN: -1 } )
error: { "$err" : "bad hint", "code" : 10113 }
```

If you create an index on ISBN numbers, this technique will be more successful:

```
> db.media.ensureIndex({ISBN: 1}, {background: true});
> db.media.find( { ISBN: "987-1-4302-3051-9"} ) . hint ( { ISBN: 1 } )

{ "_id" : ObjectId("4c45a5418e0f000000006291"), "Type" : "Book", "Title" : "Definitive Guide
to MongoDB, the", "ISBN" : "987-1-4302-3051-9", "Author" : [ "Membrey, Peter", "Plugge,
Eelco", "Hawkins, Tim" ], "Publisher" : [
        {
                "$ref" : "publisherscollection",
                "$id" : ObjectId("4c4597e98e0f000000006290")
        }
] }
```

## Constraining Query Matches

The min() and max() functions enable you to constrain query matches to only those that have index keys between the min and max keys specified. Therefore, you will need to have an index for the keys you are specifying. Also, you can either combine the two functions or use them separately. Let's begin by adding a few documents that enable you to take advantage of these functions. First, create an index on the Released field:

```
> db.media.insert( { "Type" : "DVD", "Title" : "Matrix, the", "Released" :
1999} )
> db.media.insert( { "Type" : "DVD", "Title" : "Blade Runner", "Released" :
1982 } )
> db.media.insert( { "Type" : "DVD", "Title" : "Toy Story 3", "Released" :
2010} )
> db.media.ensureIndex( { "Released": 1 } )
```

You can now use the max() and min() commands, as in this example:

```
> db.media.find() . min ( { Released: 1995 } ) . max ( { Released : 2005 } )
{ "_id" : ObjectId("4c45b5b38e0f0000000062a9"), "Type" : "DVD", "Title" :
"Matrix, the", "Released" : 1999 }
```

If no index is created, then an error message will be returned, saying that no index has been found for the specified keypattern. Obviously, you will need to define which index must be used with the hint() function:

```
> db.media.find() . min ( { Released: 1995 } ) .
max ( { Released : 2005 } ). hint ( { Released : 1 } )
{ "_id" : ObjectId("4c45b5b38e0f0000000062a9"), "Type" : "DVD", "Title" :
"Matrix, the", "Released" : 1999 }
```

---

■ **Note** The min() value will be *included* in the results, whereas the max() value will be *excluded* from the results.

---

Generally speaking, it is recommended that you use $gt and $lt (greater than and less than, respectively) rather than min() and max() because $gt and $lt don't require an index. The min() and max() functions are used primarily for compound keys.

# Summary

In this chapter, we've taken a look at the most commonly used commands and options that can be performed with the MongoDB shell to manipulate data. We also examined how to search for, add, modify, and delete data. We also looked at how to modify your collections and databases. Next, we took a quick look at Atomic Operations, how to use aggregation, and when to use operators such as $elemMatch. Finally, we explored how to create indexes and when to use them. We also examined what indexes are for, how you can drop them, how to search for your data using the indexes created, and how to check for running indexing operations.

In the next chapter, we'll look into the fundamentals of GridFS, including what it is, what it does, and how it can be used to your benefit.

CHAPTER 5

# GridFS

We live in a world of high definition video, 12MP cameras, and storage media that can hold 50GB of data on a disc the size of a CDROM. In that context, the 4MB limit for the maximum size of a MongoDB document might seem laughably inadequate. Indeed, you might wonder why MongoDB, which has been designed as a database for today's high-tech age, has such a strange limitation. The short answer: performance.

If the data were stored in the document itself, it would obviously get very large, which in turn would make the data hard to work with. For example, pulling back the whole document would require loading the files in the document, as well. You could work around this issue, but you would still need to pull back the entire file whenever you accessed it, even if you only wanted a small section of it. You can't ask for a chunk of data in the middle of a document—it's an all or nothing proposition. Fortunately, MongoDB features a somewhat unique and elegant solution to this problem. MongoDB enables you to store large files quite easily, yet also allows you to access parts of the file without retrieving the entire thing—all while maintaining extremely high performance. It achieves this by leveraging a specification known as GridFS.

---

**Note** One interesting thing about GridFS is that it isn't actually a software feature. For example, there isn't any special server-side code in MongoDB that manages GridFS. Instead, GridFS is a simple specification used by all of the supported drivers on MongoDB. The key benefit of such a specification is that files stored by one driver can be accessed by any other driver that follows the same convention.

---

This approach adheres closely to the MongoDB principle of keeping things simple. Because GridFS uses standard MongoDB features, it's easy to implement and work with the specification from the driver's point of view. It also means you can poke around by hand if you really want to as to MongoDB they are just normal collections containing documents.

## Filling in Some Background

Chapter 1 touched on the fact that we have been taught to use databases for even simple storage for many years. For example, the book I bought to help improve my PHP more than 13 years ago introduced MySQL in Chapter 3. Considering the complexity of SQL and databases in the real world (not to mention in theory), you might wonder why a book intended for beginners would practically start off with SQL. After all, it was a PHP book and not a MySQL book.

One thing most people don't appreciate until they try it is that reading and writing data directly to disk is hard. Some people don't agree with me on this point—after all, opening and reading files in Python might seem trivial. And it is: in simpler scenarios, working with files is rather painless when using PHP. If all you want to do is read in lines and process them, you're unlikely to have any trouble.

On the other hand, things become a lot harder if you want to search a file or store complicated or structured data. Even if you can work out how to do this and create a solution, your solution is unlikely to be faster or more efficient than relying on a database instead. Applications these days depend on finding and storing data quickly—and databases make this possible for those of us who can't or don't want to write such a system ourselves.

One area that is glossed over by many books is the storing of files. Most books that teach you to use a database to store your data also teach you to read and write to the filesystem instead when you need to store files. In some ways, this isn't usually a problem because it's much easier to read and write simple files than process what's in them. There are some issues, however. First, the developer must have permission to write those files in the first place and that requires giving the web server permissions to the developer to write to the local filesystem. This might not seem likely to pose a problem, but it gives system administrators nightmares—getting files onto a server is the first stage in being able to compromise it.

Databases can store binary files; typically, it's just not elegant for them to do so. MySQL has a special column type called `BLOB`. PostgreSQL requires special procedures to be followed to store such files—and the data isn't stored in the table itself. In other words, it's messy. These solutions are obviously bolt-ons. Thus it's not surprising that people choose to write data to the disk instead. But that approach also has issues. Apart from the problems with security, it adds another directory that needs to be backed up, and you must also ensure that this information is replicated to all the appropriate servers. There are filesystems that provide the ability to write to disk and have that content fully replicated (including GFS); but these solutions are complex and add additional overhead; moreover, these features typically make your solution harder to maintain.

MongoDB, on the other hand, enforces a maximum document size of 4MB. This is more than enough for storing rich documents, and it might have sufficed a few years ago for storing many other types of files as well. However, this limit is wholly inadequate for today's environment.

## Working with GridFS

Next, we'll take a brief look at how GridFS is implemented. As the MongoDB website points out, you do not need to understand or be aware of the underlying implementation of GridFS to use it. In fact, you can simply let the driver handle the heavy lifting for you. For the most part, the drivers that support GridFS implement file handling in a language-specific way. For example, the driver that enables Python in MongoDB works in a manner that is wholly consistent with Python, as you'll see shortly. But if the ins-and-outs of GridFS don't interest you, then just skip ahead to the next section. We promise you won't miss anything that enables you to use MongoDB effectively!

GridFS consists of two parts. More specifically, it consists of two collections. One collection holds the filename and related information such as size (called metadata), while the other collection holds the file data itself, usually in 256k chunks. The specification calls for these to be named *files* and *chunks* respectively. By default, the files and chunks collections are created in the fs namespace, but this can be changed. The ability to change the default namespace is useful if you want to store different types of files. For example, you might want to keep image and movie files separate.

## Getting Started with the Command-Line Tools

We have some of the background out of the way. Now let's look at how to get started with GridFS by exploring the command-line tools available to leverage it. First, we will need a file to play with. To keep things simple, let's use the dictionary file. On Ubuntu, you can find this at `/usr/share/dict/words`. However, there are various levels of symlinks, so you might want to run this command first:

```
root@core2:/usr/share/dict# cat words > /tmp/dictionary
```

---

■ **Note** In Ubuntu, you might need to use `apt-get install wbritish` to get the dictionary file installed.

---

This command copies all the contents of the file to a nice and simple path that you can use easily. Of course, you can use any file that you wish for this example; it doesn't need to be any particular size or type.

Rather than describe all the options you can use with mongofiles, let's jump right in and start playing with some of the tool's features. This book assumes that you're running mongofiles on the same machine as MongoDB. If you're not, then you'll need to use the `-h` option to specify the host that MongoDB is running on. You'll learn about the other options available in the mongofiles command after putting it through its paces.

First, let's list all the files in the database. We're not expecting any files to be in there yet, but let's make sure. The `list` command lists the files in the database so far:

```
$ mongofiles list
connected to: 127.0.0.1
$
```

OK, so that probably wasn't very exciting. Keep in mind that mongofiles is a proof-of-concept tool; it's probably not a tool you will use much with your own applications. However, mongofiles is a great learning tool. Once you create a file, you can use the tool to explore the files and chunks that are created.

Let's kick things up a notch and the `put` command to add the dictionary file created previously (remember: you can use any file that you fancy for this example):

```
$ mongofiles put /tmp/dictionary
connected to: 127.0.0.1
added file: { _id: ObjId(4c0be291e03f062f0a33a4e2), filename: "/tmp/dictionary", length:
929844,
chunkSize: 262144, uploadDate: new Date(1275847313417), md5:
 "677a9d1adf3511ffb924390b2d1ba642" } done!
$
```

This preceding example returns some useful information; however, let's double-check the information it shows by confirming that the file is there. Do so by re-running the `list` command:

```
$  mongofiles list
connected to: 127.0.0.1
/tmp/dictionary 929844
$
```

This preceding example shows the dictionary file, along with its size. The information clearly comes from the files collection, but we're getting ahead of ourselves. Let's take a moment to step back and examine the output returned from the `put` command in the preceding example.

## Using the _id Key

As you know, each document in MongoDB includes a unique identifier stored in the `_id` key. Like MySQL's `auto_increment` field, the `_id` key is not of much direct interest, apart from the fact it allows you to pick out a specific file.

## Working with Filenames

The output from the `put` command also shows a `Filename` key, which itself needs a little explanation. Generally, you will want to keep this field unique to help prevent major confusion; however, that's not entirely necessary. In fact, if you run the `put` command again, you'll end up with two documents that look identical. In this case, the files and metadata are identical, apart from the `_id` key. You might be surprised by this and wonder why MongoDB doesn't update the file that exists rather than create a new one. The reason: there could be many cases where you would have filenames that are identical. For example, if you built a system to store student assignments, then chances are that the filenames would be the same. MongoDB cannot assume identical filenames (even those with identical sizes) are in fact the same file. Thus, there are many cases where it would be a mistake for MongoDB to update the file. Of course, you can use the `_id` key to update a specific file; and you'll learn more about this topic in the upcoming Python-based experiments.

## Determining a File's Length

The `put` command also returns a file's length, which is both useful information and critical to how GridFS works. While it is nice to know how big a file is for reference, the file's size also plays a big part when you write your own applications. For example, when sending a file over the Web (through HTTP, for example), you need to specify how big the file is. Not all servers do this; for example, when downloading files from certain sites, you may have noticed that your web browser can tell you the speed you're downloading the file at, but not how long it will take to finish downloading the file. This is because the server did not provide size information.

Knowing the size of your file is important in one other respect. Earlier, we mentioned that a file is broken up into *chunks*—that is, the file is split into smaller pieces. By default, the chunk size is 256K, but that can be changed to another value if you wish. To work out how many chunks a file takes up, you need to know two things. First you must know how big each chunk is; and second, you must know the filesize, so that you can tell how many chunks there are.

You might think that this shouldn't be important. After all, if you have a 1MB file and the chunk size is 256K, then you know that you must start with chunk number four if you want to access data starting at the 800K point. Yet you still need to know how big the overall file is for the following reason: if you don't know the size, you cannot work out how many valid chunks there are. In the previous example, there's nothing to stop you asking for data that starts at 1.26MB (i.e., the sixth chunk). In this case, that chunk doesn't exist, but there is no way to know that without a reference to the filesize. Of course, the driver handles all of this for you, so there's no need to worry too much about it; however, knowing how GridFS works "behind the scenes" as it were will certainly help when it comes to debugging your applications.

## Working with Chunk Sizes

The `put` command also returns the chunk size because, although there is a default chunk size, this default can be changed on a file-by-file basis. This allows flexible sizing. If your website streams video, you might want to have many chunks so that you can easily skip to any part of a given video with ease. If you had one big file, you would have to return the whole file, and then find the starting point for the specified section in it. With GridFS, you can pull back data at the chunk level. If you're using the default size, then you can start retrieving data from any 256K chunk. Of course, you can also specify the bit of data you actually want (i.e., you might want only five minutes in the middle of a sixty-minute movie). This is a very efficient system, and 256K is a pretty good chunk size for most purposes. If you do decide to change it, you should have a good reason for doing so. And as always, don't forget to benchmark and test the performance of your custom chunk size; it's not uncommon for theoretically better systems to fail to live up to expectations.

---

▒ **Note** MongoDB has a 4MB restriction on document size. Because GridFS is simply a different way of storing files in the standard MongoDB framework, this restriction also exists in GridFS. That is, you can't create chunks larger than 4MB. This shouldn't pose a problem because the whole point of GridFS is to alleviate the need for huge document sizes. If you're worried that you're storing huge files and this will give you too many chunk documents, you needn't worry—there are MongoDB systems in production with significantly more than a billion documents!

---

## Tracking the Upload Date

The `uploadDate` key does exactly what its name suggests: it stores the date the file was created in MongoDB. This is a good time to mention that the `files` collection is just a normal MongoDB collection, containing normal documents. This means that you can add any additional key and value pairs that you need, in the same way you would for any other collection.

For example, consider the case of a real-world application that needs to store text content that you extract from various files. You might need to do this so you could perform some additional indexing and searching. To accomplish this, you might add a `file_text` key and store the text in there. The elegance of the GridFS system means that you can do anything with this system you can do with any other MongoDB documents. Elegance and power are two of the defining characteristics of working in MongoDB.

## Hashing Your Files

MongoDB ships with MD5, a hashing algorithm. You may have come across the algorithm previously when downloading software over the Internet. The theory behind md5 is that each file has a unique signature. Changing a single bit anywhere in that file will drastically change the signature. This signature is used for two reasons: security and integrity. For security, if you know what the md5 hash is supposed to be and you trust the source (perhaps a friend gave it to you), then you can be assured that the file has not been altered if the hash (or often called *checksum*) is correct. This also ensures that the file integrity has been maintained and that no data has been lost or damaged. The md5 hash of a particular file acts like a fingerprint for a file. The hash can be also used to identify files that have different filenames, but have the same contents.

**Warning** The md5 algorithm is no longer considered secure, and it has been demonstrated that it is possible to create two different files that have the same md5 checksum, even though their contents are different. In cryptographic terms, this is called a *collision*. Such collisions are bad because they mean it is possible for an attacker to alter a file in such a way that it cannot be detected. This caveat remains somewhat theoretical because a great deal of effort and time would be required to create such collisions intentionally; and even then, the files could be so different as to be obviously not the same file. For this reason, md5 is still the preferred method of determining file integrity because it is so widely supported. However, if you want to use hashing for its security benefits, you are much better off using one of the SHA family specifications—ideally SHA-256 or SHA-512. Even these hashing families have some theoretical vulnerabilities; however, no one has yet demonstrated a practical case of creating intentional collisions for the SHA family of hashes. MongoDB uses md5 to ensure file integrity, which is fine for most purposes. However, if you want to hash important data (such as user passwords), then you should probably consider using the SHA family of hashes instead.

# Looking Under MongoDB's Hood

At this point, you have some data in a MongoDB database. Now let's take a closer look at that data under the covers. To do this, you'll again use some command-line tools to connect and query the database. For example, try running the `find()` command against the file created earlier:

```
$ mongo test
MongoDB shell version: 1.4.3
url: test
connecting to: test
type "help" for help
> db.fs.files.find()
{ "_id" : ObjectId("4c0be291e03f062f0a33a4e2"), "filename" : "/tmp/dictionary", "length" :
929844,
"chunkSize" : 262144, "uploadDate" : "Sun Jun 06 2010 18:01:53 GMT+0000 (UTC)", "md5" :
"677a9d1adf3511ffb924390b2d1ba642" }

>
```

The preceding output should look familiar—after all, it's the same data that you saw earlier in this chapter. Now you can see that the information printed by mongofiles was taken from the file's entry in the `fs.files` collection.

Next, let's take a look at the chunks collection:

```
$ mongo test
MongoDB shell version: 1.4.3
url: test
connecting to: test
type "help" for help
> db.fs.chunks.find()
{ "_id" : ObjectId("4c0bd0f47404c770eadef5d7"), "files_id" :
ObjectId("4c0bd0f4659c33bb62a362ef"), "n"
```

```
: 0, "data" : BinData type: 2 len: 262148 }
{ "_id" : ObjectId("4c0bd0f47404c770eadef5d8"), "files_id" :
ObjectId("4c0bd0f4659c33bb62a362ef"), "n"
: 1, "data" : BinData type: 2 len: 262148
{ "_id" : ObjectId("4c0bd0f47404c770eadef5d9"), "files_id" :
ObjectId("4c0bd0f4659c33bb62a362ef"), "n"
: 2, "data" : BinData type: 2 len: 262148 }
{ "_id" : ObjectId("4c0bd0f47404c770eadef5da"), "files_id" :
ObjectId("4c0bd0f4659c33bb62a362ef"), "n"
: 3, "data" : BinData type: 2 len: 143416 }
{ "_id" : ObjectId("4c0bd29b7404c770eadef5db"), "files_id" :
ObjectId("4c0bd29bda73920e93347608"),
"n" : 0, "data" : BinData type: 2 len: 262148 }
{ "_id" : ObjectId("4c0bd29b7404c770eadef5dc"), "files_id" :
ObjectId("4c0bd29bda73920e93347608"),
"n" : 1, "data" : BinData type: 2 len: 262148 }
{ "_id" : ObjectId("4c0bd29b7404c770eadef5dd"), "files_id" :
ObjectId("4c0bd29bda73920e93347608"),
"n" : 2, "data" : BinData type: 2 len: 262148 }
{ "_id" : ObjectId("4c0bd29b7404c770eadef5de"), "files_id" :
ObjectId("4c0bd29bda73920e93347608"),
"n" : 3, "data" : BinData type: 2 len: 143416 }
{ "_id" : ObjectId("4c0be2917404c770eadef5df"), "files_id" :
ObjectId("4c0be291e03f062f0a33a4e2"), "n"
 : 0, "data" : BinData type: 2 len: 262148 }
{ "_id" : ObjectId("4c0be2917404c770eadef5e0"), "files_id" :
ObjectId("4c0be291e03f062f0a33a4e2"),
 "n" : 1, "data" : BinData type: 2 len: 262148 }
{ "_id" : ObjectId("4c0be2917404c770eadef5e1"), "files_id" :
ObjectId("4c0be291e03f062f0a33a4e2"),
 "n" : 2, "data" : BinData type: 2 len: 262148 }
{ "_id" : ObjectId("4c0be2917404c770eadef5e2"), "files_id" :
ObjectId("4c0be291e03f062f0a33a4e2"),
 "n" : 3, "data" : BinData type: 2 len: 143416 }
>
```

You might wonder why the preceding code has so many entries. As noted previously, GridFS is just a specification. That is, it uses what MongoDB already provides. While testing the commands for the book, the dictionary file was added a couple of times. Later, this file was deleted by emptying the `fs.files` collection. You can see for yourself what happened next! The fact some documents were removed from a collection has no bearing on what happens in another collection. Remember: MongoDB doesn't treat these documents or collections in any special way. If the file had been deleted properly through a driver or the mongofiles tool, that tool would also have cleaned up the chunks collection.

---

**Warning** Accessing documents and collections directly is a powerful feature, but you need to be careful. This feature also makes it much easier to shoot yourself in both feet at the same time. Make sure you know what you're doing and that you perform a great deal of testing if you decide to edit these documents and collections manually. Also, keep in mind that the GridFS support in MongoDB's drivers won't know anything about the customizations that you've made.

---

## Using the Search Command

Next, let's take a closer look at MongoDB's search command. Thus far, there is only a single file in the database, which greatly limits the types of searches you might conduct! So, let's add something else. The following snippet copies the dictionary to another file, and then imports that file:

```
$ cp /tmp/dictionary /tmp/hello_world
$ mongofiles put /tmp/hello_world
connected to: 127.0.0.1
added file: { _id: ObjId(4c110f266e3d814146e545ea), filename: "/tmp/hello_world", length:
929844, chunkSize: 262144, uploadDate: new Date(1276186406258), md5:
"677a9d1adf3511ffb924390b2d1ba642" }
done!root@core2:~# mongofiles list
connected to: 127.0.0.1
/tmp/dictionary    929844
/tmp/hello_world    929844
$
```

So the first line copies the file, while the second line imports it into MongoDB. As in the earlier example, the put command prints out the new document that MongoDB has created. Next, you might run the mongofiles list command to check that the files were correctly stored. If you do so, you can see that there are now two files in the collection; unsurprisingly, both files have the same filesize.

The search command works exactly as you would expect. All you need to do is tell mongofiles what you are looking for, and it will try to find it for you, as in this example:

```
$  mongofiles search hello
connected to: 127.0.0.1
/tmp/hello_world    929844
$  mongofiles search dict
connected to: 127.0.0.1
/tmp/dictionary    929844
$
```

Again, nothing too exciting happens in the preceding example. However, there is an important take away that's worth noting. MongoDB can be as simple or as complex as you need it to be. The mongofiles tool is only for reference use, and it includes very basic debugging. The good news: MongoDB makes it easy to perform simple searches against your files. The even better news: MongoDB also has your back if you want to write some insanely complicated searches.

## Deleting

The mongofiles delete command doesn't require much explanation, but it does deserve a big warning. This command deletes files based on the filename. Thus, if you have more than one file with the same name, this command will delete *all* of them. The following snippet shows you how to use the delete command:

```
$ mongofiles delete /tmp/hello_world
connected to: 127.0.0.1
$ mongofiles list
connected to: 127.0.0.1
/tmp/dictionary 929844
$
```

---

■ **Note** Many people have commented in connection with this issue that deleting multiple files with the same name is not a problem because no application would have duplicate names. This is simply not true; and in many cases, it doesn't even make sense to enforce unique names. For example, if your app lets users upload photos to their profiles, then there's a good chance half the files you receive will be called `photo.jpg` or `me.png`.

Of course, if you are unlikely to use mongofiles to manage your live data—and in truth no one ever expected it to be used that way—then you just need to be careful when deleting data in general (please see Chapter 9 for more information on this topic).

---

## Retrieving Files from MongoDB

So far, you haven't actually pulled any files out from MongoDB. The most important feature of any database is that it lets you find and retrieve data once it's been put in. The following snippet retrieves a file from MongoDB using the mongofiles `get` command:

```
$ mongofiles get /tmp/dictionary
connected to: 127.0.0.1
done write to: /tmp/dictionary
$
```

The preceding example includes an intentional mistake. Because it specifies the full name and path of the file you want to retrieve (as required), mongofiles writes the data to a file with the same name and path. Effectively, this overwrites the original dictionary file! This isn't exactly a great loss because it is being overwritten by the same file—and the dictionary file was only a temporary copy in the first place. Nevertheless, this could give you a rather nasty shock as you accidentally erase two weeks of work. Trust me, you won't figure out where all your work went until sometime after the event! As when using the `delete` command, you need to be careful when using the `get` command.

## Summing up mongofiles

The mongofiles utility is a useful tool for quickly looking at what's in your database. If you've written some software, and you suspect something might be amiss with it, then you can use mongofiles to double-check what's going on.

It's an extremely simple implementation, so it doesn't require any fancy logic that could complicate accomplishing the task at hand. Whether you would use mongofiles in a production environment is a matter of personal taste. It's not exactly a Swiss army knife; however, it does provide a useful set of commands that you'll be grateful to have if your application begins misbehaving. In short, you should be familiar with this tool because someday it might be exactly the tool you require to solve an otherwise nettlesome problem.

# Exploiting the Power of Python

At this point, you have a solid idea of how GridFS works. Next, you will learn how to access GridFS from Python. Chapter 2 covered how to install Python and PyMongo; if you have any trouble with the examples, please refer back to Chapter 2 and make sure everything is installed correctly.

If you've been following along with the previous examples in this chapter, you should have one file in GridFS. You'll also recall that the file is a dictionary file, so it contains a list of words. In this section, you will learn how to write a simple Python script that prints out all the words in the dictionary file. Sure, it would be simpler and more efficient to simply `cat` the original file—but where would the fun be in that?

Begin by firing up Python:

```
Python 2.6.5 (r265:79063, Apr 16 2010, 13:57:41)
[GCC 4.4.3] on linux2
Type "help", "copyright", "credits" or "license" for more information.
>>>
```

The standard driver for Python is called *PyMongo*, and it was written by Mike Dirolf. Because the PyMongo driver is supported directly by 10gen, the company that publishes MongoDB, you can rest assured that it will be regularly updated and maintained. So, let's go ahead and import the library. You should see something like the following:

```
>>> from pymongo import Connection
>>> import gridfs
>>>
```

If PyMongo isn't installed correctly, you will get an error similar to the following:

```
>>> import gridfs
Traceback (most recent call last):
  File "<stdin>", line 1, in <module>
ImportError: No module named gridfs
>>>
```

If you see the latter message, chances are something was missed during installation. In that case, pop back to Chapter 2 and follow the instructions to install PyMongo again.

## Connecting to the Database

Before you can retrieve information from a database, you must first establish a connection to it. When you were using the mongofiles utility earlier in this chapter, you probably noticed the reference to `127.0.0.1`. This value is also known as the *localhost*, and it represents your computer's loopback address. This value is simply a shortcut for telling a computer to talk to itself. The reason mongofiles mentioned this IP address is because it was actually connecting to MongoDB through the network. The default is to connect to the local machine on the default MongoDB port. Because you haven't changed the default settings, mongofiles can find and connect to your database without any trouble.

When using MongoDB with Python, however, you need to connect to the database and then set up GridFS. Fortunately, this is easy to do:

```
>>> db = Connection().test
>>> fs = gridfs.GridFS(db)
>>>
```

The first line opens the connection and selects the database. By default, mongofiles uses `test` database; hence, you'll find your dictionary file in `test` database. The second line sets up GridFS and prepares it for use.

## Accessing the Words

In its original implementation, the PyMongo driver used a file-like interface to leverage GridFS. This is somewhat different to what you saw in this chapter's earlier examples with mongofiles, which were more FTP-like in nature. In the original implementation of PyMongo, you could read and write data just as you do for a normal file.

This made PyMongo very pythonic to use, and it allowed for easy integration with existing scripts. However, this behavior was changed in version 1.6 of the driver, and this functionality is no longer supported. While very pythonic, the behavior had some problems that made the tool less effective overall.

Generally speaking, the PyMongo driver attempts to make GridFS files look and feel like ordinary files on the filesystem. On the one hand, this is nice because it means there's no learning curve, and the driver is usable with any method that requires a file. On the other hand, this approach is somewhat limiting and doesn't give a good feel for how powerful GridFS is. Important changes were made to how PyMongo works in version 1.6, particularly in how `get` and `put` work. You can find lots of great information on this change on Mike Dirolf's blog at `http://dirolf.com/2010/03/29/new-gridfs-implementation-for-PyMongo.html`.

---

**Note** This revised version of PyMongo isn't too dissimilar from previous versions of the tool, and many people who used the previous API have found it easy to adapt to the revised version. That said, Mike's changes haven't gone down well with everybody. For example, some people found the file-based keying in the old API to be extremely useful and easy to use. The revised version of PyMongo supports the ability to create filenames, so the missing behavior can be replicated in the revised version; however, doing so does require a bit more code.

---

# Putting Files into MongoDB

Getting files into GridFS through PyMongo is straightforward and intentionally similar to how you do so using command-line tools. MongoDB is all about throughput, and the changes to the API in the revised version of PyMongo reflect this. Not only do you get better performance, but the changes also bring the Python driver in line with the other GridFS implementations.

Let's put the dictionary into GridFS (again):

```
>>> with open("/tmp/dictionary") as dictionary:
...   uid = fs.put(dictionary)
...
>>> uid
ObjectId('4c1526a83207a8154a000000')
>>>
```

In the preceding example, you use the `put` method to insert the file. It's important that you capture the result from this method because it contains the document `_id` for your file. PyMongo takes a different approach than mongotools, which assumes the filename is effectively the key (even though you can have duplicates). Instead, PyMongo references files based on their `_id`. If you don't capture this information, then you won't be able to reliably find the file again. Actually, that's not strictly true—you could *search* for a file quite easily—but if you want to link this file to a particular user account, then you need this `_id`.

Two useful arguments that can be used in conjunction with the put command are filename and content_type. As you might expect, these arguments let you set the filename and the content type of the file, respectively. This is useful for loading files directly from disk. However, it is even handier when you're handling files received over the Internet or that have been generated in memory because, in those cases, you can use *file*-like semantics, but without actually having to create a real file on the disk.

# Retrieving Files from GridFS

At long last, you're now ready to return your data! At this point, you have your unique _id, so finding the file is easy. The get method retrieves a file from GridFS:

```
>>> new_dictionary = fs.get(uid)
```

That's it! The preceding snippet returns a file-like object; thus, you can print all the words in the dictionary using the following snippet:

```
>>> for word in new_dictionary:
...   print word
```

Now watch in awe as a list of words quickly scrolls up the screen! Okay, so this isn't exactly rocket science. However, the fact that it isn't rocket science or in any way difficult is part of the beauty of GridFS—it does work as advertised, and it does so in an intuitive and easily understood way!

# Deleting Files

Deleting a file is also easy. All you have to do is call fs.delete() and pass the _id of the file, as in the following example:

```
>>> fs.delete(uid)
>>> new_dictionary = fs.get(uid)
Traceback (most recent call last):
  File "<stdin>", line 1, in <module>
  File "/usr/local/lib/python2.6/dist-packages/pymongo-1.6-py2.6-linux-
x86_64.egg/gridfs/__init__.py", line
 114, in get
    return GridOut(self.__collection, file_id)
  File "/usr/local/lib/python2.6/dist-packages/pymongo-1.6-py2.6-linux-
x86_64.egg/gridfs/grid_file.py", line
 304, in __init__
    (root_collection, file_id))
gridfs.errors.NoFile: no file in gridfs collection Collection(Database(Connection('localhost',
27017),
u'test'), u'fs') with _id ObjectId('4c1526a83207a8154a000000')
>>>
```

The preceding results could look a bit scary, but it's just PyMongo's way of saying that it couldn't find the file. This isn't surprising because you just deleted it!

## Summary

In this chapter, you undertook a fast-paced tour of GridFS. You learned what GridFS is, how it all fits together with MongoDB, and how to use its basic syntax. This chapter didn't explore GridFS in great depth, but in the next chapter, you'll learn how to integrate GridFS with a real application using PHP. For now, it's enough to understand how GridFS can save you time and hassle when storing files and other large pieces of data.

In the next chapter, you'll start putting what you've learned to real use—specifically, you'll learn how to build a fully functional address book!

# PART II

# Developing

CHAPTER 6

■ ■ ■

# PHP and MongoDB

Through the first five chapters, you've learned how to perform all sorts of actions in the MongoDB shell. For example, you've learned how to add, modify, and delete a document. You've also learned about the workings of DBRef and GridFS, including how to use them.

Thus far, however, most of the things you've learned about have taken place in the MongoDB shell. This is a very capable application, but the MongoDB software also comes with a vast number of additional drivers (see Chapter 2 for more information on these) that let you step outside the shell to accomplish many other sorts of tasks.

One such driver is the PHP driver, which is maintained by Kristina Chodorow, and allows you to extend your PHP installation to connect, modify, and manage your MongoDB databases for when you want to use PHP rather than the shell. This can be helpful when you need to design a web application, or don't have access to the actual MongoDB shell itself. As this chapter will demonstrate, most of the actions you can perform with the PHP driver closely resemble functions you can execute in the MongoDB shell; however, the PHP driver requires that the options be specified in an array, rather than between two curly brackets. Similarities notwithstanding, you will need to be aware of quite a few *however*s when working with the PHP driver. This chapter will walk you through the benefits of using PHP with MongoDB, as well as how to overcome the aforementioned "howevers."

This chapter brings you back to the beginning in many ways. You will start by learning to navigate the database use collections in PHP. Next you will learn how to insert, modify, and delete posts in PHP. You will also learn how to use and DBRef again; this time, however, the focus will be on how to use them in PHP, rather than the theory behind these technologies.

## Comparing Documents in MongoDB and PHP

As you've learned previously, a document in a MongoDB collection is stored using a JSON-like format that consists of keys and values. This is similar to how PHP defines an associative array, so it shouldn't be too difficult to get used to this format.

For example, assume a document looks like the following in the MongoDB shell:

```
contact = ( {
    "First Name" : "Philip",
    "Last Name" : "Moran",
    "Address" : [
        {
        "Street" : "681 Hinkle Lake Road",
        "Place" : "Newton",
        "Postal Code" : "MA 02160",
        "Country" : "USA"
        }
    ],
```

```
    "E-Mail" : [
        "pm@example.com",
        "pm@office.com",
        "philip@example.com",
        "philip@office.com",
        "moran@example.com",
        "moran@office.com",
        "pmoran@example.com",
        "pmoran@office.com"
    ],
    "Phone" : "617-546-8428",
    "Age" : 60
})
```

The same document would look like this when contained in an array in PHP:

```
$contact = array(
    "First Name" => "Philip",
    "Last Name" => "Moran",
    "Address" => array(
        "Street" => "681 Hinkle Lake Road",
        "Place" => "Newton",
        "Postal Code" => "MA 02160",
        "Country" => "USA"
    )
    ,
    "E-Mail" => array(
        "pm@example.com",
        "pm@office.com"
        "philip@example.com",
        "philip@office.com",
        "moran@example.com",
        "moran@office.com",
        "pmoran@example.com",
        "pmoran@office.com"
    ),
    "Phone" => "617-546-8428",
    "Age" => 60
);
```

The two versions of the document look a lot alike. The obvious key difference is that the colon (:) is replaced by an arrow-like symbol (=>) in PHP. You will get used to these syntactical differences relatively quickly.

# MongoDB Classes

The PHP driver for MongoDB contains four core classes, a few others for dealing with GridFS, and several more to represent MongoDB datatypes. The core classes make up the most important part of the driver. Together, these classes allow you to execute a rich set of commands. The four core classes available are as follows:

- `Mongo`: Initiates a connection to the database and provides database server commands such as `connect()`, `close()`, `listDBs()`, `selectDBs()`, and `selectCollection()`.

- MongoDB: Interacts with the database and provides commands such as createCollection(), selectCollection(), createDBRef(), getDBRef(), drop(), and getGridFS().
- MongoCollection: Interacts with the collection. It includes commands such as count(), find(), findOne(), insert(), remove(), save(), and update().
- MongoCursor: Interacts with the results returned by a find() command and includes commands such as getNext(), count(), hint(), limit(), skip(), and sort().

In this chapter, we'll look at all of the preceding commands; without a doubt, you'll use these commands the most.

---

■ **Note** This chapter will not break down the preceding commands on a class-by-class basis; instead, the commands will be sorted in as logical an order as possible.

---

# Connecting and Disconnecting

Let's begin by examining how to use the MongoDB driver to connect to and select a database and a collection. You establish connections using the Mongo class, which is also used for database server commands. The following example shows how to quickly connect to your database in PHP:

```
// Connect to the database
$c = new Mongo();
// Select the database you want to connect to, e.g contacts
$c->contacts;
```

The Mongo class also includes the selectDB() function, which you can also use to select a database:

```
// Connect to the database
$c = new Mongo();
// Select the database you want to connect to, e.g. contacts
$c->selectDB("contacts");
```

The next example shows you how to select the collection you want to work with. The same rules apply as when working in the shell: if you select a collection that does not exist yet, it will be created when you save data to it. The process for selecting the collection you want to connect to is similar to the process of connecting to the database; in other words, you use the (->) syntax to literally point to the collection in question, as in the following example:

```
// Connect to the database
$c = new Mongo();
// Selecting the database ('contacts') and collection ('people') you want
// to connect to
$c->contacts->people;
```

The selectCollection() function also lets you select—or switch—collections, as in the following example:

```
// Connect to the database
$c = new Mongo();
```

```
// Selecting the database ('contacts') and collection ('people') you want
// to connect to
$c-> selectDB("contacts")->selectCollection("people ");
```

Before you can select a database or a collection, you sometimes need to find the desired database or collection. The Mongo class includes two additional commands for listing the available databases, as well as the available collections. You can acquire a list of available databases by invoking the listDBs() function and printing the output (which will be placed in an array):

```
// Connecting to the database
$c = new Mongo();
// Listing the available databases
print_r($c->listDBs());
```

Likewise, you can use listCollections() to get a list of available collections in a database:

```
// Connecting to the database
$c = new Mongo();
// Listing the available collections within the 'contacts' database
print_r($c->contacts->listCollections());
```

---

▒ **Note** The print_r command used in the preceding example is a PHP command that prints the contents of an array. The listDBs() function returns an array directly, so the command can be used as a parameter of the print_r function.

---

The Mongo class also contains a close() function that you can use to disconnect the PHP session from the database server. However, this is generally not required, except in unusual circumstances, because the driver will automatically close the connection to the database in a clean manner whenever the Mongo object goes out of scope.

Sometimes you may not want to forcefully close a connection. For example, you may not be sure of the actual state of the connection, or you may wish to ensure a new connection can be established. In this case, you can use the close() function, as shown in the following example:

```
// Connecting to the database
$c = new Mongo();
// Closing the connection
$c->close();
```

# Inserting Data

So far you've seen how to establish a connection to the database. Now it's time to learn how to insert data into your collection. The process for doing this is no different in PHP than when using the MongoDB shell. The process has two steps. First, you define the document in a variable. Second, you insert it using the insert() function.

Defining a document is not specifically related to MongoDB—instead, you create an array with keys and values stored in it, as in the following example:

```
$contact = array(
    "First Name" => "Philip",
```

```
    "Last Name" => "Moran",
    "Address" => array(
        "Street" => "681 Hinkle Lake Road",
        "Place" => "Newton",
        "Postal Code" => "MA 02160",
        "Country" => "USA"
    )
    ,
    "E-Mail" => array(
        "pm@example.com",
        "pm@office.com",
        "philip@example.com",
        "philip@office.com",
        "moran@example.com",
        "moran@office.com",
        "pmoran@example.com",
        "pmoran@office.com"
    ),
    "Phone" => "617-546-8428",
    "Age" => 60
);
```

Once you've assigned your data properly to a variable—called `$contact` in this case—you can use the `insert()` function to insert it in the `MongoCollection` class:

```
// Connect to the database
$c = new Mongo();
// Select the collection 'people'
$collection = $c->contacts->people;
// Insert the document '$contact' into the people collection '$collection'
$collection->insert($contact);
```

PHP's `insert()` function takes two options: `safe` and `fsync`. If set to `TRUE`, the `safe` option waits for the database to indicate whether the insertion was successful before proceeding with the rest of the PHP code. The `safe` option returns an array that reports the status of the insertion (assuming the option was set to `TRUE`). If the `safe` option isn't set (or it is set to the default value of `FALSE`), then the code will continue executing without waiting for a database response. The `fsync` option can be set to `TRUE` or `FALSE`; `FALSE` is the default value for this option as well. If set to `TRUE`, `fsync` forces the data to be written to the hard disk before it indicates the insertion was a success. This option is only useful if the `safe` option is set to `TRUE`; therefore, a `safe` insert is applied automatically when the `fsync` option is set to `TRUE`.

The following example illustrates how to use the `safe` option to insert data:

```
// Define another contact
$contact = array(
        "First Name" => "Victoria",
        "Last Name" => "Wood",
        "Address" => array(
                        "Street" => "50 Ash lane",
                        "Place" => "Ystradgynlais",
                        "Postal Code" => "SA9 6XS",
                        "Country" => "UK"
        )
        ,
        "E-Mail" => array(
```

```
                "vw@example.com",
                "vw@office.com"
        ),
        "Phone" => "078-8727-8049",
        "Age" => 28
);
// Connect to the database
$c = new Mongo();
// Select the collection 'people'
$collection = $c->contacts->people;
// Specify the safe option
$options = array("safe" => True);
// Insert the document '$contact' into the people collection '$collection'
$collection->insert($contact,$options);
```

And that's all there is to inserting data into your database with the PHP driver. For the most part, you will probably be working on defining the array that contains the data, rather than injecting the data into the array.

# Listing Your Data

Typically, you will use the `find()` function to query for data. The `find()` function takes a parameter that you use to specify your search criteria; once you specify your criteria, you execute `find()` to get the results. By default, the `find()` function simply returns all documents in the collection. This is similar to the shell examples discussed in Chapter 4. Most of the time, however, you will not want to do this. Instead, you will want to define specific information to return results for. The next sections will cover commonly used options and parameters that you can used with the `find()` function to filter your results.

## Returning a Single Document

Listing a single document is easy: simply executing the `findOne()` function without any parameters specified will grab the first document it finds in the collection. The `findOne` function stores the returned information in an array and leaves it for you to print it out again, as in this example:

```
// Connect to the database
$c = new Mongo();
// Select the collection 'people' from the database 'contacts'
$collection = $c->contacts->people;
// Find the very first document within the collection, and print it out
// using print_r
print_r($collection->findOne());
```

As noted previously, it's easy to list a single document in a collection: all you will need to do is define the `findOne()` function itself. Naturally, you can use the *`findOne()`* function with additional filters. For instance, if you know the last name of a person you're looking for, you can specify this as an option in the `findOne()` function:

```
// Connect to the database
$c = new Mongo();
// Select the collection 'people' from the database 'contacts'
$collection = $c->contacts->people;
// Define the last name of the person in the $lastname variable
```

```
$lastname = array("Last Name" => "Moran");
// Find the very first person in the collection with the last name "Moran"
print_r($collection->findOne($lastname));
```

Of course, many more options exist for filtering the data; you'll learn more about these additional options later in this chapter. Let's begin by looking at some sample output returned by using the `print_r()` command (the example adds a few line breaks for the sake of making the code easier to read):

```
Array (
    [_id] => MongoId Object ( )
    [First Name] => Philip
    [Last Name] => Moran
    [Address] => Array (
        [Street] => 681 Hinkle Lake Road
        [Place] => Newton
        [Postal Code] => MA 02160
        [Country] => USA
    )
    [E-Mail] => Array (
        [0] => pm@example.com
        [1] => pm@office.com
        [2] => philip@example.com
        [3] => philip@office.com
        [4] => moran@example.com
        [5] => moran@office.com
        [6] => pmoran@example.com
        [7] => pmoran@office.com
    )
    [Phone] => 617-546-8428
    [Age] => 60
)
```

# Listing All Documents

While you can use the `findOne()` function to list a single document, you will use the `find()` function for pretty much everything else. Don't misunderstand, please: you *can* find a single document with the `find()` function by limiting your results; but if you are unsure about the number of documents to be returned, or if you are expecting more than one document, then the `find()` function is your friend.

As detailed in the previous chapter, the `find()` function has many, many options that you can use to filter your results to suit just about any circumstance you can imagine. We'll start off with a few simple examples and build from there.

First, let's take a look at how you can display all the documents in a certain collection using PHP and the `find()` function. The only thing that you should be wary of when printing out multiple documents is that each document is returned in an array, and that each array needs to be printed individually. You can do this using PHP's `while()` function. As just indicated, you will need to instruct the function to print each document out before proceeding with the next document. The `getNext()` command gets the next document in the cursor from MongoDB; this command effectively returns the next object in the cursor and advances the cursor. The following snippet lists all the documents found in a collection:

```
// Connect to the database
$c = new Mongo();
// Select the collection ‘people’ from the database 'contacts'
```

```
$collection = $c->contacts->people;
// Execute the query and store it under the $cursor variable
$cursor = $collection->find();
// For each document it finds within the collection, print its contents
while ($document = $cursor->getNext())
{
        print_r($document);
}
```

---

■ **Note** You can implement the syntax for the preceding example several different ways. For example, a faster way to execute the preceding command would look like this: `$cursor = $c->contacts->people->find()`. For the sake of clarity, however, code examples like this one will be split up into two lines in this chapter, leaving more room for comments.

---

At this stage, the resulting output would still show only two arrays, assuming you have added the documents described previously in this chapter (and nothing else). If you were to add more documents, then each document would be printed in its own array. Granted, this doesn't look pretty; however, that's nothing you can't fix with a little additional PHP (you'll see examples that present the information in a more user-friendly way in Chapter 8).

# Using Query Operators

Whatever you can do in the MongoDB shell, you can also accomplish using the PHP driver. As you've seen in the previous chapter, the shell includes dozens of options for filtering your results. For example, you can use dot notation; sort or limit the results; skip, count, or group a number of items; or even use Regular Expression, among many other things. The following sections will walk you through how to use most of these options with the PHP driver.

# Querying for Specific Information

As you might remember from Chapter 4, you can use dot notation to query for specific information in an embedded object in a document. For instance, if you want to find one of your contacts for which you know a portion of the address details, you can use dot notation to find this, as in the following example:

```
// Connect to the database
$c = new Mongo();
// Select the collection 'people' from the database 'contacts'
$collection = $c->contacts->people;
// Use dot notation to search for a document in which the place
// is set to "Newton"
$address = array("Address.Place" => "Newton");
// Execute the query and store it under the $cursor variable
$cursor = $collection->find($address);
// For each document it finds within the collection, print the ID
// and its contents
while ($document = $cursor->getNext())
```

```
{
    print_r($document);
}
```

In a similar fashion, you can search for information in a document's array by specifying one of the items in that array, such as an e-mail address. Because an e-mail address is (usually) unique, the findOne() function will suffice in this example:

```
// Connect to the database
$c = new Mongo();
// Select the collection 'people' from the database 'contacts'
$collection = $c->contacts->people;
// Define the e-mail address you want to search for under $email
$email = array("E-Mail" => "vw@example.com");
// Find the very first person in the collection matching the e-mail address
print_r($collection->findOne($email));
```

As expected, the preceding example returns the first document that matches the e-mail address vw@example.com—the address of Victoria Wood in this case. The document is returned in the form of an array:

```
Array (
    [_id] => MongoId Object ( )
    [First Name] => Victoria
    [Last Name] => Wood
    [Address] => Array (
        [Street] => 50 Ash lane
        [Place] => Ystradgynlais
        [Postal Code] => SA9 6XS
        [Country] => UK
    )
    [E-Mail] => Array (
        [0] => vw@example.com
        [1] => vw@office.com
    )
    [Phone] => 078-8727-8049
    [Age] => 28
)
```

## Sorting, Limiting, and Skipping Items

The MongoCursor class provides sort(), limit(), and skip() functions that allow you to sort your results, limit the total number of returned results, and skip a specific number of results, respectively. Let's use the PHP driver to examine each function, including how that function is used.

PHP's sort() function takes one array as a parameter. In that array, you can specify which field it should sort the documents by. As when using the shell, you use the value 1 to sort the results in ascending order and -1 to sort the results in descending order. Note that you execute these functions on an existing cursor—that is, against the results of a previously executed find() command.

The following example sorts your contacts based on their age in ascending order:

```
// Connect to the database
$c = new Mongo();
// Select the collection 'people' from the database 'contacts'
$collection = $c->contacts->people;
```

```
// Execute the query and store it under the $cursor variable
$cursor = $collection->find();
// Use the sort command to sort all results in $cursor, based on their age
$cursor->sort(array('Age' => 1));
// Print the results
while($document = $cursor->getNext())
{
    print_r($document);
}
```

You execute the `limit()` function on the actual cursor; this takes a stunning total of *one* parameter, which specifies the number of results you would like to have returned. The `limit()` command returns the first number of *n* items it finds in the collection that match your search criteria. The following example returns only one document (granted, you could use the `findOne()` function for this instead, but `limit()` does the job):

```
// Connect to the database
$c = new Mongo();
// Select the collection 'people' from the database 'contacts'
$collection = $c->contacts->people;
// Execute the query and store it under the $cursor variable
$cursor = $collection->find();
// Use the limit function to limit the number of results to 1
$cursor->limit(1);
//Print the result
while($document = $cursor->getNext())
{
    print_r($document);
}
```

Finally, you can use the `skip()` function to skip the first *n* results that match your criteria. This function also works on a cursor:

```
// Connect to the database
$c = new Mongo();
// Select the collection 'people' from the database 'contacts'
$collection = $c->contacts->people;
// Execute the query and store it under the $cursor variable
$cursor = $collection->find();
// Use the skip function to skip the first result found
$cursor->skip(1);
// Print the result
while($document = $cursor->getNext())
{
    print_r($document);
}
```

The `sort()`, `limit()`, and `skip()` commands will prove especially handy later in this book when you implement a paging system in an application (see Chapter 8 for more information on this).

## Counting the Number of Matching Results

You can use PHP's `count()` function to count the number of documents matching your criteria and return the number of items in an array. This function is also part of the `MongoCursor` class and thus operates on the cursor. The following example shows how to get a count of contacts in the collection for people who live in the United States:

```
// Connect to the database
$c = new Mongo();
// Select the collection 'people' from the database 'contacts'
$collection = $c->contacts->people;
// Specify the search parameters
$country = array("Address.Country" => "USA");
// Execute the query and store under the $cursor variable for further processing
$cursor = $collection->find($country);
// Count the results and return the value
print_r($cursor->count());
```

The preceding query returns one result. Such counts can be useful for all sorts of operations, whether it's counting comments, the total number of registered users, or anything else.

# Grouping Data with Map/Reduce

Map/Reduce is easily one of the most powerful aggregation tools MongoDB has to offer. The way Map/Reduce allows you to group similar data makes it similar to MySQL's `GROUP BY` command, which lets you perform batch manipulation on your results. The `GROUP BY` command is also similar to the `group()` command shown in Chapter 4; the difference is that the `group()` command is (at the moment) incapable of dealing with sharded environments. Thus, to quote 10gen (the company that publishes MongoDB), the output from the `group()` command "has to be fairly small—less than 10,000 keys."

In cases where you need to display larger sets of results, it is absolutely recommended that you use `Map/Reduce` rather than the `group()` function for such operations; thus, this chapter will show you how to use `Map/Reduce` instead of the `group()` function. The `mapreduce()` function executes server-side in the form of a JavaScript; thus, you execute it using the `command()` function.

Let's say that you want to get a list of all contacts in your collection, grouped by the country where they live. Map/Reduce lets you do this easily, and so much more that using this command in this circumstance *almost* feels like overkill. Nevertheless, it's a fun command, we'll use it, anyway. Let's take a look at an example of how Map/Reduce can be put into practice.

As its name implies, Map/Reduce involves two steps: first, you need to *map* the data from the collection specified; and second, you need to *reduce* the results. Before executing the `mapreduce()` function itself, however, you need to define your $map and $reduce values.

You will use `$map` to format the data as a set of keys and values. You will use the country name for the key, as found in the `Address.Country` field of your document. In this example, you'll use `1` as the value because this is the number that every item should count. If you want every item to count for more than one, then you can change this to whatever value you prefer instead. Also, remember that the `mapreduce()` function is executed server-side in JavaScript; therefore, you'll use the `MongoCode` class to define the functions *$map* and *$reduce* in JavaScript format:

```
$map = new MongoCode('function()
    {
        emit(this.Address.Country, 1 );
    }
');
```

Once the data is mapped, it needs to be group together before you can get the total number of each unique occurrence in the collection. For this, you'll initialize a counter (starting at `0` or any other value you want to start at). The results from $map will be combined as each value is returned, eventually giving you a total, which is returned in the `Totals` variable:

```
$reduce = new MongoCode('function(key, value) {
    var Totals = 0;
        for(index in value) {
        Totals += value[index];
    }
    return Totals;
}');
```

Your $map and the $reduce variables have been defined, so you can start executing the code by using `mapreduce()`, the Map/Reduce database function. By default, the output of a Map/Reduce action is held in a temporary collection that is removed the moment the connection gets closed. However, you can also specify that the output be stored in a permanent collection by specifying an additional `$out` parameter when executing the code.

Now let's look at a practical example:

```
// Connect to the database
$c = new Mongo();
// Specify the database in which to work
$db = $c->contacts;
// Execute the mapreduce function via the command() function
$db->command(array(
    "mapreduce" => "people",
    "map" => $map,
    "reduce" => $reduce,
    "out" => "countries"
));
```

You might wonder what the resulting output will look like. The just-created document in the newly created `countries` collection looks like this:

```
{
    "_id" : "UK",
    "value" : 1
}
{
    "_id" : "USA",
    "value" : 1
}
```

Of course, these numbers aren't much of a shock. Just for fun, however, try adding another set of documents using the same format. Doing so will let you see these numbers increase when reloading the `mapreduce()` command.

## Specifying the Index with Hint

You use PHP's `hint()` function to specify which index should be used when querying for data; doing so can help you increase query performance. For instance, assume you have thousands of contacts in your collection, and you generally search for a person based upon his/her last name. In this case, it's recommended that you create an index on the `Last Name` key in the collection.

---

**Note** The `hint()` example shown next will not return anything if no index is created first.

---

To use the `hint()` function, you must apply it to the cursor, as in the following example:

```
// Connect to the database
$c = new Mongo();
// Select the collection 'people' from the database 'contacts'
$collection = $c->contacts->people;
// Execute the query and store it under the $cursor variable
$cursor = $collection->find(array("Last Name" => "Moran"));
// Use the hint function to specify which index to use
$cursor->hint(array("Last Name" => -1));
//Print the result
while($document = $cursor->getNext())
{
    print_r($document);
}
```

---

**Note** See Chapter 4 for more details on how to create an index. It is also possible to use the PHP driver's `ensureIndex()` function to create an index; however, that function is beyond the scope of this chapter.

---

## Refining Queries with Conditional Operators

You can use conditional operators to refine your queries. PHP comes with a nice set of default conditional operators, such as `<` (smaller than), `>` (larger than), `<=` (smaller than or equals to), and `>=` (larger than or equals to). Now for the bad news: you cannot use these operators with the PHP driver. Instead, you will need to use MongoDB's version of these operators. Fortunately, MongoDB itself comes with a vast set of conditional operators (you can see more information on these operators in Chapter 4). You can use all of these operators when querying for data through PHP, passing them on through the `find()` function.

While you can use all these operators with the PHP driver, you must use specific syntax to do so; that is, you must place them in an array, and pass this array to the `find()` function. The following sections will walk you through how to use several commonly used operators.

## Using the $lt, $gt, $lte, and $gte Operators

MongoDB's `$lt`, `$gt`, `$lte`, and `$gte` operators allow you to perform the same actions as the `<`, `>`, `<=`, and `>=` operators, respectively. These operators are useful in situations where you want to search for documents that store integer values.

You can use the `$lt` (less than) operator to find any kind of data for which the integer value is less than *n*, as shown in the following example:

```
// Connect to the database
$c = new Mongo();
// Select the collection 'people' from the database 'contacts'
$collection = $c->contacts->people;
// Specify the conditional operator
$cond = array('Age' => array('$lt' => 30));
// Execute the query and store it under the $cursor variable
$cursor = $collection->find($cond);
//Print the results
while($document = $cursor->getNext())
{
    print_r($document);
}
```

The resulting output shows only one result in the current documents: the contact information for Victoria Wood, who happens to be younger than 30:

```
Array (
    [_id] => MongoId Object ( )
    [First Name] => Victoria
    [Last Name] => Wood
        Address] => Array (
        [Street] => 50 Ash lane
        [Place] => Ystradgynlais
        [Postal Code] => SA9 6XS
        [Country] => UK
    )
    [E-Mail] => Array (
        [0] => vw@example.com
        [1] => vw@office.com
    )
    [Phone] => 078-8727-8049
    [Age] => 28
)
```

Similarly, you can use the `$gt` operator to find any contacts who are older than 30. This following example does this by changing the `$lt` variable to `$gt` (greater than), instead:

```
// Connect to the database
$c = new Mongo();
// Select the collection ‘people’ from the database 'contacts'
$collection = $c->contacts->people;
// Specify the conditional operator
$cond = array('Age' => array('$gt' => 30));
// Execute the query and store it under the $cursor variable
$cursor = $collection->find($cond);
//Print the results
```

```
while($document = $cursor->getNext())
{
    print_r($document);
}
```

This will return the document for Philip Moran because he's only a few years older than 30:

```
Array (
    [_id] => MongoId Object ( )
    [First Name] => Philip
    [Last Name] => Moran
    [Address] => Array (
        [Street] => 681 Hinkle Lake Road
        [Place] => Newton
        [Postal Code] => MA 02160
        [Country] => USA
    )
    [E-Mail] => Array (
        [0] => pm@example.com
        [1] => pm@office.com
        [2] => philip@example.com
        [3] => philip@office.com
        [4] => moran@example.com
        [5] => moran@office.com
        [6] => pmoran@example.com
        [7] => pmoran@office.com
    )
    [Phone] => 617-546-8428
    [Age] => 60
)
```

You can use the `$lte` operator to specify that the value must either match exactly or be lower than the value specified. Remember: `$lt` will find anyone who is younger than 30, but not anyone who is exactly 30. The same goes for the `$gte` operator, which finds any value that is greater than or equal to the integer specified. Now let's look at a pair of examples.

The first example will return both items from your collection to your screen:

```
// Connect to the database
$c = new Mongo();
// Select the collection 'people' from the database 'contacts'
$collection = $c->contacts->people;
// Specify the conditional operator
$cond = array('Age' => array('$lte' => 60));
// Execute the query and store it under the $cursor variable
$cursor = $collection->find($cond);
//Print the results
while($document = $cursor->getNext())
{
    print_r($document);
}
```

The second example will display only one document because the collection only holds one contact who is either 60 or older:

```
// Connect to the database
$c = new Mongo();
// Select the collection 'people' from the database 'contacts'
$collection = $c->contacts->people;
// Specify the conditional operator
$cond = array('Age' => array('$gte' => 60));
// Execute the query and store it under the $cursor variable
$cursor = $collection->find($cond);
//Print the results
while($document = $cursor->getNext())
{
    print_r($document);
}
```

## Finding Documents that *Don't* Match a Value

You can use the $ne (not equals) operator to find any documents that don't match the value specified in the $ne operator. The syntax for this operator is straightforward. The next example will display any contact whose age is not equal to 28:

```
// Connect to the database
$c = new Mongo();
// Select the collection 'people' from the database 'contacts'
$collection = $c->contacts->people;
// Specify the conditional operator
$cond = array('Age' => array('$ne' => 28));
// Execute the query and store it under the $cursor variable
$cursor = $collection->find($cond);
//Print the results
while($document = $cursor->getNext())
{
    print_r($document);
}
```

## Matching Any of Multiple Values with $in

The $in operator lets you search for documents that match any of several possible values added to an array, as in the following example:

```
// Connect to the database
$c = new Mongo();
// Select the collection ‘people’ from the database ‘contacts’
$collection = $c->contacts->people;
// Specify the conditional operator
$cond = array('Address.Country' => array('$in' => array("USA","UK")));
// Execute the query and store it under the $cursor variable
$cursor = $collection->find($cond);
//Print the results
while($document = $cursor->getNext())
{
    print_r($document);
}
```

The resulting output would show any contact information from any person you add, whether that person lives in the US or the UK. Note that the list of possibilities is actually added in an array; it cannot be typed in "just like that."

## Matching All Criteria in a Query with $all

Like the `$in` operator, the `$all` operator lets you compare against multiple values in an additional array. The difference is that the `$all` operator requires that all items in the array match a document before it returns any results. The following example shows how to conduct such a query:

```
// Connect to the database
$c = new Mongo();
// Select the collection 'people' from the database 'contacts'
$collection = $c->contacts->people;
// Specify the conditional operator
$cond = array('E-Mail' => array('$all' => array("vw@example.com","vw@office.com")));
// Execute the query and store it under the $cursor variable
$cursor = $collection->find($cond);
//Print the results
while($document = $cursor->getNext())
{
    print_r($document);
}
```

## Searching for Multiple Expressions with $or

You can use the `$or` operator to specify multiple expressions a document can contain to return a match. The difference between the two operators is that the `$in` operator doesn't allow you to specify both a key and value, whereas the `$or` operator does. You can combine the `$or` operator with any other key/value combination. Let's look at two examples.

The first example searches for and returns any document that contains either an `Age` key with the integer value of `28` or an `Address.Country` key with the value of `USA`:

```
// Connect to the database
$c = new Mongo();
// Select the collection 'people' from the database 'contacts'
$collection = $c->contacts->people;
// Specify the conditional operator
$cond = array('$or' => array(
        array("Age" => 28),
        array("Address.Country" => "USA")
) );
// Execute the query and store it under the $cursor variable
$cursor = $collection->find($cond);
//Print the results
while($document = $cursor->getNext())
{
    print_r($document);
}
```

The second example searches for and returns any document that has the `Address.Country` key set to `USA` (mandatory), as well as a key/value set either to `"Last Name" : "Moran"` or to `"E-Mail" : "vw@example.com"`:

```
// Connect to the database
$c = new Mongo();
// Select the collection 'people' from the database 'contacts'
$collection = $c->contacts->people;
// Specify the conditional operator
$cond = array(
    "Address.Country" => "USA",
    '$or' => array(
        array("Last Name" => "Moran"),
        array("E-Mail" => "vw@example.com")
    )
);
// Execute the query and store it under the $cursor variable
$cursor = $collection->find($cond);
//Print the results
while($document = $cursor->getNext())
{
    print_r($document);
}
```

The `$or` operator allows you to conduct two searches at once and then combine the resulting output, even if the searches have nothing in common.

## Retrieving a Specified Number of Items with $slice

You can use the `$slice` operator to retrieve a specified number of items from an array in your document. This function is similar to the `skip()` and `limit()` functions detailed previously in this chapter. The difference is that the `skip()` and `limit()` functions work on full documents, whereas the `$slice` operator allows you to work on an array rather than a single document.

The `$slice` operator is a great method for limiting the number of items per page (this is generally known as *paging*). The next example shows how to limit the number of e-mail addresses returned from one of the contacts specified earlier (Philip Moran); in this case, you only return the first three e-mail addresses:

```
// Connect to the database
$c = new Mongo();
// Select the collection 'people' from the database 'contacts'
$collection = $c->contacts->people;
// Specify our search operator
$query = array("Last Name" => "Moran");
// Specify the conditional operator
$cond = (object)array('E-Mail' => array('$slice' => 3));
// Execute the query and store it under the $cursor variable
$cursor = $collection->find($query, $cond);
// For each document it finds within the collection, print its contents
while ($document = $cursor->getNext())
{
        print_r($document);
}
```

Similarly, you can get only the *last* three e-mail addresses in the list by making the integer negative, as shown in the following example:

```
// Connect to the database
$c = new Mongo();
// Select the collection 'people' from the database 'contacts'
$collection = $c->contacts->people;
// Specify our search operator
$query = array("Last Name" => "Moran");
// Specify the conditional operator
$cond = (object)array('E-Mail' => array('$slice' => -3));
// Execute the query and store it under the $cursor variable
$cursor = $collection->find($query, $cond);
// For each document it finds within the collection, print its contents
while ($document = $cursor->getNext())
{
        print_r($document);
}
```

Or, you can skip the first two entries and limit the results to three:

```
// Connect to the database
$c = new Mongo();
// Select the collection 'people' from the database 'contacts'
$collection = $c->contacts->people;
// Specify our search operator
$query = array("Last Name" => "Moran");
// Specify the conditional operator
$cond = (object)array('E-Mail' => array('$slice' => [2, 3]));
// Execute the query and store it under the $cursor variable
$cursor = $collection->find($query, $cond);
// For each document it finds within the collection, print its contents
while ($document = $cursor->getNext())
{
        print_r($document);
}
```

The `$slice` operator is a great method for limiting the number of items in an array; you'll definitely want to keep this operator in mind when programming with the MongoDB driver and PHP.

## Determining Whether a Field Has a Value

You can use the `$exists` operator to return a result based on whether a field holds a value (regardless of the value of this field). As illogical as this may sound, it's actually very handy. For example, you can search for contacts where the `Age` field has not been set yet; or you can search for contacts for whom you have a street name.

The following example returns any contacts that do not have an `Age` field set:

```
// Connect to the database
$c = new Mongo();
// Select the collection 'people' from the database 'contacts'
$collection = $c->contacts->people;
// Specify the conditional operator
$cond = array('Age' => array('$exists' => false));
```

```
// Execute the query and store it under the $cursor variable
$cursor = $collection->find($cond);
//Print the results
while($document = $cursor->getNext())
{
    print_r($document);
}
```

Similarly, the next example returns any contacts that have the `Country` field set:

```
// Connect to the database
$c = new Mongo();
// Select the collection 'people' from the database 'contacts'
$collection = $c->contacts->people;
// Specify the conditional operator
$cond = array("Address.Street" => array('$exists' => true));
// Execute the query and store it under the $cursor variable
$cursor = $collection->find($cond);
//Print the results
while($document = $cursor->getNext())
{
    print_r($document);
}
```

## Regular Expressions

Regular Expressions are neat. You can use them for just about everything (except for making coffee, perhaps); and they can greatly simplify your life when searching for data. The PHP driver comes with its own class for Regular Expressions: the `MongoRegex` class. You can use this class to create Regular Expressions, and then use them to find data.

The `MongoRegex` class knows six regular expression flags that you can use to query your data. You may already be familiar with some of them:

- `i`: Triggers case insensitivity.
- `m`: Searches for content that is spread over multiple lines (linebreaks).
- `x`: Allows your search to contain #comments.
- `l`: Specifies a locale.
- `s`: dotall, "." can be specified to match everything, including new lines.
- `u`: Matches Unicode.

Now let's take a closer look at how to use Regular Expressions in PHP to search for data in your collection. Obviously, this is best demonstrated with a simple example.

For example, assume you want to search for a contact about whom you know only a small portion of information. For example, you may vaguely recall the place where the person lives and that it contains something like stradgynl in the middle somewhere. Regular Expressions give you a simple yet elegant way to search for such a person:

```
// Connect to the database
$c = new Mongo();
// Select the collection 'people' from the database 'contacts'
$collection = $c->contacts->people;
```

```
// Specify the Regular Expression
$regex = new MongoRegex("/stradgynl/i");
// Execute the query and store it under the $cursor variable
$cursor = $collection->find(array("Address.Place" => $regex));
//Print the results
while($document = $cursor->getNext())
{
    print_r($document);
}
```

When creating a PHP application, you'll typically want to search for specific data. In the preceding example, you would probably replace the text ("stradgynl", in this case) with a $_POST variable. You will see an example that shows how to do this in Chapter 8.

# Modifying Data with PHP

If we lived in a world where all data remained static and humans never made any typos, we would never need to update our documents. But the world is a little more flexible than that, and there are times when we make mistakes that we'd like to correct.

For such situations, you can use a set of modifier functions in MongoDB to update (and therefore change) your existing data. You can do this in several ways. For example, you might use the update() function to update existing information, and then use the save() function to save your changes. The following sections look at a handful of these and other modifier operators, illustrating how to use them effectively.

## Updating via update()

As detailed in Chapter 4, you use the update() function to perform most document updates. Like the version of update() in the MongoDB shell, the update() function that comes with the PHP driver allows you to use an assortment of modifier operators to update your documents quickly and easily. PHP's version of the update() function operates almost identically; nevertheless, using the PHP version successfully requires a significantly different approach. The upcoming section will walk you through how to use the function successfully with PHP.

PHP's update() function takes a minimum of two parameters: the first describes the object(s) to update, and the second describes the object you want to update the matching record(s) with. Additionally, you can specify a third parameter for an expanded set of options.

The options parameter provides four additional flags you can use with the update() function; this list explains what they are and how to use them:

- *upsert*: If set to true, this Boolean option causes a new document to be created if the search criteria is not matched.
- *multiple*: If set to true, this Boolean option causes all documents matching the search criteria to be updated.
- *safe*: If set to true, this option instructs the application to wait for a database response to confirm whether an update was successful. If it wasn't successful, an exception is thrown. If the safe option is set to an integer *n*, then it will replicate the update to *n* number of machines before returning success.
- *fsync*: If set to true, this Boolean option causes the data to be synced to disk before returning a success. If this option is set to true, then it's implied that safe is also set to true, even if it's set to false.

Now let's look at a common example that changes Victoria Wood's first name to "Vicky" without using any of the modifier operators (these will be discussed momentarily):

```
// Connect to the database
$c = new Mongo();
// Select the collection 'people' from the database 'contacts'
$collection = $c->contacts->people;
// Specify the search criteria
$criteria = array("Last Name" => "Wood");
// Specify the information to be changed
$update = array(
        "First Name" => "Vicky",
        "Last Name" => "Wood",
        "Address" => array(
                        "Street" => "50 Ash lane",
                        "Place" => "Ystradgynlais",
                        "Postal Code" => "SA9 6XS",
                        "Country" => "UK"
        )
        ,
        "E-Mail" => array(
                "vw@example.com",
                "vw@office.com"
        ),
        "Phone" => "078-8727-8049",
        "Age" => 28
);
// Options
$options = array("upsert" => true);
// Perform the update
$collection->update($criteria,$update,$options);
// Show the result
print_r($collection->findOne($criteria));
```

The resulting output would look like this:

```
Array (
    [Address] => Array (
         [Street] => 50 Ash lane
         [Place] => Ystradgynlais
         [Postal Code] => SA9 6XS
         [Country] => UK
    )
     [Age] => 28
     [E-Mail] => Array (
         [0] => vw@example.com
         [1] => vw@office.com
    )
     [First Name] => Vicky
     [Last Name] => Wood
     [Phone] => 078-8727-8049
     [_id] => MongoId Object ( )
)
```

This is a lot of work just to change one value—not exactly what you'd want to be doing to make a living. However, this is precisely what you would have to do if you didn't use PHP's modifier operators. Now let's look at how you can use these operators in PHP to make life easier and consume less time.

---

■ **Warning** If you don't specify any of the conditional operators when applying the change, the data in the matching document(s) will be replaced by the information in the array. Generally, it's best to use `$set` if you want to change only one field.

---

# Saving Time with Modifier Operators

The modifier operations are going to save you loads of typing. As you'll probably agree, the preceding example is just not feasible to work with. Fortunately, the PHP driver includes about half a dozen modifier operators for quickly updating your data, without going through the trouble of writing it out fully. The purpose of each operator will be briefly summarized again, although you are probably familiar with most of them at this point (you can find more information about all the modifier operators discussed in this section in Chapter 4). However, the way you use them in PHP differs significantly, as do the options associated with them. We'll look at examples for each of these operators, not least so you can familiarize you with their syntax in PHP.

---

■ **Note** None of the modifier operators that follow will include PHP code to review the changes made; rather, the examples that follow only apply the changes. It's suggested that you fire up the MongoDB shell alongside of the PHP code, so you can perform searches and confirm that the desired changes have applied. Alternatively, you can write additional PHP code to perform these checks.

---

## Increasing the Value of a Specific Key with $inc

The `$inc` operator allows you to increase the value of a specific key by *n*, assuming that the key exists. If the key does not exist, it will be created instead. The following example increases the age of each person younger than 40 by three years:

```
// Connect to the database
$c = new Mongo();
// Select the collection 'people' from the database 'contacts'
$collection = $c->contacts->people;
// Search for anyone that's younger than 40
$criteria = array("Age" => array('$lt' => 40));
// Use $inc to increase their age by 3 years
$update = array('$inc' => array('Age' => 3));
// Options
$options = array("upsert" => true);
// Perform the update
$collection->update($criteria,$update,$options);
```

## Changing the Value of a Key with $set

The $set operator lets you change the value of a key while ignoring any other fields. As noted previously, this would have been a much better choice for updating Victoria's first name to "Vicky" in the earlier example. The following example shows how to use the $set operator to change the contact's name to "Vicky":

```
// Connect to the database
$c = new Mongo();
// Select the collection 'people' from the database 'contacts'
$collection = $c->contacts->people;
// Specify the search criteria
$criteria = array("Last Name" => "Wood");
// Specify the information to be changed
$update = array('$set' => array("First Name" => "Vicky"));
// Options
$options = array("upsert" => true);
// Perform the update
$collection->update($criteria,$update,$options);
```

You can also use $set to add a field for every occurrence found matching your query:

```
// Connect to the database
$c = new Mongo();
// Select the collection ‘people’ from the database ‘contacts’
$collection = $c->contacts->people;
// Specify the search criteria using Regular Expressions
$criteria = array("E-Mail" => new MongoRegex("/@office.com/i"));
// Add “Category => Work” into every occurrence found
$update = array('$set' => array('Category' => 'Work'));
// Options
$options = array('upsert' => true, 'multi' => true);
// Perform the upsert via save()
$collection->update($criteria,$update,$options);
```

## Deleting a Field with $unset

The $unset operator works similarly to the $set operator. The difference is that $unset lets you delete a given field from a document. For instance, the following example removes the Phone field and its associated data from the contact information for Victoria Wood:

```
// Connect to the database
$c = new Mongo();
// Select the collection 'people' from the database 'contacts'
$collection = $c->contacts->people;
// Specify the search criteria
$criteria = array("Last Name" => "Wood");
// Specify the information to be removed
$update = array('$unset' => array("Phone" => 1));
// Perform the update
$collection->update($criteria,$update);
```

## Appending a Value to a Specified Field with $push

PHP's $push operator lets you append a value to a specified field. If the field is an existing array, the data will be added; if the field does not exist, it will be created. If the field exists, but it is not an array, then an error condition will be raised. The following example shows how to use $push to add some data into an already existing array:

```
// Connect to the database
$c = new Mongo();
// Select the collection 'people' from the database 'contacts'
$collection = $c->contacts->people;
// Specify the search criteria
$criteria = array("Last Name" => "Wood");
// Specify the information to be added
$update = array('$push' => array("E-Mail" => "vw@mongo.db"));
// Perform the update
$collection->update($criteria,$update);
```

## Adding Multiple Values to a Key with $pushAll

Similarly, the $pushAll operator allows you to add multiple values to a key. The same rules apply for this operator: if the field exists, and it is an array, then the data will be added; if it does not exist, then it will be created; if it exists, but it isn't an array, then an error condition will be raised. The following example illustrates how to use the $pushAll operator:

```
// Connect to the database
$c = new Mongo();
// Select the collection ‘people’ from the database ‘contacts’
$collection = $c->contacts->people;
// Specify the search criteria
$criteria = array("Last Name" => "Wood");
// Specify the information to be added
$update = array(
        '$pushAll' => array(
                "E-Mail" => array("vicwo@mongo.db","vicwo@example.com")
        )
);
// Perform the update
$collection->update($criteria,$update);
```

## Adding Data to an Array with $addToSet

The $addToSet operator is similar to the $push and $pushAll operators, with one important difference: $addToSet ensures that data is added to an array only if the data is not in there already (neither the $push nor $pushAll operators check for this condition). The $addToSet operator takes one array as a parameter:

```
// Connect to the database
$c = new Mongo();
// Select the collection 'people' from the database 'contacts'
$collection = $c->contacts->people;
// Specify the search criteria
$criteria = array("Last Name" => "Wood");
```

```
// Specify the information to be added (successful because it doesn't exist yet)
$update = array('$addToSet' => array("E-Mail" => "vicwo@example.com"));
// Perform the update
$collection->update($criteria,$update);
```

Similarly, you can add a number of items that don't exist yet by combining the $addToSet operator with the $each operator:

```
// Connect to the database
$c = new Mongo();
// Select the collection 'people' from the database 'contacts'
$collection = $c->contacts->people;
// Specify the search criteria
$criteria = array("Last Name" => "Wood");
// Specify the information to be added (partially successful, some
// examples were already there)
$update = array(
    '$addToSet' => array
        (
        "E-Mail" => array
            (
            '$each' => array
                (
                "vw@mongo.db",
                "vicky@mongo.db",
                "vicky@example.com"
                )
            )
        )
);
// Perform the update
$collection->update($criteria,$update);
```

## Removing an Element from an Array with $pop

PHP's $pop operator lets you remove an element from an array. Keep in mind that you can remove only the first or last element in the array—and nothing in between. You remove the first element by specifying a value of -1; similarly, you remove the last element by specifying a value of 1:

```
// Connect to the database
$c = new Mongo();
// Select the collection 'people' from the database 'contacts'
$collection = $c->contacts->people;
// Specify the search criteria
$criteria = array("Last Name" => "Wood");
// Pop out the first e-mail address found in the list
$update = array('$pop' => array("E-Mail" => -1));
// Perform the update
$collection->update($criteria,$update);
```

---

■ **Note** Specifying a value of -2 or 1000 wouldn't change which element gets removed. Any negative number will remove the first element, whereas any positive number removes the last element. Using a value of 0 removes the last element from the array.

---

## Removing Each Occurrence of a Value with $pull

You can use PHP's $pull operator to remove each occurrence of a given value from an array. For example, this is handy if you've accidentally added duplicates to an array when using $push or $pushAll. The following example removes any duplicate occurrence of an e-mail address:

```
// Connect to the database
$c = new Mongo();
// Select the collection 'people' from the database 'contacts'
$collection = $c->contacts->people;
// Specify the search criteria
$criteria = array("Last Name" => "Wood");
// Pull out each occurrence of the e-mail address "vicky@example.com"
$update = array('$pull' => array("E-Mail" => "vicky@example.com"));
// Perform the update
$collection->update($criteria,$update);
```

## Removing Each Occurrence of Multiple Elements

Similarly, you can use the $pullAll operator to remove each occurrence of multiple elements from your documents, as shown in the following example:

```
// Connect to the database
$c = new Mongo();
// Select the collection 'people' from the database 'contacts'
$collection = $c->contacts->people;
// Specify the search criteria
$criteria = array("Last Name" => "Wood");
// Pull out each occurrence of the e-mail addresses below
$update = array(
        '$pullAll' => array(
                "E-Mail" => array("vw@mongo.db","vw@office.com")
        )
);
// Perform the update
$collection->update($criteria,$update);
```

# Upserting Data with save()

Like the insert() function, the save() function allows you to insert data into your collection. The only difference is that you can also use save() to update a field that already holds data. As you might recall, this is called an *upsert*. The way you execute the save() function shouldn't come as a surprise by this point. As when using save() in the MongoDB shell, PHP's save() takes only one parameter: an array that contains the information you wish to save. The syntax for PHP's version is similar, as the following example illustrates:

```
// Specify the document to be saved
$contact = array(
        "First Name" => "Kenji",
        "Last Name" => "Kitahara",
        "Address" => array(
                        "Street" => "149 Bartlett Avenue",
                        "Place" => "Southfield",
                        "Postal Code" => "MI 48075",
                        "Country" => "USA"
        )
        ,
        "E-Mail" => array(
                "kk@example.com",
                "kk@office.com"
        ),
        "Phone" => "248-510-1562",
        "Age" => 34
);
// Connect to the database
$c = new Mongo();
// Select the collection 'people'
$collection = $c->contacts->people;
// Save via the save() function
$collection->save($contact);
// Realizing you forgot something, let's upsert this contact:
$contact['Category'] = 'Work';
// Perform the upsert
$collection->save($contact);
```

## Modifying a Document Atomically

Like the `save()` and `update()` functions, the `findAndModify()` function can be invoked from the PHP driver. Remember that you can use the `findAndModify()` function to atomically modify a document and return the results after the update executes successfully. The PHP driver currently does not have a helper method for this, however, so you need to execute this function as a database command (as you did previously with the `mapreduce()` function). Fortunately, the `findAndModify()` function is much less complicated than the `mapreduce()` function; unfortunately, it is not quite simple enough that we can skip explaining how to use it.

You use the `findAndModify()` function to update a single document—and nothing more. You may recall that, by default, the document returned will *not* show the modifications made—returning the document with the modifications made would require specifying an additional argument: the `new` parameter.

The `findAndModify` function takes about half a dozen parameters; of these, you must include either the `update` or `remove` parameter. The following list details the available parameters, some of which are optional:

- `query`: Specifies a filter for the query. If this parameter isn't specified, then all documents in the collection will be seen as possible candidates, and the first document encountered will be updated or removed.
- `sort`: Sorts the matching documents in a specified order.

- remove: If set to true, the first matching document will be removed.
- update: Specifies the information to update the document. Note that any of the modifier operators specified previously can be used to accomplish this.
- new: If set to true, returns the updated document, rather than the selected document. Note that this parameter is not set by default, which might be a bit confusing in some circumstances.
- fields: Specifies the fields you would like to see returned, rather than the entire document. This parameter behaves identically to the identically named parameter in the find() function. Note that the _id field will always be returned, even if that field isn't included in your list of fields to return.
- upsert: If set to true, performs an upsert.

Now let's look at a set of examples that elaborate on how to use these parameters. The first example searches for a contact with the last name "Kitahara" and adds an e-mail address to his contact card by combining an update() with the $push operator. The new parameter is not set in the following example, so the resulting output still displays the *old* information:

```
// Connect to the database
$c = new Mongo();
// Specify the database in which to work
$db = $c->contacts;
// Perform a findAndModify()
print_r($db->command(
    array(
        "findandmodify" => "people",
        "query" => array("Last Name" => "Kitahara"),
        "update" => array('$push' => array("E-Mail" => "kitahara@mongo.db"))
    )
));
```

The result returned looks like this:

```
Array (
    [value] => Array (
        [First Name] => Kenji
        [Last Name] => Kitahara
        [Address] => Array (
            [Street] => 149 Bartlett Avenue
            [Place] => Southfield
            [Postal Code] => MI 48075
            [Country] => USA
            )
            [E-Mail] => Array (
                [0] => kk@example.com
                [1] => kk@office.com
           )
            [Phone] => 248-510-1562
            [Age] => 34
            [_id] => MongoId Object ( )
            [Category] => Work
    )
    [ok] => 1
)
```

The following example shows how to use the remove and sort parameters:

```
// Connect to the database
$c = new Mongo();
// Specify the database in which to work
$db = $c->contacts;
// Perform a findAndModify()
print_r($db->command(
    array(
        "findandmodify" => "people",
        "query" => array("Category" => "Work"),
        "sort" => array("Age" => -1),
        "remove" => true
    )
));
```

The resulting output shows that Philip has been removed from the collection:

```
Array (
    [value] => Array (
    [Address] => Array (
        [Street] => 681 Hinkle Lake Road
        [Place] => Newton
        [Postal Code] => MA 02160
        [Country] => USA
    )
    [Age] => 60
    [Category] => Work
    [E-Mail] => Array (
        [0] => pm@example.com
        [1] => pm@office.com
        [2] => philip@example.com
        [3] => philip@office.com
        [4] => moran@example.com
        [5] => moran@office.com
        [6] => pmoran@example.com
        [7] => pmoran@office.com
    )
    [First Name] => Philip
    [Last Name] => Moran
    [Phone] => 617-546-8428
    [_id] => MongoId Object ( )
    )
     [ok] => 1
)
```

# Deleting Data

You can use the remove() function to remove a document like the preceding one from the MongoDB shell. The PHP driver also includes a remove() function you can use to remove data. The PHP version of this function takes two parameters: one contains the description of the record or records to remove, while the other specifies additional options governing the removal process.

There are three options available: justOne, which specifies that at most only one record matching the criteria must be removed; safe, which specifies that the PHP code must wait for a response from the database that confirms the removal went successfully before proceeding with the rest of the PHP code; and fsync, which forces the update to be synced to disk before returning a success. The last option will automatically assume that safe is also set to true when enabled.

Now let's look at a couple of code examples that illustrate how to remove a document:

```
// Connect to the database
$c = new Mongo();
// Select the collection 'people' from the database 'contacts'
$collection = $c->contacts->people;
// Specify the search criteria
$criteria = array("Last Name" => "Wood");
// Specify the options
$options = array('justOne' => true, 'safe' => true);
// Perform the removal
$collection->remove($criteria,$options);
```

Similarly, the next example removes multiple documents at the same time:

```
// Connect to the database
$c = new Mongo();
// Select the collection 'people' from the database 'contacts'
$collection = $c->contacts->people;
// Specify the search criteria using Regular Expressions
$criteria = array("E-Mail" => new MongoRegex("/@office.com/i"));
// Specify the options
$options = array("justOne" => false);
// Perform the removal
$collection->remove($criteria,$options);
```

---

■ **Warning** When you remove a document, remember that any reference to that document will remain in the database. Make sure that you also manually delete or update references to the deleted document; otherwise, these references will return null when evaluated.

---

Similarly, you can drop an entire collection using the drop() function. This following example returns an array with the removal results:

```
// Connect to the database
$c = new Mongo();
// Select the collection to remove
$collection = $c->contacts->people;
// Remove the collection and return the results
print_r($collection->drop());
```

The results returned look like this:

```
Array (
    [nIndexesWas] => 1
    [msg] => indexes dropped for collection
    [ns] => contacts.people
    [ok] => 1
)
```

Last but not least, you can use PHP to drop entire databases. You accomplish this by using the drop() function in the MongoDB class, as shown in the following example:

```
// Connect to the database
$c = new Mongo();
// Select the database to remove
$db = $c->contacts;
// Remove the database and return the results
print_r($db->drop());
```

The results returned show the name of the database dropped:

```
Array (
[dropped] => contacts
[ok] => 1
)
```

# DBRef

DBRef enables you to create links between two different documents stored in different locations; this functionality lets you implement behavior similar to that found in a relational database. This functionality can be particularly handy if you want to store the addresses from the people in an addresses collection, rather than include that information in your people collection.

There are two ways to do this. First, you can use a simple link (e.g., *manual referencing*); in this case, you include the _id of a document into another document. Second, you can use DBRef to create such links automatically.

First, let's look at how you implement manual referencing. In the following example, you add a contact and, under its address information, specify the _id of another document:

```
// Connect to the database
$c = new Mongo();
$db = $c->contacts;
// Select the collections we want to store our contacts and addresses in
$people = $db->people;
$addresses = $db->addresses;
// Specify an address:
$address = array(
    "Street" => "St. Annastraat 44",
    "Place" => "Monster",
    "Postal Code" => "2681 SR",
    "Country" => "Netherlands"
);
// Save the address
$addresses->insert($address);
```

```
// Add a contact living at the address
$contact = array(
    "First Name" => "Melvyn",
    "Last Name" => "Babel",
    "Age" => 35,
    "Address" => $address['_id']
);
$people->insert($contact);
```

Now assume you want to find the preceding contact's address information. To do this, simply query for the `Object ID` in the address field; you can find this information in the addresses collection (assuming you know the name of this collection).

This works, but the preferred method for referencing another document relies on DBRef. This is because DBRef relies on a common format that the database and all the drivers understand. We'll look at a DBRef version of the preceding example momentarily. Before doing so, however, let's take a look at the `create()` function of the `DBRef` class; you will use this class to create the desired reference.

The `create()` function takes three parameters:

- `collection`: Specifies the name of the collection where the information resides (without the database name).
- `id`: Specifies the ID of the document to link to.
- `database`: Specifies the name of the database in which the document resides.

The following example uses the `create()` function to create a reference to an address in another document:

```
// Connect to the database
$c = new Mongo();
$db = $c->contacts;

// Select the collections we want to store our contacts and addresses in
$people = $db->people;
$addresses = $db->addresses;

// Specify an address:
$address = array(
    "Street" => "WA Visser het Hooftlaan 2621",
    "Place" => "Driebergen",
    "Postal Code" => "3972 SR",
    "Country" => "Netherlands"
);

// Save the address
$addresses->insert($address);

// Create a reference to the address
$addressRef = MongoDBRef::create($addresses->getName(), $address['_id']);

// Add a contact living at the address
$contact = array(
    "First Name" => "Ivo",
    "Last Name" => "Lauw",
    "Age" => 24,
    "Address" => $addressRef
);
$people->insert($contact);
```

---

**Note** The `getName()` function in the preceding example is used to get the name of the collection.

---

## Retrieving the Information

So far you've used DBRef to create a reference. Now it's time to look at how to retrieve the information referenced, so that you can display the contents again correctly. You do this using MongoDBRef's `get()` function.

MongoDBRef's `get()` function takes two parameters. The first parameter specifies the database to use, while the second provides the reference to fetch:

```
// Connect to the database
$c = new Mongo();
// Select the collection 'people' from the database 'contacts'
$people = $c->contacts->people;
// Define the search parameters
$lastname = array("Last Name" => "Lauw");
// Find our contact, and store under the $person variable
$person = $people->findOne(array("Last Name" => "Lauw"));
// Dereference the address
$address = MongoDBRef::get($people->db, $person['Address']);
// Print out the address from the matching contact
print_r($address);
```

The resulting output shows the document being referred to:

```
Array (
    [_id] => MongoId Object ( )
    [Street] => WA Visser het Hooftlaan 2621
    [Place] => Driebergen
    [Postal Code] => 3972 SR
    [Country] => Netherlands
)
```

DBRef provides a great way to store data you want to reference, not least because it permits flexible naming of the collection and database names.

# GridFS and the PHP Driver

The previous chapter elaborated on GridFS and its benefits. For example, it explained how to use this technology to store data and retrieve data, in addition to other GridFS-related techniques. In this section, you'll learn how to use the PHP driver to store and retrieve files using GridFS.

The PHP driver contains its own classes for dealing with GridFS; here are three of its most important classes and what they do:

- `MongoGridFS`: Stores and retrieves files from the database. This class contains several methods, including `delete()`, `find()`, `storeUpload()`, and about a half dozen others.
- `MongoGridFSFile`: Works on a specific file in the database. It includes functions such as `__construct()`, `getFilename()`, `getSize()`, and `write()`.
- `MongoGridFSCursor`: Works on the cursor. It contains a handful of functions, such as `__construct()`, `current()`, `getNext()`, and `key()`.

Let's have a look at how we can use PHP to upload files into the database.

---

■ **Note** The code in the following example will not work without a HTML form that uploads data. Such code is beyond the scope of this chapter, however, so it is not shown here.

---

## Storing Files

You use the `storeUpload()` function to store files into your database with GridFS. This function takes two parameters: one indicates the name of the file to be uploaded, and the other specifies the filename you'd like to use in the database. Once used, the function reports back the _id of the file stored.

The following simple code example shows how to use the `storeUpload()` function:

```
// Connect to the database
$c = new Mongo();
// Select the name of the database
$db = $c->contacts;
// Define the GridFS class to ensure we can handle the files
$gridFS = $db->getGridFS();
// Specify the parameters of the filename to be stored (optional)
$name = $_FILES['File']['name'];
// Upload the file into the database
$id = $gridFS->storeUpload('File',$name);
```

And that's all there is to it. As you can see, `$id` is used as a parameter to store the file in the database. You might also use this parameter to reference the data with DBRef.

## Adding More Metadata to Stored Files

Sometimes you may want to add more metadata to your stored files. By default, the only other data that's added is the `_id` field, which you might use to reference the data when you're storing a picture to a contact card. Unfortunately, that might prove to be more of a restriction than a benefit when you want to start searching for your data through these tags.

The following example shows how to store metadata for your uploaded data. This example builds on the previous code block and the `$id` parameter in particular. Obviously, you can customize this yourself, using any other desired search criteria:

```
// Specify the metadata to be added
$metadata = array('$set' => array("Tag" => "Avatar"));
// Specify the search criteria to which to apply the metadata
$criteria = array('_id' => $id);
// Insert the metadata
$db->grid->update($criteria, $metadata);
```

## Retrieving Files

Of course, the ability to store your files in a database wouldn't do you any good if you weren't able to retrieve these files later. Retrieving files is about as hard (read: easy!) as storing them. Let's look at two examples: the first retrieves the filenames stored, while the second retrieves the files themselves.

The following example shows how to retrieve the filenames stored, which you accomplish using the getFilename() function:

```
// Connect to the database
$c = new Mongo();
$db = $c->contacts;
// Initialize GridFS
$gridFS = $db->getGridFS();
// Find all files in the GridFS storage and store under the $cursor parameter
$cursor = $gridFS->find();
// Return all the names of the files
foreach ($cursor as $object) {
    echo "Filename:".$object->getFilename();
}
```

That was easy! Of course, the preceding example assumes that you have some data stored in your database. You might also want to add more search parameters to the find() function after you've added a little more data or if you want to search for more specific data. Note that the find() function searches through the metadata added to each uploaded file (as detailed earlier in this chapter).

You might wonder how you go about retrieving the files themselves. After all, retrieving the data is probably what you'll be using the most in the end. You accomplish this by using the getBytes() function to send it to your browser. The next example uses the getBytes() function to retrieve a previously stored image. Note that you can retrieve the _id parameter by querying the database (the following example just makes up some parameters). Also, it's mandatory to specify the content type because, logically, this is not recognized by the browser when you build up the data again:

```
// Connect to the database
$c = new Mongo();
// Specify the database name
$db = $c->contacts;
// Initialize the GridFS files collection
$gridFS = $db->getGridFS();
// Specify the search parameter for the file
$id = new MongoId('4c555c70be90968001080000');
// Retrieve the file
$file = $gridFS->findOne(array('_id' => $id));
// Specify the header for the file and write the data to it
header('Content-Type: image/jpeg');
echo $file->getBytes();
exit;
```

## Deleting Data

You can ensure that any previously stored data gets removed by using the delete() function. This function takes one parameter: the _id of the file itself. The following example illustrates how to use the delete() function to delete the file matching the Object ID 4c555c70be90968001080000:

```
// Connect to the database
$c = new Mongo();
// Specify the database name
$db = $c->contacts;
// Initialize GridFS
$gridFS = $db->getGridFS();
// Specify the file via it's ID
$id = new MongoId('4c555c70be90968001080000');
$file = $gridFS->findOne(array('_id' => $id));
// Remove the file using the remove() function
$gridFS->delete($id);
```

# Summary

In this chapter, you've taken an in-depth look at how to work with MongoDB's PHP driver. For example, you've seen how to use the most commonly used functions with the PHP driver, including the insert(), update(), and modify() functions. You've also learned how to search your documents by using the PHP driver's equivalent of the find() function. Finally, you've learned how to use leverage DBRef's functionality, as well as how to store and retrieve files with GridFS.

One chapter couldn't possibly cover everything there is to know about using the PHP driver for MongoDB; nonetheless, this chapter should provide the necessary basics to perform most of the actions you'd want to accomplish with this driver. Along the way, you've also learned enough to use the server-side commands whenever the going gets a little more complicated.

In the next chapter, you'll explore the same concepts, but for the Python driver instead.

CHAPTER 7

# Python and MongoDB

Python is by far one of the easier programming languages to learn and master. It's an especially great language to start with if you are relatively new to programming. And you'll pick it up that much more quickly if you're already quite familiar with programming.

Python can be used to quickly develop an application while ensuring the code itself remains perfectly readable. With that in mind, this chapter will show you how to write simple yet elegant, clear, and powerful code that works with MongoDB through the Python driver (AKA, the PyMongo driver).

First, you'll look at the `Connection()` function, which enables you to establish a connection to the database. Second, you'll learn how to write documents, or *dictionaries*, as well as how to insert them. Third, you'll learn how to use either the `find()` or `find_one()` command to retrieve documents using the Python driver. Both of these commands optionally take a rich set of query modifiers to narrow down your search and make your query a little easier to implement. Fourth, you'll learn about the wide variety of operators that exist for performing updates. Finally, you'll take a look at how to use PyMongo to delete your data at the document or even the database level. As an added bonus, you'll learn how to use `DBRef` module to refer to data stored elsewhere.

Throughout the chapter, you'll see many practical code examples that illustrate the examples discussed. The code itself will be preceded with a greater than (>) symbol to indicate the command gets written in the Python shell. The query code will be styled in **bold**, whereas the resulting output will be rendered in plaintext. Let's get started.

## Working with Documents in Python

As mentioned in earlier chapters, MongoDB uses BSON-styled documents, and PHP uses associative arrays. In a similar vein, Python has what it calls *dictionaries*. If you've already played around with the MongoDB console, we're confident you are absolutely going to *love* Python. After all, the syntax is so similar that the learning curve for the language syntax will be negligible.

We've already covered the structure of a MongoDB document in the preceding chapter, so we won't get into that again now. Instead, let's examine what a document looks like in the Python shell:

```
item = {
    "Type" : "Laptop",
    "ItemNumber" : "1234EXD",
    "Status" : "In use",
    "Location" : {
        "Department" : "Development",
    "Building" : "2B",
        "Floor" : 12,
        "Desk" : 120101,
        "Owner" : "Anderson, Thomas"
    },
    "Tags" : ["Laptop","Development","In Use"]
}
```

While you should keep the Python term *dictionary* in mind, in most cases this chapter will refer to its MongoDB equivalent, *document*. After all, most of the time, we will be working with MongoDB documents.

## Using PyMongo Modules

The Python driver works with modules. You can treat these much as you treat the classes in the PHP driver. Each module within the PyMongo driver is responsible for a set of operations. There's an individual module for each of the following tasks (and quite a few more): establishing connections, working with databases, leveraging collections, manipulating the cursor, working with the `DBRef` module, converting the `Object ID`, and running server-side JavaScript code.

This chapter will walk you through the most basic yet useful set of operations needed to work with the PyMongo driver. Step-by-step, you learn how to use commands with simple and easy-to-understand pieces of code that you can copy and paste directly into your Python shell (or script). From there, it's a short step to managing your MongoDB database.

---

▒ **Note** Commands will be styled in **bold** in code and have a prefix that is preceded by three greater than symbols (**>>>**). This convention indicates that the line introduces a new command that is typed into the shell. Code that starts with three dots (...) indicates that the code is continued from the preceding line. The resulting output will not be styled.

---

## Connecting and Disconnecting

Establishing a connection to the database requires that you first import the PyMongo driver into Python itself. This is an absolute prerequisite; otherwise, none of the modules will be loaded, and your code will fail.

To import the driver, type the following command in your shell:

```
>>> import pymongo
```

Once the driver has been loaded and is known to the Python shell, you can start loading the module you want to work with. The `Connection` module enables you to establish connections. Type the following statement in the shell to load the `Connection` module:

```
>>> from pymongo import Connection
```

Once your MongoDB service is up and running (this is mandatory if you wish to connect), then you can go ahead and establish a connection to the service by calling the `Connection` function.

If no additional parameters are given, then the function assumes you want to connect to the service on the localhost (the default port number for the localhost is 27017). The following line establishes the connection:

```
>>> c = Connection()
```

You can see the connection coming in through the MongoDB service shell. Once you establish a connection, you can use the c dictionary to refer to the connection, just as you did in the shell with db and in PHP with $c. Next, select the database that you want to work with, storing that database under the db dictionary. You can do this just as you would in the MongoDB shell—in this example, you use the inventory database:

```
>>> db = c.inventory
>>> db
Database(Connection('localhost', 27017), u'inventory')
```

The output in the preceding example shows that you that you are connected to the localhost and that you are using the inventory database.

Now that the database has been selected, you can select your MongoDB collection in the exact same way. Because you've already stored the database name under the db dictionary, you can use that to select the collection's name, which is called items in this case:

```
>>> collection = db.items
```

# Inserting Data

All that remains is to define the document by storing it in a dictionary. Let's take the preceding example and insert that into the shell:

```
>>> item = {
...     "Type" : "Laptop",
...     "ItemNumber" : "1234EXD",
...     "Status" : "In use",
...     "Location" : {
...             "Department" : "Development",
...             "Building" : "2B",
...             "Floor" : 12,
...             "Desk" : 120101,
...             "Owner" : "Anderson, Thomas"
...     },
...     "Tags" : ["Laptop","Development","In Use"]
... }
```

Once you define the document, you can insert it using the same insert function that is available in the MongoDB shell:

```
>>> collection.insert(item)
ObjectId('4c57207b4abffe0e0c000000')
```

That's all there is to it: you define the document and insert it using the insert function.

There's one more interesting trick you can take advantage of when inserting documents: inserting multiple documents at the same time. You can do this by specifying both documents in a single dictionary, and then inserting that document afterwards. The result will return two Object IDs; pay careful attention to how the brackets are used in the following example:

```
>>> two = [{
...     "Type" : "Laptop",
...     "ItemNumber" : "2345FDX",
```

```
...     "Status" : "In use",
...     "Location" : {
...             "Department" : "Development",
...             "Building" : "2B",
...             "Floor" : 12,
...             "Desk" : 120102,
...             "Owner" : "Smith, Simon"
...     },
...     "Tags" : ["Laptop","Development","In Use"]
... },
... {
...     "Type" : "Laptop",
...     "ItemNumber" : "3456TFS",
...     "Status" : "In use",
...     "Location" : {
...             "Department" : "Development",
...             "Building" : "2B",
...             "Floor" : 12,
...             "Desk" : 120103,
...             "Owner" : "Walker, Jan"
...     },
...     "Tags" : ["Laptop","Development","In Use"]
... }]
>>> collection.insert(two)
[ObjectId('4c57234c4abffe0e0c000001'), ObjectId('4c57234c4abffe0e0c000002')]
```

# Finding Your Data

PyMongo provides two functions for finding your data: `find_one()`, which finds a single document in your collection that matches specified criteria; and `find()`, which can find multiple documents based on the supplied parameters (if you do not specify any parameters, `find()` returns all documents in the collection). Let's look at some examples.

## Finding a Single Document

As just mentioned, you use the `find_one()` function to find a single document. The function is similar to the `findOne()` function in the MongoDB shell, so mastering how it works shouldn't present much of a challenge for you. By default, this function will return the first document in your collection if it is executed without any parameters, as in the following example:

```
>>> collection.find_one()
    {
    u'Status': u'In use',
    u'Tags': [u'Laptop', u'Development', u'In Use'],
    u'ItemNumber': u'1234EXD',
    u'Location':{
        u'Department': u'Development',
        u'Building': u'2B',
        u'Floor': 12,
        u'Owner': u'Anderson, Thomas',
```

```
        u'Desk': 120101
        },
    u'_id': ObjectId('4c57207b4abffe0e0c000000'),
    u'Type': u'Laptop'
    }
```

You can specify additional parameters to ensure that the first document returned matches your query. The query parameters need to be written just as they would if you were defining them in the shell; that is, you need to specify a key and its value (or a number of values). For instance, assume you want to find a document for which an `ItemNumber` has the value of `3456TFS`. The following query accomplishes that, returning the output as shown:

```
>>> collection.find_one({"ItemNumber" : "3456TFS"})
{
    u'Status': u'In use',
    u'Tags': [u'Laptop', u'Development', u'In Use'],
    u'ItemNumber': u'3456TFS',
    u'Location': {
        u'Department': u'Development',
        u'Building': u'2B',
        u'Floor': 12,
        u'Owner': u'Walker, Jan',
        u'Desk': 120103
    },
        '_id': ObjectId('4c57234c4abffe0e0c000002'),
    u'Type': u'Laptop'
}
```

If the search criteria are relatively common for a document, you can also specify additional query operators. For example, imagine querying for `{"Department" : "Development"}`, which would return more than one result. We'll look at such an example momentarily; however, first let's determine how to return multiple documents, rather than just one. This may actually be a little different than you suspect.

# Finding Multiple Documents

You need to use the `find()` function to return more than a single document. You've probably used this command in MongoDB hundreds of times by this point in the book, so you're probably feeling rather comfortable with it. The concept is the same in Python: you specify the query parameters between the brackets to find the actual information.

Getting the results back to your screen, however, works a little differently. Just as when working with PHP and in the shell, querying for a set of documents will return a cursor instance to you. Unlike when typing in the shell, however, you can't simply type in `db.items.find()` to have all results presented to you. Instead, you need to retrieve all documents using the cursor. The following example shows how to display all documents from the `items` collection (note that you previously defined `collection` to match the collection's name; the results are left out for the sake of clarity):

```
>>> for doc in collection.find():
...             doc
...
```

Pay close attention to the indentation before the word `doc`. If this indentation is not used, then an error message will be displayed stating that an expected indented block didn't occur. It's one of Python's strengths that it uses such an indentation method for block delimiters because this approach keeps the code well ordered. Rest assured, you'll get used to this *Pythonic* coding convention relatively quickly. If you do happen to forget about the indentation, however, you'll see an error message that looks something like this:

```
File "<stdin>", line 2
    doc
      ^
IndentationError: expected an indented block
```

Next, let's look at how to specify a query operator using the `find()` function. The methods used for this are identical to the ones seen previously in the book:

```
>>> for doc in collection.find({"Location.Owner" : "Walker, Jan"}):
...             doc
...
{
    u'Status': u'In use',
    u'Tags': [u'Laptop', u'Development', u'In Use'],
    u'ItemNumber': u'3456TFS',
    u'Location': {
        u'Department': u'Development',
        u'Building': u'2B',
        u'Floor': 12,
        u'Owner': u'Walker, Jan',
        u'Desk': 120103
    },
    u'_id': ObjectId('4c57234c4abffe0e0c000002'),
    u'Type': u'Laptop'
}
```

# Using Dot Notation

*Dot notation* is used to search for matching elements in an embedded object. The preceding snippet actually shows an example of how to do this. When using this technique, you simply specify the key name for an item within the embedded object to search for it, as in the following example:

```
>>> for doc in collection.find({"Location.Department" : "Development"}):
...             doc
...
```

The preceding example returns any document that has the `Development` department set. When searching for information in a simple array (for instance, the tags applied), you only need to fill in any of the matching tags:

```
>>> for doc in collection.find({"Tags" : "Laptop"}):
...             doc
...
```

# Returning Fields

If your documents are relatively large, and you do not want to return all key/value information stored in a document, you can include an additional parameter in the `find()` function to specify that only a certain set of fields need to be returned. You do this by providing a list of field names after the search criteria.

The following example returns the only current owner's name, the item number, and the object ID (this will always be returned, even if you tell it to not show up):

```
>>> for doc in collection.find({'Status' : 'In use'} , {'ItemNumber' : 'true',
'Location.Owner':'true'}):
...             doc
...
{
        u'ItemNumber': u'1234EXD',
        u'_id': ObjectId('4c57207b4abffe0e0c000000'),
        u'Location': {
                u'Owner': u'Anderson, Thomas'
        }
}
{
        u'ItemNumber': u'2345FDX',
        u'_id': ObjectId('4c57234c4abffe0e0c000001'),
        u'Location': {
                u'Owner': u'Smith, Simon'
        }
}
{
        u'ItemNumber': u'3456TFS',
        u'_id': ObjectId('4c57234c4abffe0e0c000002'),
        u'Location': {
                u'Owner': u'Walker, Jan'
        }
}
```

I suspect you'll agree this approach to specifying criteria is quite handy.

## Simplifying Queries with Sort, Limit, and Skip

The `sort()`, `limit()`, and `skip()` functions will make implementing your queries much easier. Individually, each of these functions has its charms, but combining them makes them even better and more powerful. You can use the `sort()` function to sort the results by a specific key; the `limit()` function to limit the total number of results returned; and the `skip()` function to skip the first *n* number of items found before returning the remainder of the documents that match your query.

Let's look at a set of individual examples, beginning with the `sort()` function. To save some space, the following example includes another parameter to ensure only a few fields are returned:

```
>>> for doc in collection.find ({"Status" : "In use"},
...     {"ItemNumber":"true", "Location.Owner" : "True"})
...    .sort("ItemNumber"):
...             doc
...
{
        u'ItemNumber': u'1234EXD',
        u'_id': ObjectId('4c57207b4abffe0e0c000000'),
        u'Location': {
                u'Owner': u'Anderson, Thomas'
```

```
        }
}
{
        u'ItemNumber': u'2345FDX',
        u'_id': ObjectId('4c57234c4abffe0e0c000001'),
        u'Location': {
                u'Owner': u'Smith, Simon'
        }
}
{
        u'ItemNumber': u'3456TFS',
        u'_id': ObjectId('4c57234c4abffe0e0c000002'),
        u'Location': {
                u'Owner': u'Walker, Jan'
        }
}
```

Next, let's look at the limit() function in action. In this case, you tell the function to return only the ItemNumber from the first two items it finds in the collection (note that no search criteria are specified in this example):

```
>>> for doc in collection.find({}, {"ItemNumber" : "true"}).limit(2):
...             doc
...
{u'ItemNumber': u'1234EXD', u'_id': ObjectId('4c57207b4abffe0e0c000000')}
{u'ItemNumber': u'2345FDX', u'_id': ObjectId('4c57234c4abffe0e0c000001')}
```

You can use the skip() function to skip a few items before returning a set of documents, as in the following example:

```
>>> for doc in collection.find({}, {"ItemNumber" : "true"}).skip(2):
...     doc
...
{u'ItemNumber': u'3456TFS', u'_id': ObjectId('4c57234c4abffe0e0c000002')}
```

You can also combine the three functions to select only a certain amount of items found, while simultaneously specifying a specific number of items to skip and sorting them:

```
>>> for doc in collection.find( {'Status' : 'In use'},
...     {'ItemNumber':'true', 'Location.Owner':'true'} )
...     .limit(2).skip(1).sort("ItemNumber"):
...             doc
...
{
        u'ItemNumber': u'2345FDX',
        u'_id': ObjectId('4c57234c4abffe0e0c000001'),
        u'Location': {
                u'Owner': u'Smith, Simon'
                }
```

```
}
{
        u'ItemNumber': u'3456TFS',
        u'_id': ObjectId('4c57234c4abffe0e0c000002'),
        u'Location': {
                u'Owner': u'Walker, Jan'
        }
}
```

What you just did—limiting the results returned and skipping a certain number of items—is generally known as *paging*. You can accomplish this in a slightly more simplistic way with the `$slice` operator, which will be covered later in this chapter.

# Aggregating Queries

As previously noted, MongoDB comes with a powerful set of aggregation tools (see Chapter 4 for more information on these tools). The cool part: you can use all these tools with the Python driver. These tools make it possible to using the `count()` function to perform a count on your data; using the `distinct()` function to get a list of distinct values with no duplicates; and, last but not least, use the `map_reduce()` function to group your data and batch manipulate the results or simply to perform counts.

This set of commands, used separately or together, enables you to effectively query for the information you need to know—and nothing else.

## Counting Items with Count()

You can use the `count()` function if all you want is to perform a count on the total number of items matching your criteria,. The function doesn't return all the information the way the `find()` function does; instead, it returns an integer value with the total of items found.

Let's have a look at some simple examples. Let's begin by returning the total number of documents in the entire collection, without specifying any criteria.

```
>>> collection.find({}).count()
3
```

You can also specify these count queries more precisely, as in this example:

```
>>> collection.find({"Status" : "In use", "Location.Owner" : "Walker, Jan"}).count()
1
```

The `count()` function can be great when all you need is a quick count of the total number of documents that match your criteria.

## Counting Unique Items with Distinct()

The `count()` function is a great way to get the total number of items returned. However, sometimes you might accidentally add duplicates to your collection because you simply forget to remove or change an old document, and you want to get an accurate count that shows no duplicates. This is where the `distinct()` function can help you out. This function ensures that only unique items will be returned. Let's set up an example by adding another item to the collection with an `ItemNumber` used previously:

```
>>> dup = ( {
    "ItemNumber" : "2345FDX",
```

```
    "Status" : "Not used",
    "Type" : "Laptop",
    "Location" : {
        "Department" : "Storage",
        "Building" : "1A"
    },
    "Tags" : ["Not used","Laptop","Storage"]
} )
>>> collection.insert(dup)
ObjectId('4c592eb84abffe0e0c000004')
```

When you use the `count()` function at this juncture, the number of *unique* items won't be correct:

```
>>> collection.find({}).count()
4
```

Instead, you can use the `distinct()` function to ensure that any duplicates get ignored:

```
>>> collection.distinct("ItemNumber")
[u'1234EXD', u'2345FDX', u'3456TFS']
```

## Grouping Data with map_reduce()

The map_reduce() function is great for grouping your data by a certain tag and performing counts or other type of manipulation on it. The `map_reduce()` function is called from the `Code` module; therefore it needs to be invoked first. Let's have a look at a practical example that counts the occurrence of each tag and returns the results.

Begin by loading the `Code` module; you do this the same way you loaded the `Connection` module at the beginning of this chapter:

```
>>> from pymongo.code import Code
```

Now you're ready to define the `map` dictionary itself. You tell this object to format the data it finds as a set of keys and values. The following example uses the `Tags` key, setting the value of it to `1` because you want every item to count as just one object (this helps keep things simple). Naturally, you can change this number if you want to, but let's leave it as-is for now. The following snippet defines the `map` dictionary:

```
>>> map = Code("function() {"
...     "this.Tags.forEach(function(t) {"
...     "        emit(t, 1);"
...     "});"
...     "}")
```

You've defined the `map` dictionary; next, you need to specify the `reduce` dictionary, so you can accomplish the actual grouping. This requires an initial counter called `Total`, which you set to `0`. This is your default value. If you want to start off with 20 tags each, then you can change this value from `0` to `20`.

The following code specifies the `reduce` dictionary:

```
>>> reduce = Code("function (key, values) {"
...     "        var Total = 0;"
...     "        for (var i = 0; i < values.length; i++) {"
...     "                Total += values[i];"
...     "        }"
...     "        return Total;"
...     "}")
```

Now that the map and reduce dictionaries have been defined, you can go ahead and invoke the map_reduce() command, specifying map and reduce as its parameters. The results will be returned in a cursor, which you will need to treat like any other cursor to return the contents, as in the following example:

```
>>> result = collection.map_reduce(map, reduce)
>>> for tag in result.find():
...             tag
...
{u'_id': u'Development', u'value': 3.0}
{u'_id': u'In Use', u'value': 3.0}
{u'_id': u'Laptop', u'value': 4.0}
{u'_id': u'Not used', u'value': 1.0}
{u'_id': u'Storage', u'value': 1.0}
```

You can also use additional parameters as desired. For instance, you can use the out parameter to define the output collection; the query parameter to define your query; or the limit parameter to limit the total number of results returned. The next example applies these parameters. You don't need to redefine the map or reduce dictionaries this time, so you can skip ahead to executing the map_reduce command itself:

```
>>> result = collection.map_reduce(map, reduce, query={"Status" : "In use"}, limit=4,
out="Tags")
>>> for tag in result.find():
...             tag
...
{u'_id': u'Development', u'value': 3.0}
{u'_id': u'In Use', u'value': 3.0}
{u'_id': u'Laptop', u'value': 3.0}
```

# Specifying an Index with Hint()

You can use the hint() function to specify which index ought to be used when querying for data. Using this function helps you to increase the query's performance. In Python, the hint() function also executes on the cursor. However, you should keep in mind that the hint name you specify in Python needs to be the same as the one you passed to the create_index() function.

In the next example, you will create an index first, and then search for the data that specifies the index. Before you can sort in ascending order, however, you will need to use the import() function to import the ASCENDING method. Finally, you need to execute the create_index() function:

```
>>> from pymongo import ASCENDING
>>> collection.create_index([("ItemNumber", ASCENDING)])
u'ItemNumber_1'

>>> for doc in collection.find({"Location.Owner" : "Walker, Jan"}) .hint([("ItemNumber",
ASCENDING)]):
...             doc
...
{
    u'Status': u'In use',
    u'Tags': [u'Laptop', u'Development', u'In Use'],
    u'ItemNumber': u'3456TFS',
    u'Location': {
```

```
        u'Department': u'Development',
        u'Building': u'2B',
        u'Floor': 12,
        u'Owner': u'Walker, Jan',
        u'Desk': 120103
    },
    u'_id': ObjectId('4c57234c4abffe0e0c000002'),
    u'Type': u'Laptop'
}
```

Using indexes can help you significantly increase performance when the size of your collections keeps growing (see Chapter 10 for more details on performance tuning).

# Refining Queries with Conditional Operators

You can use conditional operators to refine your query. Python includes more than a half dozen conditional operators; these are identical to the conditional operators you've seen in the previous chapters. The following sections walk you through the conditional operators available in Python, as well as how you can use them to refine your queries in Python.

## Using the $lt, $gt, $lte, and $gte Operators

Let's begin by looking at the `$lt`, `$gt`, `$lte`, and `$gte` conditional operators. You can use the `$lt` operator to search for any numerical information that is *less than n*. The operator only takes one parameter: the number `n`, which specifies the limit. The following example finds any entries that have a desk number lower than 120102. Note that the `n` parameter itself is *not* included:

```
>>> for doc in collection.find({"Location.Desk" : {"$lt" : 120102} }):
...             doc
...
{
    u'Status': u'In use',
    u'Tags': [u'Laptop', u'Development', u'In Use'],
    u'ItemNumber': u'1234EXD',
    u'Location': {
        u'Department': u'Development',
        u'Building': u'2B',
        u'Floor': 12,
        u'Owner': u'Anderson, Thomas',
        u'Desk': 120101
    },
    u'_id': ObjectId('4c57207b4abffe0e0c000000'),
    u'Type': u'Laptop'
}
```

In a similar vein, you can use the `$gt` operator to find any items with a value *higher than n*. Again, note that the `n` parameter itself is not included:

```
>>> for doc in collection.find({"Location.Desk" : {"$gt" : 120102} }):
...             doc
...
{
```

```
    u'Status': u'In use',
    u'Tags': [u'Laptop', u'Development', u'In Use'],
    u'ItemNumber': u'3456TFS',
    u'Location': {
        u'Department': u'Development',
        u'Building': u'2B',
        u'Floor': 12,
        u'Owner': u'Walker, Jan',
        u'Desk': 120103
    },
    u'_id': ObjectId('4c57234c4abffe0e0c000002'),
    u'Type': u'Laptop'
}
```

If you want to include the value of the n parameters in your results, then you can use either the $lte or $gte operators to find any values *less than or equal to n* or *greater than or equal to n,* respectively. The following examples illustrate how to use these operators:

```
>>> for doc in collection.find({"Location.Desk" : {"$lte" : 120102} }):
...             doc
...
{
    u'Status': u'In use',
    u'Tags': [u'Laptop', u'Development', u'In Use'],
    u'ItemNumber': u'1234EXD',
    u'Location': {
        u'Department': u'Development',
        u'Building': u'2B',
        u'Floor': 12,
        u'Owner': u'Anderson, Thomas',
        u'Desk': 120101
    },
    u'_id': ObjectId('4c57207b4abffe0e0c000000'),
    u'Type': u'Laptop'
}
{
    u'Status': u'In use',
    u'Tags': [u'Laptop', u'Development', u'In Use'],
    u'ItemNumber': u'2345FDX',
    u'Location': {
        u'Department': u'Development',
        u'Building': u'2B',
        u'Floor': 12,
        u'Owner': u'Smith, Simon',
        u'Desk': 120102
    },
    u'_id': ObjectId('4c57234c4abffe0e0c000001'),
    u'Type': u'Laptop'
}

>>> for doc in collection.find({"Location.Desk" : {"$gte" : 120102} }):
...             doc
...
{
```

```
    u'Status': u'In use',
    u'Tags': [u'Laptop', u'Development', u'In Use'],
    u'ItemNumber': u'2345FDX',
    u'Location': {
        u'Department': u'Development',
        u'Building': u'2B',
        u'Floor': 12,
        u'Owner': u'Smith, Simon',
        u'Desk': 120102
    },
    u'_id': ObjectId('4c57234c4abffe0e0c000001'),
    u'Type': u'Laptop'
}
{
    u'Status': u'In use',
    u'Tags': [u'Laptop', u'Development', u'In Use'],
    u'ItemNumber': u'3456TFS',
    u'Location': {
        u'Department': u'Development',
        u'Building': u'2B',
        u'Floor': 12,
        u'Owner': u'Walker, Jan',
        u'Desk': 120103
    },
    u'_id': ObjectId('4c57234c4abffe0e0c000002'),
    u'Type': u'Laptop'
}
```

## Searching for Non-Matching Values with $ne

You can use the `$ne` (not equals) operator to search for any documents in a collection that do *not* match specified criteria. This operator requires one parameter, the key and value information that a document should not have for the result to return a match:

```
>>> collection.find({"Status" : {"$ne" : "In use"}}).count()
1
```

## Specifying an Array of Matches with $in

The `$in` operator lets you specify an array of possible matches; the SQL equivalent of this operator is `IN`.

For instance, assume you're looking for only two different kinds of development computers: not used or with `Development`. Also assume that you want to limit the results to two items, returning only the ItemNumber:

```
>>> for doc in collection.find({"Tags" : {"$in" : ["Not used","Development"]}} ,
{"ItemNumber":"true"}).limit(2):
...             doc
...
{u'ItemNumber': u'1234EXD', u'_id': ObjectId('4c57207b4abffe0e0c000000')}
{u'ItemNumber': u'2345FDX', u'_id': ObjectId('4c57234c4abffe0e0c000001')}
```

## Specifying Against an Array of Matches with $nin

You use the $nin operator exactly as you use the $in operator; the difference is that this operator *excludes* any documents that match any of the values specified in the given array. For example, the following query finds any items that are currently *not* used in the Development department:

```
>>> for doc in collection.find({"Tags" : {"$nin" : ["Development"]}}, {"ItemNumber":"true"}):
...             doc
...
{u'ItemNumber': u'2345FDX', u'_id': ObjectId('4c592eb84abffe0e0c000004')}
```

## Finding Documents that Match an Array's Values

Whereas the $in operator can be used to find any document that matches *any* of the values specified in an array, the $all operator lets you find any document that matches *all* of the values specified in an array. The syntax to accomplish this looks exactly the same:

```
>>> for doc in collection.find({"Tags" : {"$all" : ["Storage","Not used"]}},
{"ItemNumber":"true"}):
...             doc
...
{u'ItemNumber': u'2345FDX', u'_id': ObjectId('4c592eb84abffe0e0c000004')}
```

## Specifying Multiple Expressions to Match with $or

You can use the $or operator to specify multiple values that a document can have to qualify as a match. This is similar to the $in operator; the difference is that the $or operator lets you specify the key, as well as the value. You can also combine the $or operator with another key/value combination. Let's look at a few examples.

This example returns all documents that either have the location set to Storage or have the owner set to Anderson, Thomas:

```
>>> for doc in collection.find({"$or" : [ { "Location.Department" : "Storage" },
...     { "Location.Owner" : "Anderson, Thomas"} ] } ):
...             doc
...
```

You can also combine the preceding code with another key/value pair, as in this example:

```
>>> for doc in collection.find({ "Location.Building" : "2B", "$or" : [ { "Location.Department"
: "Storage" },
...     { "Location.Owner" : "Anderson, Thomas"} ] } ):
...             doc
...
```

The $or operator basically allows you to conduct two searches simultaneously and combine the resulting output, even if the individual searches have nothing in common with each other.

## Retrieving Items from an Array with $slice

You can use the `$slice` operator to retrieve a certain number of items from a given array in your document. This operator provides functionality similar to the `skip()` and `limit()` functions; the difference is that those two functions work on full documents, whereas the `$slice` operator works on an array in a *single* document.

Before looking at an example, let's add a new document that will enable us to take a better look at this operator. Assume that your company is maniacally obsessed with tracking its chair inventory, tracking chairs wherever they might go. Naturally, every chair has its own history of desks to which it once belonged. The `$slice` example operator is great for tracking that kind of inventory.

Begin by adding the following document:

```
>>> chair =  ({
...     "Status" : "Not used",
...     "Tags" : ["Chair","Not used","Storage"],
...     "ItemNumber" : "6789SID",
...     "Location" : {
...     "Department" : "Storage",
...     "Building" : "2B"
...     },
...     "PreviousLocation" :
...     [ "120100","120101","120102","120103","120104","120105",
...     "120106","120107","120108","120109","120110" ]
...     })
```

```
>>> collection.insert(chair)
ObjectId('4c5973554abffe0e0c000005')
```

Now assume you want to see all the information available for the chair returned in the preceding example, with one caveat: you don't want to see all the previous location information, but only the first three desks it belonged to:

```
>>> collection.find_one({"ItemNumber" : "6789SID"}, {"PreviousLocation" : {"$slice" : 3} })
{
    u'Status': u'Not used',
    u'PreviousLocation': [u'120100', u'120101', u'120102'],
    u'Tags': [u'Chair', u'Not used', u'Storage'],
    u'ItemNumber': u'6789SID',
    u'Location': {
        u'Department': u'Storage',
        u'Building': u'2B'
    },
    u'_id': ObjectId('4c5973554abffe0e0c000005')
}
```

Similarly, you can see its three most recent locations by making the integer value negative:

```
>>> collection.find_one({"ItemNumber" : "6789SID"}, {"PreviousLocation" : {"$slice" : -3} })
{
    u'Status': u'Not used',
    u'PreviousLocation': [u'120108', u'120109', u'120110'],
    u'Tags': [u'Chair', u'Not used', u'Storage'],
    u'ItemNumber': u'6789SID',
    u'Location': {
```

```
        u'Department': u'Storage',
        u'Building': u'2B'
    },
    u'_id': ObjectId('4c5973554abffe0e0c000005')
}
```

Or, you could skip the first five locations for the chair and limit the number of results returned to three (pay special attention to the brackets, here):

```
>>> collection.find_one({"ItemNumber" : "6789SID"}, {"PreviousLocation" : {"$slice" : [5, 3] }
})
{
    u'Status': u'Not used',
    u'PreviousLocation': [u'120105', u'120106', u'120107'],
    u'Tags': [u'Chair', u'Not used', u'Storage'],
    u'ItemNumber': u'6789SID',
    u'Location': {
        u'Department': u'Storage',
        u'Building': u'2B'
    },
    u'_id': ObjectId('4c5973554abffe0e0c000005')
}
```

You probably get the idea. The preceding example might seem a tad unusual, but inventory control systems often veer into the unorthodox; and the `$slice` operator is intrinsically good at helping you account for unusual or complex circumstances. For example, the `$slice` operator might prove an especially effective tool for implementing the paging system for a website's Comments section, as you see in the next chapter.

## Conducting Searches with Regular Expression

One useful tool for conducting searches is Regular Expression. The default Regular Expression module for Python is called re. Performing a search with the re module requires that you first load the module, as in this example:

```
>>> import re
```

After you load the module, you can specify the Regular Expression query in the `value` field of your search criteria. The following example shows how to search for any document where `ItemNumber` has a value that contains a 4 (for the sake of keeping things simple, this example returns only the values in `ItemNumber`):

```
>>> for doc in collection.find({"ItemNumber" : re.compile("4")}, {"ItemNumber" : "true"}):
...             doc
...
{u'ItemNumber': u'1234EXD', u'_id': ObjectId('4c57207b4abffe0e0c000000')}
{u'ItemNumber': u'2345FDX', u'_id': ObjectId('4c57234c4abffe0e0c000001')}
{u'ItemNumber': u'2345FDX', u'_id': ObjectId('4c592eb84abffe0e0c000004')}
{u'ItemNumber': u'3456TFS', u'_id': ObjectId('4c57234c4abffe0e0c000002')}
```

You can further define a Regular Expression. At this stage, your query is case sensitive, and it will match any document that has a 4 in the value of `ItemNumber`, regardless of its position. However, assume you want to find a document where the value of `ItemNumber` ends with FS, is preceded by an unknown value, and can contain no additional data after the FS:

```
>>> for doc in collection.find({"ItemNumber" : re.compile(".FS$")}, {"ItemNumber" : "true"}):
...             doc
...
{u'ItemNumber': u'3456TFS', u'_id': ObjectId('4c57234c4abffe0e0c000002')}
```

You can also to search for information in a case-insensitive way, but first you must add another function, as in this example:

```
>>> for doc in collection.find({"Location.Owner" : re.compile("^anderson.", re.IGNORECASE)},
...     {"ItemNumber" : "true", "Location.Owner" : "true"}):
...             doc
...
{
     u'ItemNumber': u'1234EXD',
     u'_id': ObjectId('4c57207b4abffe0e0c000000'),
     u'Location': {
         u'Owner': u'Anderson, Thomas'
     }
}
```

Regular Expression can be an extremely powerful tool, as long as you utilize it properly. For more details on how the re module works and which functions it includes, please refer to the module's official documentation at http://docs.python.org/library/re.html.

# Modifying the Data

So far you've learned how to use conditional operators and Regular Expression in Python to query for information in your database. In the next part of this chapter, we'll examine how to use Python to modify the existing data in your collections. We can use Python to accomplish this task in several different ways. The upcoming sections will build on the previously used query operators to find the documents that ought to match your modifications. In a couple cases, you may need to skip back to earlier parts of this chapter to brush up on particular aspects of using query operators—but that's a normal part of the learning process, and it will reinforce the lessons taught so far.

## Updating Your Data

The way you use Python's `update()` function doesn't vary much from how you use the identically named function in the MongoDB shell or the PHP driver. In this case, you provide two mandatory parameters to update your data: arg and doc. The arg parameter specifies the key/value information used to match a document, while the doc parameter contains the updated information. You can also specify four optional parameters. The following list covers Python's list of parameters to update information, including what they do:

- `arg`: Specifies the search arguments (key/value information) that a document must contain to qualify for the update. These arguments can be either a dictionary or a set of key/value information that is stored in a SON object.
- `doc`: Comprises either a *dictionary* or a *SON* object that contains the information to update the matching document with.
- `upsert` *(optional)*: If set to `true`, performs an upsert.

- manipulate *(optional)*: If set to true, indicates the document will be manipulated *before* performing the update using all instances of the *SONManipulator*.
- safe *(optional)*: If set to true, performs a check to see whether the update succeeded.
- multi *(optional)*: If set to true, updates any matching document, rather than just the first document it finds (the default action). It is recommended that you always set this to true or false, rather than relying on the default behavior (which could always change in the future).

If you do not specify any of the modifier operators when updating a document, then by default all information in the document will be replaced with whatever data you inserted in the doc parameter. It is best to avoid relying on the default behavior; instead, you should use the aforementioned operators to specify your desired updates explicitly (you'll learn how to do this momentarily).

You can see why it's best to use conditional operators with the update() command by looking at a case where you don't use any conditional operators with the command:

```
// Define the updated data
>>> update = ( {
    "Type" : "Chair",
    "Status" : "In use",
    "Tags" : ["Chair","In use","Marketing"],
    "ItemNumber" : "6789SID",
    "Location" : {
        "Department" : "Marketing",
        "Building" : "2B",
        "DeskNumber" : 131131,
        "Owner" : "Martin, Lisa"
    }
} )

// Now, perform the update
>>> collection.update({"ItemNumber" : "6789SID"}, update)

// Confirm the update was successful
>>> collection.find_one({"Type" : "Chair"})
{
    u'Status': u'In use',
    u'Tags': [u'Chair', u'In use', u'Marketing'],
    u'ItemNumber': u'6789SID',
    u'Location': {
        u'Department': u'Marketing',
        u'Building': u'2B',
        u'DeskNumber': 131131,
        u'Owner': u'Martin, Lisa'
    },
    u'_id': ObjectId('4c5973554abffe0e0c000005'),
    u'Type': u'Chair'
}
```

One big minus about the preceding example: it's somewhat lengthy, and it updates only a few fields. Next, we'll look at what the modifier operators can be used to accomplish.

## Modifier Operators

Chapter 4 detailed how the MongoDB shell includes a large set of modifier operators that you can use to manipulate your data more easily, but without needing to rewrite the entire document to change a single field's value (as seen in the preceding example).

The modifier operators let you do everything from changing one existing value in a document, to inserting an entire array, to removing all entries from multiple items specified in an array. As a group, these operators make it easy to modify data. Now let's take a look at what the operators do and how you use them.

### Increasing an Integer Value with $inc

You use the `$inc` operator to increase an integer value in a document by the given number, *n*. The following example shows how to increase the integer value of `Location.Desknumber` by 20:

```
>>> collection.update({"ItemNumber" : "6789SID"}, {"$inc" : {"Location.DeskNumber" : 20}})
```

Next, check to see whether the update was successful:

```
>>> collection.find_one({"Type" : "Chair"}, {"Location" : "True"})
{
     u'_id': ObjectId('4c5973554abffe0e0c000005'),
     u'Location': {
          u'Department': u'Marketing',
          u'Building': u'2B',
          u'Owner': u'Martin, Lisa',
          u'DeskNumber': 131151
     }
}
```

Note that the `$inc` operator only works on integer values (i.e., numeric values), but not on any string values or even numeric values added as a string (e.g., `"123"` vs. `123`).

### Changing an Existing Value with $set

You use the `$set` operator to change an existing value in any matching document. This is an operator you'll use frequently. The next example changes the value from `"Building"` in any item currently matching the key/value `"Location.Department / Development"`.

You use `$set` to perform the update, ensuring that all documents are updated and all upserts are performed:

```
>>> collection.update({"Location.Department" : "Development"},
...     {"$set" : {"Location.Building" : "3B"} },
...     upsert = True, multi = True )
```

Next, use the find_one() command to confirm all went well:

```
>>> collection.find_one({"Location.Department" : "Development"}, {"Location.Building" : True})
{
     u'_id': ObjectId('4c57207b4abffe0e0c000000'),
     u'Location': {u'Building': u'3B'}
}
```

## Removing a Key/Value Field with $unset

Likewise, you use the $unset operator to remove a key/value field from a document, as shown in the following example:

```
>>> collection.update({"Status" : "Not used", "ItemNumber" : "2345FDX"},
...      {"$unset" : {"Location.Building" : 1 } } )
```

Next, use the find_one() command to confirm all went well:

```
>>> collection.find_one({"Status" : "Not used", "ItemNumber" : "2345FDX"}, {"Location" :
"True"})
{
     u'_id': ObjectId('4c592eb84abffe0e0c000004'),
     u'Location': {u'Department': u'Storage'}
}
```

## Adding a Value to an Array with $push

The $push operator lets you add a value to an array, assuming the array exists. If the array does not exist, then it will be created with the value specified.

---

■ **Warning** If you use $push to update an existing field that isn't an array, an error message will pop up.

---

Now you're ready to add a value to an already existing array and confirm whether all went well. First, perform the update:

```
>>> collection.update({"Location.Owner" : "Anderson, Thomas"},
...     {"$push" : {"Tags" : "Anderson"} }, multi = True )
```

Now, execute find_one() to confirm whether the update(s) went well:

```
>>> collection.find_one({"Location.Owner" : "Anderson, Thomas"}, {"Tags" : "True"})
{
     u'_id': ObjectId('4c57207b4abffe0e0c000000'),
     u'Tags': [u'Laptop', u'Development', u'In Use', u'Anderson']
}
```

## Adding Multiple Values to an Array with $pushAll

The $pushAll operator is similar to the $push operator, with one essential difference: it lets you add multiple values to an existing array. Again, the array must already exist, or you will receive an error. The following example uses $pushAll in conjunction with Regular Expression to perform a search; this enables you to apply a change to all matching queries:

```
>>> collection.update({"Location.Owner" : re.compile("^Walker,")},
...     {"$pushAll" : {"Tags" : ["Walker","Warranty"] } } )
```

Next, execute find_one() to see whether all went well:

```
>>> collection.find_one({"Location.Owner" : re.compile("^Walker,")}, {"Tags" : "True"})
{
     u'_id': ObjectId('4c57234c4abffe0e0c000002'),
     u'Tags': [u'Laptop', u'Development', u'In Use', u'Walker', u'Warranty']
}
```

## Adding a Value to an Existing Array with $addToSet

The $addToSet operator also lets you add a value to an already existing array. The difference is that this method checks whether the array already exists before attempting the update (the $push and $pushAll operators do not check for this condition).

This operator only takes one additional value; however, it's also good to know that you can combine this operator with the $each operator. Let's look at two examples. First, let's perform the update using the $addToSet operator on any object matching "Type : Chair" and then check whether all went well using the find_one() function:

```
>>> collection.update({"Type" : "Chair"}, {"$addToSet" : {"Tags" : "Warranty"} }, multi =
True)

>>> collection.find_one({"Type" : "Chair"}, {"Tags" : "True"})
{
     u'_id': ObjectId('4c5973554abffe0e0c000005'),
     u'Tags': [u'Chair', u'In use', u'Marketing', u'Warranty']
}
```

You can also use the $each statement to add multiple tags. Note that you perform this search using a Regular Expression. Also, one of the tags in the list has been previously added; fortunately, it won't be added again because this is what $addToSet specifically prevents:

```
// Use the $each operator to add multiple tags, including one that was already added
>>> collection.update({"Type" : "Chair", "Location.Owner" : re.compile("^Martin,")},
...     {"$addToSet" : { "Tags" : {"$each" : ["Martin","Warranty","Chair","In use"] } } } )
```

Now it's time to check whether all went well; specifically, you want to verify that the duplicate Warranty tag has not been added again:

```
>>> collection.find_one({"Type" : "Chair", "Location.Owner" : re.compile("^Martin,")}, {"Tags"
: "True"})
{
     u'_id': ObjectId('4c5973554abffe0e0c000005'),
     u'Tags': [u'Chair', u'In use', u'Marketing', u'Warranty', u'Martin']
}
```

## Removing an Element from an Array with $pop

So far, you've seen how to use the update() function to add values to an existing document. Now let's turn this around and look at how to remove data instead. We'll begin by look into the $pop operator.

This operator allows you to delete either the first or last value from an array, but nothing in between. The following example removes the first value in the Tags array from the first document it finds that matches the "Type" : "Chair" criteria; the example then uses the find_one() command to confirm all went well with the update:

```
>>> collection.update({"Type" : "Chair"}, {"$pop" : {"Tags" : -1}})

>>> collection.find_one({"Type" : "Chair"}, {"Tags" : "True"})
{
    u'_id': ObjectId('4c5973554abffe0e0c000005'),
    u'Tags': [u'In use', u'Marketing', u'Warranty', u'Martin']
}
```

Giving the Tags array a positive value instead removes the last occurrence in an array, as in the following example:

```
>>> collection.update({"Type" : "Chair"}, {"$pop" : {"Tags" :  1}})
```

Next, execute the find_one() function again to confirm that all went well:

```
>>> collection.find_one({"Type" : "Chair"}, {"Tags" : "True"})
{
    u'_id': ObjectId('4c5973554abffe0e0c000005'),
    u'Tags': [u'In use', u'Marketing', u'Warranty']
}
```

## Removing a Specific Value with $pull

The $pull operator lets you remove each occurrence of a specific value from an array, regardless of how many times the value occurs; as long as the value is the same, it will be removed.

Let's look at an example. Begin by using the $push operator to add identical tags with the value Double to the Tags array:

```
>>> collection.update({"Type" : "Chair"}, {"$push" : {"Tags" : "Double"} }, multi = False )
>>> collection.update({"Type" : "Chair"}, {"$push" : {"Tags" : "Double"} }, multi = False )
```

Next, ensure that the tag was added twice by executing the find_one() command. Once you confirm the tag exists twice, use the $pull operator to remove both instances of the tag:

```
>>> collection.find_one({"Type" : "Chair"}, {"Tags" : "True"})
{
    u'_id': ObjectId('4c5973554abffe0e0c000005'),
    u'Tags': [u'In use', u'Marketing', u'Warranty', u'Double', u'Double']
}

>>> collection.update({"Type" : "Chair"}, {"$pull" : {"Tags" : "Double"} }, multi = False)
```

To confirm all went well, execute find_one() command again, this time making sure that the result no longer lists Double tag:

```
>>> collection.find_one({"Type" : "Chair"}, {"Tags" : "True"})
{
     u'_id': ObjectId('4c5973554abffe0e0c000005'),
     u'Tags': [u'In use', u'Marketing', u'Warranty']
}
```

You can use the $pullAll operator to perform the same action; the difference is that the $pullAll operator lets you remove multiple tags. Again, let's look at an example. First, you need to add multiple items into the Tags array again and confirm that they have been added:

```
>>> collection.update({"Type" : "Chair"}, {"$addToSet" : { "Tags" : {"$each" :
["Bacon","Spam"] } } } )
>>> collection.find_one({"Type" : "Chair"}, {"Tags" : "True"})
{
     u'_id': ObjectId('4c5973554abffe0e0c000005'),
     u'Tags': [u'In use', u'Marketing', u'Warranty', u'Bacon', u'Spam']
}
```

Now you can use $pullAll operator to remove the multiple tags. The following example shows how to use this operator; the example also executes a find_one() command immediately afterward to confirm that the Bacon and Spam tags have been removed:

```
>>> collection.update({"Type" : "Chair"}, {"$pullAll" : {"Tags" : ["Bacon","Spam"] } }, multi
= False)
>>> collection.find_one({"Type" : "Chair"}, {"Tags" : "True"})
{
     u'_id': ObjectId('4c5973554abffe0e0c000005'),
     u'Tags': [u'In use', u'Marketing', u'Warranty']
}
```

## Saving Documents Quickly with Save()

You can use the save() function to quickly add a document through the upsert method. For this to work, you must also define the value of the _id field. If the document you want to save already exists, then the document will be updated; if it does not exist already, then it will be created.

Let's look at an example that saves a dictionary called Desktop. Begin by specifying the dictionary by typing it into the shell with an identifier, after which you can save it with the save() function. Executing the save() function returns the Object ID from the document once the save is successful:

```
>>> Desktop = ( {
    "Status" : "In use",
    "Tags" : ["Desktop","In use","Marketing","Warranty"],
    "ItemNumber" : "4532FOO",
    "Location" : {
        "Department" : "Marketing",
        "Building" : "2B",
        "Desknumber" : 131131,
        "Owner" : "Martin, Lisa",
    }
} )
>>> collection.save(Desktop)
ObjectId('4c5ddbe24abffe0f34000001')
```

Now assume you realize that you forgot to specify a key/value pair in the dictionary. You can easily add this information to the dictionary by defining the dictionary's name, followed by its key between brackets, and then including the desired contents. Once you do this, you can perform the upsert by simply saving the entire dictionary again; doing so returns the `Object ID` again from the document:

```
>>> Desktop[ "Type" ] = "Desktop"
>>> collection.save(Desktop)
ObjectId('4c5ddbe24abffe0f34000001')
```

As you can see, the value of the `Object ID` returned is unchanged.

## Modifying a Document Atomically

You can use the `findAndModify()` function to modify a document atomically and return the results. The Python driver currently does not have a helper method for this function, however, so it needs to be executed as a database command (see Chapter 4 for more information on atomic updates).

The `findAndModify()` function can be used to update only a single document—and nothing more. You should also keep in mind the fact that the document returned will not include the modifications made by default; getting this information requires that you specify an additional argument.

The `findAndModify()` function can be used with seven parameters, and you must include either the `update` parameter or the `remove` parameter. The following list covers all the available parameters, explaining what they are and what they do:

- `query`: Specifies a filter for the query. If this isn't specified, then all documents in the collection will be seen as possible candidates, after which the first document it encounters will be updated or removed.
- `sort`: Sorts the matching documents in a specified order.
- `remove`: If set to `true`, removes the first matching document.
- `update`: Specifies the information to update the document with. Note that any of the modifying operators specified previously can be used for this.
- `new`: If set to `true`, returns the updated document rather than the *selected* document. This is not set by default, however, which might be a bit confusing sometimes.
- `fields`: Specifies the fields you would like to see returned, rather than the entire document. This works identically to the `find()` function. Note that the `_id` field will always be returned.
- `upsert` *(optional)*: If set to `true`, performs an upsert.

## Putting the Parameters to Work

You know what the parameters do; now it's time to use them in a real-world example in conjunction with the `findAndModify()` function. Begin by using the `findAndModify()` function to search for any document that has a key/value pair of `"Type" : "Desktop"`—and then update each document that matches the query by setting an additional key/value pair of `"Status" : "In repair"`. Finally, you want to ensure that the updated document(s) gets returned, rather than the old document(s) matching the query:

```
>>> db.command("findandmodify", "items", query = {"Type" : "Desktop"},
...     update = {"$set" : {"Status" : "In repair"} }, new = True  )
```

```
{
    u'ok': 1.0,
    u'value': {
        u'Status': u'In repair',
        u'Tags': [u'Desktop', u'In use', u'Marketing', u'Warranty'],
        u'ItemNumber': u'4532FOO',
        u'Location': {
            u'Department': u'Marketing',
            u'Building': u'2B',
            u'Owner': u'Martin, Lisa',
            u'Desknumber': 131131
        },
        u'_id': ObjectId('4c5dda114abffe0f34000000'),
        u'Type': u'Desktop'
    }
}
```

Let's look at another example. This time, you will use `findAndModify()` to remove a document; in this case, the output will show which document was removed:

```
>>> db.command("findandmodify", "items", query = {"Type" : "Desktop"},
...     sort = {"ItemNumber" : -1}, remove = True  )
{
    u'ok': 1.0,
    u'value': {
        u'Status': u'In use',
        u'Tags': [u'Desktop', u'In use', u'Marketing', u'Warranty'],
        u'ItemNumber': u'4532FOO',
        u'Location': {
            u'Department': u'Marketing',
            u'Building': u'2B',
            u'Owner': u'Martin, Lisa',
            u'Desknumber': 131131
        },
        u'_id': ObjectId('4c5ddbe24abffe0f34000001'),
        u'Type': u'Desktop'
    }
}
```

# Deleting Data

In most cases, you will use the Python driver to add or modify your data. However, it's also important to understand how to *delete* data. The Python driver provides several methods for deleting data. First, you can use the `remove()` function to delete a single document from a collection. Second, you can use the `drop()` or `drop_collection()` function to delete an entire collection. Finally, you can use the `drop_database()` function to drop an entire database (it seems unlikely you'll be using this function frequently!).

Nevertheless, we will take a closer look at each of these functions, looking at examples for all of them.

Let's begin by looking at the `remove()` function. This function allows you to specify an argument as a parameter that will be used to find and delete any matching documents in your current collection. In this example, you use the `remove()` function to remove each document that has a key/value pair of `"Status" : "In use"`; afterward, you use the `find_one` command to confirm the results:

```
>>> collection.remove({"Status" : "In use"})
>>> collection.find_one({"Status" : "In use"})
>>>
```

You need to be careful what kind of criteria you specify with this function. Usually, you should execute a `find()` first, so you can see exactly which documents will get removed. Alternatively, you can use the `Object ID` to remove an item.

If you get tired of an entire collection, you can look into using either the `drop()` or the `drop_collection()` function to remove it. Both functions work the same way (one is just an alias for the other, really); specifically, both expect only one parameter, the collection's name:

```
>>> db.items.drop()
```

Last (and far from least because of its potential destructiveness), the `drop_database()` function enables you to delete an entire database. You call this function using the `Connection` module, as in the following example:

```
>>> c.drop_database("inventory")
```

# Creating a Link Between Two Documents

Database references can be used to create a link between two documents that reside in different locations. For example, you might create one collection for all employees and another collection for all the items—and then use the `DBRef()` function to create a reference between the employees and the location of the items, rather than typing them in manually for each item.

As you may recall from the previous chapters, you can reference data in one of two ways. First, you can add a simple reference (*manual referencing*) that uses the `_id` field from one document to store a reference to it in another. Second, you can use the `DBRef` module, which brings a few more options with it than you get with manual referencing.

Let's create a manual reference first. Begin by saving a document. For example, assume you want to save the information for a person into a specific collection. The following example defines a `jan` dictionary and saves it into the `people` collection to get back an `Object ID`:

```
>>> jan = {
...     "First Name" : "Jan",
...     "Last Name" : "Walker",
...     "Display Name" : "Walker, Jan",
...     "Department" : "Development",
...     "Building" : "2B",
...     "Floor" : 12,
...     "Desk" : 120103,
...     "E-Mail" : "jw@example.com"
... }

>>> people = db.people
>>> people.insert(jan)
ObjectId('4c5e5f104abffe0f34000002')
```

After you add an item and get its ID back, you can use this information to link the item to another document in another collection:

```
>>> laptop = {
...     "Type" : "Laptop",
```

```
...     "Status" : "In use",
...     "ItemNumber" : "12345ABC",
...     "Tags" : ["Warranty","In use","Laptop"],
...     "Owner" : jan[ "_id" ]
... }
>>> items = db.items
>>> items.insert(laptop)
ObjectId('4c5e6f6b4abffe0f34000003')
```

Now assume you want to find out the owner's information. In this case, all you have to do is query for the Object ID given in the Owner field; obviously, this is only possible if you know which collection the data is stored in.

But assume that you don't know where this information is stored. It was for handling precisely such scenarios that the DBRef() function was created. You can use this function even when you do not know which collection holds the original data. This fact means you don't have to worry so much about the collection names when searching for the information.

The DBRef() function takes three arguments; it can take a fourth argument that you can use to specify additional keyword arguments. Here's a list of the three main arguments and what they let you do:

- collection *(mandatory)*: Specifies the collection the original data resides in (e.g., people).
- id *(mandatory)*: Specifies the _id value of the document that should be referred to.
- database *(optional)*: Specifies the name of the database to reference.

The DBRef module must be loaded before you can use the DBRef method, so let's load the module before going any further:

```
>>> from pymongo.dbref import DBRef
```

At this point, you're ready to look at a practical example that leverages the DBRef() function. In the following example, you insert a person into the people collection and add an item to the items collection, using DBRef to reference the owner:

```
>>> mike = {
...     "First Name" : "Mike",
...     "Last Name" : "Wazowski",
...     "Display Name" : "Wazowski, Mike",
...     "Department" : "Entertainment",
...     "Building" : "2B",
...     "Floor" : 10,
...     "Desk" : 120789,
...     "E-Mail" : "mw@monsters.inc"
... }

>>> people.save(mike)
ObjectId('4c5e73714abffe0f34000004')
```

At this point, nothing interesting has happened. Yes, you added a document, but you did so without adding a reference to it. However, you do have the Object ID of the document, so now you can add your next document to the collection, and then use DBRef() to point the owner field at the value of the previously inserted document. Pay special attention to the syntax of the DBRef() function; in particular, you should note how the first parameter given is the collection name where your previously specified document resides, while the second parameter is nothing more than a reference to the _id key in the mike dictionary:

```
>>> laptop = {
...     "Type" : "Laptop",
...     "Status" : "In use",
...     "ItemNumber" : "2345DEF",
...     "Tags" : ["Warranty","In use","Laptop"],
...     "Owner" : DBRef('people', mike[ "_id" ])
... }


>>> items.save(laptop)
ObjectId('4c5e740a4abffe0f34000005')
```

As you probably noticed, this code isn't massively different from the code you used to create a manual reference. However, we recommend that you use the DBRef method just in case you need to reference specific information, rather than embedding it. Adopting this approach gives you the additional flexibility of not having to look up the collection's name whenever you query for the referenced information.

## Retrieving the Information

You know how to reference information with DBRef(); now let's assume that you want to retrieve the previously referenced information. You can accomplish this using the Python driver's dereference() function. All you need to do is define the field previously specified that contains the referenced information as an argument, and then press the Return key.

Next, let's walk through the process of referencing and retrieving information from one document to another from start to finish. Let's begin by finding the document that contains the referenced data, and then retrieving that document for display. The first step is to create a query that finds a random document with the reference information in it:

```
>>> items.find_one({"ItemNumber" : "2345DEF"})
{
    u'Status': u'In use',
    u'Tags': [u'Warranty', u'In use', u'Laptop'],
    u'ItemNumber': u'2345DEF',
    u'Owner': DBRef(u'people', ObjectId('4c5e73714abffe0f34000004')),
    u'_id': ObjectId('4c5e740a4abffe0f34000005'),
    u'Type': u'Laptop'
}
```

Next, you want to store this item under a person dictionary:

```
>>> person = items.find_one({"ItemNumber" : "2345DEF"})
```

At this point, you can use the dereference() function to dereference the Owner field to the person["Owner"] field as an argument. This is possible because the Owner field is linked to the data you want to retrieve:

```
>>> db.dereference(person["Owner"])

{
    u'Building': u'2B',
```

```
    u'Floor': 10,
    u'Last Name': u'Wazowski',
    u'Desk': 120789,
    u'E-Mail': u'mw@monsters.inc',
    u'First Name': u'Mike',
    u'Display Name': u'Wazowski, Mike',
    u'Department': u'Entertainment',
    u'_id': ObjectId('4c5e73714abffe0f34000004')
}
```

That wasn't so bad! The point to take away from this example is that `DBRef` provides a great way for storing data you want to reference. Additionally, `DBRef` permits some flexibility in how you specify the collection and database names. You'll find yourself using this feature frequently if you want to keep your database tidy, especially in cases where the data really shouldn't be embedded.

# Summary

In this chapter, we've explored the basics of how MongoDB's Python driver (PyMongo) can be used for the most frequently used operations. Along the way, we've covered how to search for, store, update, and delete data.

We've also looked at how to reference documents contained in another collection using two methods: manual referencing and `DBRef`. When looking at these approaches, we've seen how their syntax is remarkably similar, but the `DBRef` approach provides a bit more robustness in terms of its functionality, so is preferable in most circumstances.

The next chapter will delve into how MongoDB's innate flexibility can be used to leverage the PHP driver to create a simple web application.

CHAPTER 8

■ ■ ■

# Creating a Blog Application with the PHP Driver

In the previous pair of chapters, we discussed how to use MongoDB to store all sorts of data, as well as how to update data in a MongoDB database. We also covered a pair of drivers that you can use to extend MongoDB: the PHP driver and the Python driver.

At this point, you know what these drivers are, as well as some of the things you can do with them. In this chapter, you'll see a small but practical use for the MongoDB PHP driver. Granted, the previous chapters included some practical, real-world code snippets that can be used to accomplish nearly anything you might want to use MongoDB for. However, you haven't seen MongoDB used to create a basic application yet. To demonstrate the capabilities of MongoDB as a backend application, this chapter will walk you through how simple it is to create an easy-to-expand blog application using the PHP driver.

The application, named *blog*, will demonstrate the following functions:

- Adding, deleting, and modifying posts.
- Viewing posts on the front page.
- Searching for a post using regular expressions.
- Retrieving author names through DBRef.

The blog applications will contain the following pair of collections:

- `posts`: Contains the posts added to the database. Each post will contain a title, date, and author info that is accessed through DBRef. Each post can also contain a range of comments added by people who view the posts.
- `authors`: Contains any information related to the posts' authors, assuming there is more than one author. You use DBRef to query this information.

Before you begin writing the code for the application, you need to design how you want it to look and behave. So let's get started.

---

**Note** This chapter's example won't pay much attention to either design or security. Nor will the example contain any difficult-to-understand PHP code. The purpose of this code is to demonstrate how to combine the PHP's basic functions to create a real-world application. Think of this chapter as a sort of cookbook for writing the code in a practical example. That said, following the steps described in this chapter (and in the "Recapping the *blog* Application" section at the end of this chapter) will enable you to put a complete database application together.

---

# Designing the Application

The first thing to consider is the general structure of a document, or *post*. Each document will contain a basic set of keys that will not differ much on a per document basis. After all, there's no need to use many different kinds of key fields in this kind of example. And, while we already know that MongoDB is extremely flexible and that it does not limit a collection to only predefined keys, the example in this chapter doesn't require anything quite so advanced.

Each document will look approximately as follows:

```
{
        "Title" : "This is a blogtitle",
        "Author" :
                {
                        "$ref" : "authors",
                        "$id" : ObjectId("4c612fa7747400000000034b5")
                },
        "Date" : "Tue Aug 10 2010 13:14:08 GMT+0200",
        "Message" : "Hooray! This is a blog",
        "Comments" : [
                {
                        "Name" : "Louis",
                        "Comment" : "First!"
                },
                {
                        "Name" : "Stewie",
                        "Comment" : "Second"
                }
        ]
}
```

Specifically, the post documents have a title field that displays the title of the post; an author field that shows a DBRef for an entry in the authors collection; a date field specified through a date() function; comments placed in a nested array; and the actual message itself, which is stored under the Message key.

The authors documents will look something like this:

```
{
        "Name" : "Eelco",
        "E-Mail" : "eelco@mongo.db",
```

```
        "Interests" : "MongoDB",
        "_id" : ObjectId("4c612fa774740000000034b5")
}
```

This is an admittedly basic example; however, you're free to expand this yourself as much as you'd like to.

Next, let's add these two example documents to the database (this will ensure that the database holds some data when we attempt to list the data in the documents later in the chapter). Start up your MongoDB shell and add a document to the blog database's authors collection:

```
> use blog
switched to db blog

> author = ({ "Name" : "Eelco", "E-Mail" : "eelco@mongo.db", "Interests" : "MongoDB" })
{ "Name" : "Eelco", "E-Mail" : "eelco@mongo.db", "Interests" : "MongoDB" }

> db.authors.save(author)
```

Next, you need to add a document to the posts collection:

```
> post = ( {
    "Title" : "This is a blogtitle",
    "Author" : new DBRef ('authors', author._id),
    "Date" : new Date(),
    "Message" : "Hooray! This is a blog",
    "Comments" : [{
        "Name" : "Louis",
        "Comment" : "First!"
    },
    {
        "Name" : "Stewie",
        "Comment" : "Second"
    }]
} )

> db.posts.save(post)
```

So far, so good. Now let's begin working on the database's layout and design.

---

■ **Note** This design doesn't address trying to make the application look nice, so you won't be seeing many CSS entries or any fancy-looking tables simply because that's not the primary focus of this chapter. However, you're free to add eye-pleasing elements yourself, if you feel like it.

---

# Listing the Posts

So far you've added at least one document to your posts collection (you may have added more). This means you can start writing some simple PHP code to display this post; this will enable you to see what the application will look like.

The following snippet keeps things simple by telling PHP to list the 10 most recent posts on the frontpage:

```
<?php
// Let's define some variables!
$db = "blog";                            // This is the name of the database
$col_authors = "authors";                // This is the name of the authors collection
$col_posts = "posts";                    // This is the name of the posts collection
$limit = 10;                             // This is the total number of posts displayed

// Connect to the database
$c = new Mongo();

// Execute a search and store the posts under the cursor variable
$cursor = $c->$db->$col_posts->find()->limit($limit)->sort(array('_id'=>-1));

// For each document it finds within the collection, print it's contents
while ($document = $cursor->getNext())
{
    print_r($document);
}
```

You can add the preceding code to a new file called `posts.php`. Admittedly, this example doesn't look very user friendly; then again, all it does is print out the array and all its contents. You can make changes to the `while` statement to make it look a little better. Note that the following snippet changes only the `while` statement; the rest stays the same:

```
while ($document = $cursor->getNext())
{
    // Get the author's name via MongoDBRef
    $ref = $c->$db->getDBRef($document["Author"]);
    $author = $ref["Name"];
    // Translate the date back using date()
    $date = date('M d, Y @ h:i', $document["Date"]->sec);

    // Show the title, author, date and message
    print "<h1>$document[Title]</h1><br>";
    print "<i>By $author on $date</i>";
    print "<p>$document[Message]</p>";

    // Show clickable link to view the comments when found, and count them
    $postid = new MongoId($document['_id']);
    if(isset($document["Comments"]))
    {
        $count = count($document["Comments"]);
    }
    else {
        $count = 0;
    }
    $count = count($document["Comments"]);
    print "<a href='view.php?id=$postid'>View Comments ($count)</a>";
}
```

That should look a little better. At this point, you should be able to see the last 10 items added to the posts collection, including the date and name of the person who has added it.

## Paging with PHP and MongoDB

Now assume more than 10 posts have been added. Obviously, the first posts added will no longer be displayed (note the sorting happens on _id in descending order), so you will need to make sure that older posts remain visible in case you want to find these later. The skip() function makes it easy to do this.

Begin by adding a check to the PHP page that will determine whether a certain variable called $page has been set. If $page has been set, then that variable will be used to define the offset; in other words, it will specify how many posts should be skipped before you start requesting posts and printing them out. After all, if you know which page a document is on, and the limit per page has been set to 10, then it's a simple matter to determine how many records you need to skip. For example, assume you are on page 3. A limit of 10 means that you want to skip the first 20 posts, and retrieve the 10 posts (or less if no more are found) immediately prior to the skipped posts. If the $page variable has not been set, however, you can force it to carry the value of 1, so it will display the latest 10 posts added by default.

To do this, add the following code block either just under or just above your currently defined variables. The following example places this code just under them:

```
// Set up some PHP code to check if the $page is set and if not, set $page to '1'.
if(isset($_GET['page'])){
    $page = $_GET['page'];
}
else {
    $page = 1;
}
```

Next, you'll need to define one more variable to specify the offset, and two more variables that can either increase or decrease the $page value. You can place these directly under the if/else statement shown previously:

```
// Let's define some more variables for paging
$offset = ($page -1) * $limit;
$nextpage = ($page +1);
$prevpage = ($page -1);
```

We're almost finished. The $offset parameter has been specified (the page number minus one times the limit, 10), so you can pass this integer on to the skip() function. The previously defined $cursor value was derived like this:

```
$cursor = $c->$db->$col_posts->find()->limit($limit)->sort(array('_id'=>-1));
```

You need to update it so it looks like this:

```
$cursor = $c->$db->$col_posts->find()->skip($offset)->limit($limit)->sort(array('_id'=>-1));
```

The final step is to add two hyperlinks at the bottom of your page. These links let you navigate either one page back, or one page forward, whichever is applicable. Note that the links will not be displayed if the number of posts found can be displayed on a single page:

```
// Perform a count on all posts within the collection and add links based upon the outcome
$posts = $c->$db->$col_posts->find()->count();
if ($page > 1)
    {
        print "<a href='?page=$prevpage'>Previous Page</a>";
```

```
        if ($page * $limit < $posts)
        {
            print "<a href='?page=$nextpage'>Next page</a>";
        }
    }
else {
    if ($page * $limit < $posts) {
        print "<a href='?page=$nextpage'>Next page</a>";
    }
}
?>
```

That's it for paging. In the next section, you'll learn how to use another paging method that relies on the `$slice` operator for the comments array. For now, you are done with this page, and you can save it as `posts.php`.

---

**Tip** Don't worry if you lose track about where you are in the example. You can use the code listing at the end of this chapter to review the entire code for the project.

---

# Looking at a Single Post

So far you've gotten a basic overview of all posts. Next, you will learn how to view a single post instead. Generally speaking, you want this to work in the same way that viewing multiple documents does. One difference is that viewing a single document also lets you see comments associated with that post (if any), as well as a form for adding any *new* comments.

Let's start off with a new document called `view.php`. You start the document with a number of variables that define the connection details that you'll use throughout this page, as in the following example:

```
<?php
// Let's define some variables!
$c = new Mongo();                    // Used to connect to the db
$db= "blog";                         // This is the name of the database
$col_authors = "authors";            // This is the name of the authors collection
$col_posts = "posts";                // This is the name of the posts collection
```

Now that you've defined your variables, you need to add an `if` statement that checks whether the post ID has been specified in the URL (e.g., `view.php?id=xxx`). If so, you need to perform another check to see whether any page variable has been specified for paging the comments. If the paging variable `$_GET[p]` hasn't been specified, then it will be set to `1`, assuming this is the default page you'd want to start at for adding any comments:

```
if (isset($_GET['id']))
{
    if (isset($_GET['p']))
    {
        $commentpage = $_GET['p'];
    }
else
    {
```

```
        $commentpage = 1;
    }
```

You probably noticed that this code block isn't finished. At this stage, it will do nothing useful, unless you enjoy observing the error messages.

## Specifying Additional Variables

Let's continue building on this code block. Begin by specifying a number of additional variables needed for the paging:

```
// Add some more variables for paging the comments
$id = new MongoId($_GET['id']);
$limit = 5;                                  // Used to define the max no. of comments
$offset = ($commentpage -1) * $limit;        // This is our comments offset
$nextpage = ($commentpage +1);               // Used to increasing the commentspage
$prevpage = ($commentpage -1);               // Used to decreasing the commentspage
```

Next, you need to specify the query, the `$slice` operator, and the operator's parameters. The query is rather straightforward: you specify that the only post that you would like to see returned must have the `_id` field set to whatever the `$id` variable is set to (this variable was specified earlier in the URL of the page). Because the `_id` is unique, you can be quite certain that the resulting document is the correct one. Using the `$slice` operator enables you to tell the database to query for only a small amount of items in the nested comments, as well as to skip a certain number of them depending on the page set. You use the `$offset` parameter to specify the number of items to skip, and you use the `$limit` parameter to specify the number of items to show (i.e., limit):

```
// Define the query  parameters that we want to use
$query = array('_id' => $id);
$cond = (object)array('Comments' => array('$slice' => array($offset, $limit) ) );
```

You've specified the query parameters, so now you can perform the search operation itself. Of course, you'll use the `findOne()` function to accomplish this. This code looks simple now that you've specified the query parameters:

```
// Connect to the database, and perform the findOne
$document = $c->$db->$col_posts->findOne($query, $cond);
```

Next, you use DBRef to retrieve the author's username. You can also print the document's contents in the `$document` array from the previously executed `findOne()` function:

```
// Now get the author's name via MongoDBRef, and translate the date
$ref = $c->$db->getDBRef($document["Author"]);
$author = $ref["Name"];
$date = date('M d, Y @ h:i', $document["Date"]->sec);

// ..and print all the keys and values out
print "<h1>$document[Title]</h1>";
print "<i>By $author on $date</i>";
print "<p>$document[Message]</p>";
```

You're halfway there, but so far the page wouldn't look much different to what you'd see on the previously created page. The next step is to add the code that enables you to view and add paging for the comments (assuming there are any). Adding another `if` statement can help you accomplish this: you simply tell it to display any comments that may exist. Note that at this stage the code block is not yet finished so it will not be closed off yet with a closing bracket at the end; instead this is done in the next code block. Here is the code snippet:

```
// If there are any comments, then show them here
if (isset($document['Comments']))
{
    // Show a header to announce the comments
    print "<h3>Comments</h3>";
    // Set each comment that gets found in the $document array to $comm
    foreach ($document['Comments'] as $comm)
    {
        // For each of these, print the name and comment
        print "<b>$comm[Name]</b></br>";
        print "<i>$comm[Comment]</i></br>";
    }
```

## Viewing and Adding Comments

The next step is to add hyperlinks so that the comments can be navigated. At the beginning of the first PHP page, you specified a limit for these comments by setting the `$limit` parameter to `5` (see the "Specifying Additional Variables" section for the full context). You also defined the offset using the `$p` variable, which is set to 1 by default, unless otherwise modified using the hyperlinks that will be added shortly.

To calculate the number of comment pages to list, you will first need to perform a count of the comments. Based on this count, you will need to let the PHP code decide whether the navigation links need to be added. You will also add an HTML form at the end of the page. This page will allow visiting users to add their own comments to the post. The form will be quite simple. It will contain a total of two visible input fields, one for the user's name and another for the comment. The form will also include a hidden third field that contains the Object ID of the post. Finally, you need to add a `submit` button for submitting the information to the current PHP page itself.

Here is the code snippet that does this:

```
// Perform a count on the comments to create paging
$doc = $c->$db->$col_posts->findOne($query);
$count = count($doc["Comments"]);

// Add some links for paging the comments
if ($commentpage > 1)
{
    print "<a href='?id=$id&p=$prevpage'>Previous Page</a> ";
    if ($commentpage * $limit < $count)
    {
        print "<a href='?id=$id&p=$nextpage'>Next page</a><br/>";
    }
}
else
{
    if ($commentpage * $limit < $count)
    {
        print "<a href='?id=$id&p=$nextpage'>Next page</a><br/>";
    }
}
}
```

```
// Let's add a simple HTML form
print "<form name='addcomment' action='view.php' method='post'>";
print "Your name:<input type='text' name='commentauthor'><br>";
print "Comment:<textarea cols='20' rows='4'name='comment'></textarea>";
print "<input type='hidden' value=$id name='id'/>";
print "<input type='submit' value='Add Comment' name='addcomment'/>";
print "</form>";
}
```

You still need to specify the submit behavior of this form. This will require creating two more variables: `$criteria` and `$update`. You will use `$criteria` to specify the criteria a document must match to be updated, based on the submitted Object ID information. You will use `$update` to contain the information that performs the update itself. The information in the `$update` variable will consist of an array that contains the `$addToSet` variable for one, as well as an embedded array that contains the submitted data.

Once you gather all information, you will process it using an `if` statement that calls MongoDB's `update()` function to update the document, as in the following example:

```
if(isset($_POST["addcomment"]))
{
    // Specify the update criteria
    $criteria = array("_id" => new MongoId($_POST['id']));
    // Specify the update that should be performed
    $update = array(
        '$addToSet' => array
            (
            "Comments" => array
                (
                "Name" => $_POST['commentauthor'],
                "Comment" => addslashes($_POST['comment'])
                )
            )
        );
    // Perform the update
    $c->$db->$col_posts->update($criteria, $update);
    // Thanks
    print "Thanks for your comment!";
}
?>
```

# Searching the Posts

So far you've learned how to view all posts or a single one. You've also learned how to implement paging for both examples. The more posts you get, the harder it is to find them again. You can simplify the process of finding such posts again by creating an HTML form that passes on the input to the `find()` function. This is also a case where Regular Expression can help.

Let's begin by adding another `if` statement to the original `posts.php` page saved earlier. You can place this statement under the first listing of defined variables, and it will work like this: if a search has been performed using the HTML form, then the search value will be used to specify the query. If no search parameter has been specified, then the search query will remain empty. The code to accomplish this is as follows:

```
if(isset($_POST["search"]))
{
    // Use MongoRegEx to specify the search criteria
    $regex = new MongoRegex("/$_POST[search]/i");
    $query = array("Message" => $regex);
}
else
{
    // If no search criteria is specified, $query will be set to an empty array
    $query = array();
}
```

You also need to make the find() command itself aware of this change. After all, the $cursor currently looks like this, so it isn't aware of any $query:

```
$cursor = $c->$db->$col_posts->find()->skip($offset)->limit($limit)->sort(array('_id'=>-1));
```

The next step is to change $cursor variable so that it takes the $query variable as a parameter for the find() function, as in the following example:

```
$cursor = $c->$db->$col_posts->find($query)->skip($offset)->limit($limit)->sort(array('_id'=>-
1));
```

You still need to add the form to input the search criteria. You can do this by adding a HTML form with one input field and naming it search. Add this field somewhere at the top of the page, before any of the documents will be printed. For example, you might place it after the paging variables and before the $c variable:

```
// Add a form for searching the posts
print "<form method='post' name='search' action='posts.php'>";
print "<input type='text' name='search'>";
print "<input type='submit' value='Search'>";
print "</form>";
```

# Adding, Deleting, and Modifying Posts

So far you've created the end-user code. The next step is to work on the code that administers the blog itself. Specifically, you need to write code that creates, updates, and deletes posts. Of course, you'll also make some cosmetic changes, such as adding links that initiate these actions.

Begin by creating a new folder called admin. You also want to create a new PHP file (also called posts.php, just to keep things simple). The first thing you will want to see when going into Admin mode is an overview of the posts themselves, as well as links to either delete or edit individual posts. It would also be a good idea to create a link that lets you add an additional post.

It's best to be "lazy" and avoid doing work that you've already done before. Therefore, writing another page from scratch to show all the posts available would be unnecessary because you've already written code that does this. A simple copy/paste will suffice to start. Once you do this, you can augment the page with a few additional if statements, as well as a few hyperlinks that add, modify, or delete a post. Begin by creating a copy of the posts.php page and ensure that it gets saved in the previously mentioned admin folder.

For now, it's enough to add the links for adding, removing, or modifying a post. For example, you could add a link that adds new posts under the search box, as in the following example:

```
// Add a form for searching the posts
print "<form method='post' name='search' action='posts.php'>";
print "<input type='text' name='search'>";
print "<input type='submit' value='Search'>";
print "</form>";

// Add a link to add a post
print "<a href='add.php'>Add a post</a>";
```

You will write the add.php page momentarily, and you will use this page to add documents (i.e., *posts*) to the collection by combining an HTML form and the insert() function. Before you write that code, however, first you want to add the two links for either modifying or deleting a post. A good place to put these links would be next to the Comments link, which will also need to be changed slightly:

```
print "<a href='../view.php?id=$postid'>View Comments ($count)</a> ";
// Show clickable links to modify or delete the post
print "<a href='?modify=$postid'>Modify</a> ";
print "<a href='?del=$postid'>Delete</a>";
```

Later in this chapter, you'll define actual actions to be performed whenever these links are clicked. For now, you can leave things like this and continue on to the PHP page that adds a new post.

## Adding a New Post

You will need to create a new page so you can add any new posts through a simple HTML form. You already know what the fieldnames will be (the title, the message, and a dropdown box to identify who will add the post), so it's easy to construct the HTML form in a new PHP page named add.php.

Before creating this HTML form, however, you can make your life a little easier by first adding a handful of new variables:

```
<?php

// First, lets connect to the database
$c = new Mongo();
$db = "blog";
$col_posts = "posts";
$col_authors = "authors";
```

Adding the preceding variables ensures that the form will have the information needed to create a dropdown menu that contains the author names, which you retrieved with the following query against the authors collection:

```
// Get the list of authors
$cursor = $c->$db->$col_authors->find();
```

The authors' names are now listed under the cursor, so you can now build the HTML form:

```
print "<form action='add.php'  name='addpost' method='posts'>";
print "<input type='text' name='Title' value='Fill in the title'><br>";
print "Post as: <select name='names'>";
while ($names = $cursor->getNext())
{
    print "<option value=$names[_id]>$names[Name]";
}
print "</select><br>";
```

```
print "<textarea cols='40' rows='8' name='Message'>Type here</textarea>";
print "<input type='submit' name='addpost' value='Add'/>";
print "</form>";
```

To submit the post itself, you need to add a section in the file that gets triggered by a `$_GET['addpost']`. This section will create a new array called `$arr`. You will fill this array with a set of keys called `Title`, `Message`, `Author`, and `Date`. The values of these keys will be set to whatever has been inserted into the HTML form previously, with one exception: the date value will be added through the `MongoDate()` function, which will set the `date` field to current date and time.

Once all information has been successfully inserted into the array, the data will be injected into the `posts` collection with MongoDB's `insert()` function. This function takes the array name (`$arr`) as an argument, as shown in the following example:

```
// Specify the behavior when clicking on Add
if(isset($_GET["addpost"]))
{
    // Create a new array to store the changed values in
    $arr = array();
    $arr['Title'] = addslashes($_GET['Title']);
    $arr['Message'] = addslashes($_GET['Message']);
    $arr['Author'] = MongoDBRef::create(
        $c->$db->$col_authors->getName(),
        new MongoId($_GET['names'])
    );
    $arr['Date'] = new MongoDate();
    $c->$db->$col_posts->insert($arr);
    print "Post added. You can leave this page.";
}

?>
```

*Et voilà!* Notice that the resulting output will be extremely basic. It consists only of a message stating that the post has been added. Of course, you can make this fancier as you go along. At this point, you're ready to save this document; name it `add.php`.

## Editing a Post

Sometimes you may need to modify an existing post. For example, perhaps the post's author used language inappropriate for your site, and you want to strip that out, but leave the post itself. In this circumstance, you'd probably prefer to modify the original post without removing it, editing it, adding it back again, and then manually adding the comments back again. The preceding approach isn't exactly flexible, nor is it a good idea. For these kinds of actions, you may prefer to use the `update()` function instead.

In the `posts.php` page, you previously added a link to deal with changing a document. Currently, this link doesn't do anything other than respond when the `$_GET['modify']` variable is called; however, you're now ready to add in some code to deal with editing a post.

Begin by creating an HTML form and fetching the document from the collection. You will place the values retrieved from the collection into the fields of the HTML form, which will make it easier to change any existing data. Once you do this, you will be only a click away from using the `update()` function to update the document. The `update()` function takes two parameters: `_id`, which specifies the ID of the document that needs to be changed; and `$set`, which holds the new information the document needs to show instead.

You need to add the following code at the bottom of the `posts.php` page, just beneath the `if` statement and just before the PHP closing tag:

```
// Specify what ought to happen when the Modify link has been clicked
if(isset($_GET["modify"]))
{
    // Use the posted ID to retrieve the data, and input it in a form
    $filter = array("_id" => new MongoId($_GET["modify"]));
    $post = $c->$db->$col_posts->findOne($filter);
    // Start writing the form
    print "<form action='posts.php' name='modifypost' method='post'>";
    print "Title<input type='text' name='Title' value='$post[Title] '/><br>";
    print "Message<textarea rows='5' cols='40' name='Message'>$post[Message]</textarea>";
    print "<input type='hidden' name='id' value='$_GET[modify]'/>";
    print "<input type='submit' name='modifypost' value='Change'/>";
    print "</form>";
}
```

You've added the HTML form; next, you can specify the submission behavior:

```
// Specify the behavior when clicking on Change
else if(isset($_POST["modifypost"]))
{
    // Create a new array to store the changed values in
    $arr = array();
    $arr['Title'] = addslashes($_POST['Title']);
    $arr['Message'] = addslashes($_POST['Message']);
    $id = new MongoId($_POST['id']);
    $c->$db->$col_posts->update(array("_id" => $id),array('$set' => $arr));
    // Hooray
    print "The post has been updated. Hooray";
}
```

# Deleting a Post

Deleting a post doesn't take much effort. There's hardly any server-client communication involved because the process of deleting a post doesn't require that you query and return the values from all fields in the post. This means that it's a relatively low-bandwidth task to perform. Similarly, the code itself is simple and can be covered quickly.

You probably recall that you also added a Delete link to the `post.php` page, but didn't supply any implementation code at the time. To delete a post, you set the URL to `?del=<id>`, where `<id>` specifies the `_id` field's value from the post you want to delete. The `ID` value is also perfect for removing documents; all that you need to do to remove a document is another `if` statement.

This new `if` statement will convert the received `ID` into a MongoDB type `ID` value, and store this in the `$id` variable. Next, you need to establish a connection to the database, and then use the `remove()` function to complete the removal process. The `remove()` function takes the `$id` variable as an argument.

What follows is the last piece of PHP code; you can place this under the same `if()` statement that you used to modify the posts:

```
// Specify what ought to happen when the Delete link has been clicked
if(isset($_GET["del"]))
{
    // Use the posted ID as the _id, and convert it via MongoId
    $id = array("_id" => new MongoId($_GET["del"]));
    // Specify the options
    $options = array('justOne' => true, 'safe' => true);
    // Connect to the database and remove the document
```

```
    $c->$db->$col_posts->remove($id, $options);
    // In case the document was deleted successfully, report a success
    print "Post removed successfully";
}
```

# Creating the Index Pages

You've finished creating the basic code of your blog application. At this point, you should be able to add, modify, and delete posts. You should also be able to use paging to navigate the posts, as well as to read, add, modify, and delete comments. The only problem is that all your code is spread across a couple of pages, and clicking certain actions (e.g., submitting a post) currently navigates you away from the page, which is undesirable behavior. To counter this, you can design a simple index page (`index.html`) that contains a *frameset*, or table with the earlier pages embedded. Or you can add all the blog's contents into a single page—the choice is yours.

This section walks you through the easier of the two approaches: creating a frameset where a single page holds two frames. The first frame contains another HTML page with some navigation links, while the second frame contains the posts overview (`posts.php`). You can place the following lines of HTML code in either the root's index or in the `admin` directory:

```
<html>
<head>
    <title>MongoDB PHP Example</title>
</head>
<body>
    <frameset cols="15%,85%">
        <frame src="nav.html"/>
        <frame src="posts.php" name="contents"/>
    </frameset>
</body>
</html>
```

The page containing the navigation links isn't exactly rocket science. But remember: the aim in this chapter is to keep things simple and show what MongoDB can do for you, not to become a PHP guru. The following snippet shows the contents from the `nav.html` file, which you place in the root:

```
<html>
<body>
    <a href='posts.php' target='contents'>View Posts</a><br/>
    <a href='admin/index.html' target='blank'>Manage posts</a><br/>
</body>
</html>
```

You can adjust the hyperlinks in the `admin` section to your liking; the following snippet shows an example of the `nav.html` page for the `admin` folder:

```
<html>
<body>
    <a href='posts.php' target='contents'>View Posts</a><br/>
    <a href='add.php' target='contents'>Add Posts</a><br/>
</body>
</html>
```

At this point, you have a basic sample application that allows you to add, modify, and delete documents through a simple PHP interface. You are free to expand this sample application with additional code, as your preferences and needs require.

# Recapping the *blog* Application

Throughout this chapter, you've seen code examples designed to help you get the blog application up and running. These code examples rely on basic, yet practical functions. Because it can be hard to keep track of which code goes where—and because the code doesn't always do what you expect it to—the following sections will provide the complete and finished versions of the code examples again, along with a short commentary that explains what you see in each code sample.

The first code example you'll review (Listing 8–1) shows the code for the `index.html` file that contains the frontpage information. The index file is generally the first file to be loaded; therefore, it includes the information a visitor must see first when visiting the page. This following code snippet includes a standard, uncomplicated frameset that loads both the navigation menu (`nav.html`) on the left part of the screen and the posts overview (`posts.php`) on the right. You can adjust the percentages in the `frameset` tag based on your preferences:

***Listing 8–1.** index.html*

```
<html>
<head>
    <title>MongoDB PHP</title>
</head>
<body>
    <frameset cols="15%,85%">
        <frame src="nav.html"/>
        <frame src="posts.php" name="contents"/>
    </frameset>
</body>
</html>
```

Next comes the `nav.html` file shown in Listing 8–2, which contains two hyperlinks to other pages. The first link is a reference to the aforementioned `posts.php` page, and it ensures that this page will be loaded in the right-hand frame. The second is a link to the `admin` section, which lets you modify and/or add posts:

***Listing 8–2.** nav.html*

```
<html>
<body>
    <a href='posts.php' target='contents'>View Posts</a><br/>
    <a href='admin/index.html' target='blank'>Manage posts</a><br/>
</body>
</html>
```

The next page, `posts.php` (Listing 8–3), contains the necessary PHP and MongoDB code needed to get a list of all available posts and to display their contents. At the top of this page, you define a set of variables to control a variety of tasks, such as which database and collections need to be connected to successfully obtain the posts. You also specify the limit, which indicates the maximum number of posts to display per page.

This page also contains a number of `if` statements that control the behavior of the PHP page. The first one specifies that, if a search is being requested through the search form, then the query parameters must be changed to match the terms specified in the search box.

Next, the MongoDB `find()` command is used to fetch and display all the posts. You use this function to match the search criteria specified and limit the results to the value specified previously. Finally, the `posts.php` page adds hyperlinks to facilitate navigating the blog posts if the `find()` function returns more than the maximum number of posts per page:

***Listing 8–3.*** *posts.php*

```
<?php

// Let's define some variables!
$db = "blog";                          // This is the name of the database
$col_authors = "authors";              // This is the name of the authors collection
$col_posts = "posts";                  // This is the name of the posts collection
$limit = 10;                           // This is the total number of posts displayed

// Set up some PHP code to check if the $page is set and if not, set $page to '1'.
if(isset($_GET['page'])){
    $page = $_GET['page'];
}
else {
    $page = 1;
}

if(isset($_POST["search"]))
{
    // Use MongoRegEx to specify the search criteria
    $regex = new MongoRegex("/$_POST[search]/i");
    $query = array("Message" => $regex);
}
else
{
    $query = array();
}

// Let's define some more variables for paging
$offset = ($page -1) * $limit;
$nextpage = ($page +1);
$prevpage = ($page -1);

// Add a form for searching the posts
print "<form method='post' name='search' action='posts.php'>";
print "<input type='text' name='search'>";
print "<input type='submit' value='Search'>";
print "</form>";

// Connect to the database
$c = new Mongo();

// Execute a search and store the posts under the cursor variable
```

```
$cursor = $c->$db->$col_posts->find($query)->skip($offset)->limit($limit)->sort(array('_id'=>-
1));

// For each document it finds within the collection, print it's contents
while ($document = $cursor->getNext())
{
    // Get the author's name via MongoDBRef
    $ref = $c->$db->getDBRef($document["Author"]);
    $author = $ref["Name"];
    // Translate the date back using date()
    $date = date('M d, Y @ h:i', $document["Date"]->sec);

    // Show the title, author, date and message
    print "<h1>$document[Title]</h1><br>";
    print "<i>By $author on $date</i>";
    print "<p>$document[Message]</p>";

    // Show clickable link to view the comments, and count them
    $postid = new MongoId($document['_id']);
    if(isset($document["Comments"]))
    {
        $count = count($document["Comments"]);
    }
    else {
        $count = 0;
    }
    print "<a href='view.php?id=$postid'>View Comments ($count)</a>";
}

$posts = $c->$db->$col_posts->find()->count();
if ($page > 1)
    {
        print "<a href='?page=$prevpage'>Previous Page</a>";
        if ($page * $limit < $posts)
        {
            print "<a href='?page=$nextpage'>Next page</a>";
        }
    }
else {
    if ($page * $limit < $posts) {
        print "<a href='?page=$nextpage'>Next page</a>";
    }
}

?>
```

You use the next page, view.php (Listing 8–4), solely to display a single post, as well as its associated comments. This page also contains a set of variables that you use to connect to and obtain the right information from the right database.

If the Object ID is given in the URL, then the code in view.php implements paging for the comments added to the post, assuming the number of comments to display exceeds the limit specified per page. The page also includes hyperlinks to navigate between comments when the number of comments exceeds the maximum number of comments per page.

This page also includes an additional query that uses DBRef to target the authors collection. Specifically, this query obtains information about the author of a given post. Once all the appropriate information has been gathered, the post and its comments are displayed on the screen, followed by an HTML form that allows the user to add new comments to the post:

***Listing 8–4.** view.php*

```
<?php

// Let's define some variables!
$c = new Mongo();                          // Used to connect to the db
$db= "blog";                               // This is the name of the database
$col_authors = "authors";                  // This is the name of the authors collection
$col_posts = "posts";                      // This is the name of the posts collection

if (isset($_GET['id']))
{
    if (isset($_GET['p']))
    {
        $commentpage = $_GET['p'];
    }
        else
    {
        $commentpage = 1;
    }

    // Add some more variables for paging the comments
    $id = new MongoId($_GET['id']);
    $limit = 5;                              // Used to define the max no. of comments
    $offset = ($commentpage -1) * $limit;    // This is our comments offset
    $nextpage = ($commentpage +1);
    $prevpage = ($commentpage -1);

    // Define the query  parameters that we want to use
    $query = array('_id' => $id);
    $cond = (object)array('Comments' => array('$slice' => array($offset, $limit) ) );

    // Connect to the database, and perform the findOne
    $document = $c->$db->$col_posts->findOne($query, $cond);

    // Now get the author's name via MongoDBRef, and translate the date
    $ref = $c->$db->getDBRef($document["Author"]);
    $author = $ref["Name"];
    $date = date('M d, Y @ h:i', $document["Date"]->sec);

    // ..and print all the keys and values out
    print "<h1>$document[Title]</h1>";
    print "<i>By $author on $date</i>";
    print "<p>$document[Message]</p>";

    // If there are any comments, then show them here
    if (isset($document['Comments']))
```

```
    {
        // Show a header to announce the comments
        print "<h3>Comments</h3>";
        // Set each comment that gets found in the $document array to $comm
        foreach ($document['Comments'] as $comm)
        {
            // For each of these, print the name and comment
            print "<b>$comm[Name]</b></br>";
            print "<i>$comm[Comment]</i></br>";
        }

        // Perform a count on the comments to create paging
        $doc = $c->$db->$col_posts->findOne($query);
        $count = count($doc["Comments"]);

        // Add some links for paging the comments
        if ($commentpage > 1)
        {
            print "<a href='?id=$id&p=$prevpage'>Previous Page</a> ";
            if ($commentpage * $limit < $count)
            {
                print "<a href='?id=$id&p=$nextpage'>Next page</a><br/>";
            }
        }
        else
        {
            if ($commentpage * $limit < $count)
            {
                print "<a href='?id=$id&p=$nextpage'>Next page</a><br/>";
            }
        }
    }

    // Let's add a simple HTML form
    print "<form name='addcomment' action='view.php' method='post'>";
    print "Your name: <input type='text' name='commentauthor'><br>";
    print "Comment: <textarea cols='20' rows='4' name='comment'></textarea>";
    print "<input type='hidden' value=$id name='id'/>";
    print "<input type='submit' value='Add Comment' name='addcomment'/>";
    print "</form>";
}

if(isset($_POST["addcomment"]))
{
    // Specify the update criteria
    $criteria = array("_id" => new MongoId($_POST['id']));
    // Specify the update that should be performed
    $update = array(
        '$addToSet' => array
            (
            "Comments" => array
                (
                "Name" => $_POST['commentauthor'],
                "Comment" => addslashes($_POST['comment'])
```

```
                )
            )
        );
    // Perform the update
    $c->$db->$col_posts->update($criteria, $update);
    // Thanks
    print "Thanks for your comment!";
}
?>
```

The admin/index.html page (Listing 8–5) is the first page to load when you navigate to the admin/ directory of the website. This page contains a frameset that consists of two columns. The first column embeds the Navigation menu, while the second column embeds the posts overview (posts.php):

***Listing 8–5.** admin/index.html*

```
<html>
<head>
    <title>MongoDB PHP</title>
</head>
<body>
    <frameset cols="15%,85%">
        <frame src="nav.html"/>
        <frame src="posts.php" name="contents"/>
    </frameset>
</body>
</html>
```

The admin/nav.html page(Listing 8–6) contains a set of hyperlinks that display in the left column of the website. One of these links navigates you back to the posts overview (assuming you have navigated away from it). The second link navigates you to a page used to add more posts to the database:

***Listing 8–6.** admin/nav.html*

```
<html>
<body>
    <a href='posts.php' target='contents'>View Posts</a><br/>
    <a href='add.php' target='contents'>Add Posts</a><br/>
</body>
</html>
```

The next page, admin.posts/php (Listing 8–7), does not differ much from the previously mentioned posts.php page that is used to display all posts: the difference is that this page adds the functionality to modify and/or delete a post.

The page begins by defining a set of variables to specify the database information used to connect and retrieve all information. Next, the page includes code to search for specific posts. This code consists of regular expressions and a simple HTML form. The paging parameters are added next, including the functionality that enables you to find, retrieve, and list all posts, including the information about the authors.

All this is followed by a section that defines what ought to happen when the modify link is clicked. Clicking this link shows an HTML form with the post's information filled in, making it easy to modify the data and save it again. Naturally, the submit behavior is specified next, followed by code that implements a delete button. Clicking the delete button invokes MongoDB's remove() function, which removes the document in question, based on the Object ID:

*Listing 8–7. admin/posts.php*

```
<?php

// Let's define some variables!
$db = "blog";                         // This is the name of the database
$col_authors = "authors";             // This is the name of the authors collection
$col_posts = "posts";                 // This is the name of the posts collection
$limit = 10;                          // This is the total number of posts displayed

// Set up some PHP code to check if the $page is set and if not, set $page to '1'.
if(isset($_GET['page'])){
    $page = $_GET['page'];
}
else {
    $page = 1;
}

if(isset($_POST["search"]))
{
    // Use MongoRegEx to specify the search criteria
    $regex = new MongoRegex("/$_POST[search]/i");
    $query = array("Message" => $regex);
}
else
{
    $query = array();
}

// Let's define some more variables for paging
$offset = ($page -1) * $limit;
$nextpage = ($page +1);
$prevpage = ($page -1);

// Add a form for searching the posts
print "<form method='post' name='search' action='posts.php'>";
print "<input type='text' name='search'>";
print "<input type='submit' value='Search'>";
print "</form>";

// Add a link to add a post
print "<a href='add.php'>Add a post</a>";

// Connect to the database
$c = new Mongo();

// Execute a search and store the posts under the cursor variable
$cursor = $c->$db->$col_posts->find($query)->skip($offset)->limit($limit)->sort(array('_id'=>-
1));

// For each document it finds within the collection, print it's contents
while ($document = $cursor->getNext())
```

```
{
    // Get the author's name via MongoDBRef
    $ref = $c->$db->getDBRef($document["Author"]);
    $author = $ref["Name"];
    // Translate the date back using date()
    $date = date('M d, Y @ h:i', $document["Date"]->sec);

    // Show the title, author, date and message
    print "<h1>$document[Title]</h1><br>";
    print "<i>By $author on $date</i>";
    print "<p>$document[Message]</p>";

    // Show clickable link to view the comments, and count them
    $postid = new MongoId($document['_id']);
    if(isset($document["Comments"]))
    {
        $count = count($document["Comments"]);
    }
    else {
        $count = 0;
    }
    print "<a href='../view.php?id=$postid'>View Comments ($count)</a> ";
    // Show clickable links to modify or delete the post
    print "<a href='?modify=$postid'>Modify</a> ";
    print "<a href='?del=$postid'>Delete</a>";
}

$posts = $c->$db->$col_posts->find()->count();
if ($page > 1)
    {
        print "<a href='?page=$prevpage'>Previous Page</a>";
        if ($page * $limit < $posts)
        {
            print "<a href='?page=$nextpage'>Next page</a>";
        }
    }
else {
    if ($page * $limit < $posts) {
        print "<a href='?page=$nextpage'>Next page</a>";
    }
}

// Specify what ought to happen when the Modify link has been clicked
if(isset($_GET["modify"]))
{
    // Use the posted ID to retrieve the data, and input it in a form
    $filter = array("_id" => new MongoId($_GET["modify"]));
    $post  = $c->$db->$col_posts->findOne($filter);
    print "<form action='posts.php' name='modifypost' method='post'>";
    print "Title<input type='text' name='Title' value='$post[Title]'/><br>";
    print "Message <textarea rows='5' cols='40' name='Message'>$post[Message]</textarea>";
    print "<input type='hidden' name='id' value='$_GET[modify]'/>";
    print "<input type='submit' name='modifypost' value='Change'/>";
    print "</form>";
```

```
}

// Specify the behavior when clicking on Change
if(isset($_POST["modifypost"]))
{
    // Create a new array to store the changed values in
    $arr = array();
    $arr['Title'] = addslashes($_POST['Title']);
    $arr['Message'] = addslashes($_POST['Message']);
    $id = new MongoId($_POST['id']);
    $c->$db->$col_posts->update(array("_id" => $id),array('$set' => $arr));
    // Hooray
    print "The post has been updated. Hooray";
}

// Specify what ought to happen when the Delete link has been clicked
if(isset($_GET["del"]))
{
    // Use the posted ID as the _id, and convert it via MongoId
    $id = array("_id" => new MongoId($_GET["del"]));
    // Specify the options
    $options = array('justOne' => true, 'safe' => true);
    // Connect to the database and remove the document
    $c->$db->$col_posts->remove($id, $options);
    // In case the document was deleted successfully, report a success
    print "Post removed successfully";
}
?>
```

The final page of the application, `admin/add.php` (Listing 8–8), adds new documents to the collection. The code starts by specifying a number of variables that mostly contain database- and collection-specific information used to connect to the database. Next, the `find()` command fetches a list of existing authors added to the database previously.

The code continues with an HTML form used to input the information for a new post. The add button submits this information; this button's behavior is specified directly below an `if` statement. The `if` statement specifies that the information is to be added in the defined collection:

***Listing 8–8.** admin/add.php*

```
<?php

// First, lets connect to the database and get a list of authors
$c = new Mongo();
$db = "blog";
$col_posts = "posts";
$col_authors = "authors";
$cursor = $c->$db->$col_authors->find();

print "<h1>Let's add a post!</h1>";
print "<form action='add.php'  name='addpost' method='posts'>";
print "<input type='text' name='Title' value='Fill in the title'><br>";
print "Post as: <select name='names'>";
while ($names = $cursor->getNext())
```

```
{
    print "<option value=$names[_id]>$names[Name]";
}
print "</select><br>";
print "<textarea cols='40' rows='8' name='Message'>Type here</textarea>";
print "<input type='submit' name='addpost' value='Add'/>";
print "</form>";

// Specify the behavior when clicking on Add
if(isset($_GET["addpost"]))
{
    // Create a new array to store the changed values in
    $arr = array();
    $arr['Title'] = addslashes($_GET['Title']);
    $arr['Message'] = addslashes($_GET['Message']);
    $arr['Author'] = MongoDBRef::create(
        $c->$db->$col_authors->getName(),
        new MongoId($_GET['names'])
    );
    $arr['Date'] = new MongoDate();
    $c->$db->$col_posts->insert($arr);
    print "Post added. You can leave this page.";
}
?>
```

# Summary

In this chapter, you learned how to use the PHP MongoDB driver to create a small and simple web application. This admittedly simple application demonstrated just how little code you need to use to add, delete, or modify documents in a collection. You also saw a practical example that showed how to use Regular Expression to perform searches, as well as how to use DBRef to reference information.

In the next chapter, we'll leave the PHP driver behind us and start focusing on administration of the MongoDB installation.

# PART III

# Advanced

CHAPTER 9

# Database Administration

In this chapter, we will walk you through some of the basic administrative operations you can perform on a MongoDB server. We will also show you how to automate some of those activities, such as backing up your server.

The nature of MongoDB means that many of the more traditional functions that a DB Administrator would perform are not required. For example, creating new databases, collections, and fields on the server are not necessary because MongoDB will create these elements on-the-fly as you access them. Therefore, managing databases and schemas is not required for the vast majority of cases.

However, this freedom from having to predefine everything can result in the unintended creation of elements, such as extraneous collections and fields in documents. Administrators and developers will occasionally need to clear out unused data elements on databases, particularly during the development phase of a project where change is often rapid. They may have to try out many approaches before settling on a final solution before cleaning up the databases. MongoDB's ease of use encourages this *explorative* mode of development; however, it can also result in clutter in your datastores because the amount of effort required to create data structures has fallen almost to nothing.

A contributing factor to this clutter and one of the more significant differences between MongoDB and SQL databases is that all object and element names in MongoDB are case sensitive on all platforms. Thus, the `foo` and `Foo` database names refer to two completely different databases. Therefore, you need to be careful with your database and collection naming to avoid accidentally creating multiple databases that differ only in the case of the name.

The different versions of these databases will fill up your disk, and they can create a lot of confusion for developers and end users of the system by allowing them to connect to incomplete or unintended sets of data.

In this chapter, you will learn how to perform all the following tasks:

- Back up and restore your MongoDB system.
- Use the supplied `MongoDB` shell to perform common tasks.
- Control access to your server with authentication.
- Monitor your database instances.

Before diving into those tasks, however, we'll begin by looking at the tools used to carry out many of the tasks listed above.

---

**Note** The examples in this chapter are based on the Blog application introduced in Chapter 8.

---

# Using Administrative Tools

An administrator needs tools suitable for performing the day-to-day tasks of keeping the server running smoothly. There are some very good tools available in the MongoDB package, as well as an evolving collection of useful third-party tools. The following sections cover some of the more important tools available, as well as how to use them.

## mongo, the MongoDB Console

The main tool you will use as an administrator is mongo, the MongoDB console tool. mongo is a command-line console utility based on JavaScript. It is similar to many of the query tools supplied with mainstream relational databases. However, mongo has one unique trick up its sleeve: it can run programs written in JavaScript that interact directly with the MongoDB database.

This console allows you to script all of your interactions with MongoDB in JavaScript, and then store those scripts in `.js` files to run when you need them to. In fact, many of the built-in commands in the mongo console are themselves written in JavaScript.

You can place any commands that you would type into the command shell into a file with a .js extension, and run them by simply adding the file name to the command line when starting up the shell, the shell will execute the contents of the file and then exit. This is useful for running lists of repetitive commands.

We will be using the mongo console to demonstrate many of the administrative tasks that you can perform on a MongoDB server, and, because it is distributed with the MongoDB server, we can guarantee it will be there.

## Using Third-Party Administration Tools

There are a several third-party administration (admin) tools available for MongoDB. 10gen maintains a page on the MongoDB website that lists currently available third-party tools. You can find this list at `www.mongodb.org/display/DOCS/Admin+UIs`. Most of these tools are web-based and similar in principle to phpMyAdmin for Mysql.

# Backing up the MongoDB Server

As a new MongoDB administrator, the first skill you should learn is how to back up and restore your MongoDB server. Arming yourself with this knowledge should make you feel more comfortable with exploring some of the more advanced administrative functions. This is because you know that your precious data is stored away safely somewhere.

## Creating a Backup 101

Let's begin by performing a simple backup then restoring it. Along the way, you will make sure the backup is intact, and you will look at some practical examples that illustrate how the backup and restoration features work. Once you have a solid understanding of how to use these features, you will be able to move on to exploring the more advanced administrative features of MongoDB.

In this simple backup example, we will assume the following:

- Your MongoDB server is running on the same machine that you are currently logged into.
- You have enough disk space for dump files that could be, at most, the same size as your database.
- Your backup will be made in your home directory. This means you won't have to deal with any issues related to permissions.

The MongoDB backup utility is called mongodump; this utility is supplied as part of the standard distribution. The following example performs a simple backup of the running MongoDB server to a designated disk directory:

```
$> cd ~
$> mkdir testmongobackup
$> cd testmongobackup
$> mongodump
```

When mongodump is running, you should see it output something that looks like the following:

```
$ mongodump
connected to: 127.0.0.1
all dbs
DATABASE: blog to dump/blog
    blog.authors to dump/blog/authors.bson
        2 objects
    blog.system.indexes to dump/blog/system.indexes.bson
         3 objects
    blog.posts to dump/blog/posts.bson
        1 objects
    blog.tagcloud to dump/blog/tagcloud.bson
        4 objects
DATABASE: admin to dump/admin
```

If your output doesn't look very similar to this, then you should double-check that your environment matches up with the assumptions stated previously.

If you do see the correct output, then your database has been backed up to the `testmongobackup/dump` directory. The following snippet restores your database to its state at the time you performed the backup:

```
$> cd ~/testmongobackup
$> mongorestore --drop
connected to: 127.0.0.1
Thu Aug 12 13:31:20    dump/blog/authors.bson
Thu Aug 12 13:31:20    going into namespace [blog.authors]
Thu Aug 12 13:31:20    dropping
Thu Aug 12 13:31:20    2 objects found
Thu Aug 12 13:31:20    dump/blog/posts.bson
Thu Aug 12 13:31:20    going into namespace [blog.posts]
Thu Aug 12 13:31:20    dropping
Thu Aug 12 13:31:20    1 objects found
Thu Aug 12 13:31:20    dump/blog/system.indexes.bson
Thu Aug 12 13:31:20    going into namespace [blog.system.indexes]
Thu Aug 12 13:31:20    dropping
Thu Aug 12 13:31:20    3 objects found
```

```
Thu Aug 12 13:31:20    dump/blog/tagcloud.bson
Thu Aug 12 13:31:20    going into namespace [blog.tagcloud]
Thu Aug 12 13:31:20    dropping
Thu Aug 12 13:31:20    4 objects found
```

The --drop option tells the mongorestore utility to discard each collection in the database before restoring it. Consequently, the backed-up data replaces the data currently in the database. If you were to choose not to use the --drop option, then the restored data would be appended to the end of each collection, which would result in duplicated items.

Let's examine what happened in the preceding example more closely.

By default, the mongodump utility connects to the local database using the default port, and pulls out all of the datafiles associated with each database and collection and stores them in a predefined folder structure.

The default folder structure created by mongodump takes this form:

```
./dump/[databasename]/[collectionname].bson
```

The database system used in the preceding example consists of a single database called `blog`. The `blog` database contains three collections: `authors`, `posts`, and `tagcloud`.

The `mongodump` saves the data it retrieves from the database server in `.bson` files that are just a copy of the internal BSON format that MongoDB uses internally to store documents. You can also see the `MongoTest.system.indexes` collection backed up and restored in the preceding example. This collection is maintained by the MongoDB server, and it records which elements of each collection are indexed. It is this collection that allows you to rebuild the indexes when restoring from a backup.

Once you have dumped the database, you can archive and store the folder on to any online or offline media, such as CD, USB Drive, Tape, or S3 format.

---

■ **Note** The mongodump utility does not empty the contents of the `output` directory before it writes the backup files to it. If you have existing contents in this directory, then these contents won't be removed unless they match the name of a file (*`collectionname`*`.bson`) that mongodump has been instructed to back up. This is good if you want to add multiple collection dumps to the same dump directory; however, it could cause some issues if you use the same dump directory each time you back up data, but don't clear it out. For example, assume you have a database that you back up regularly, and at some point you decide to delete a collection from this database, unless you either clear out the directory where you are performing your backup, or manually remove the file associated with the deleted collection, then the next time you restore the data the deleted collection will reappear. Unless you want to overlay data in your backups, you should make sure you clear out the destination directory before you use mongodump.

---

## Backing up a Single Database

When you have multiple applications running on the same server, often you may find yourself wanting to back up each database individually, rather than all at once, as in the preceding example.

With mongodump, you can do this by adding the `-d` databasename option to the command line. This causes mongodump to create the `./dump` folder; however, this folder will contain only the backup files for a single database.

## Backing up a Single Collection

Imagine you have a blog site where the contents of the `authors` collection does not change much. Instead, the rapidly changing content of the blog site is contained in the `posts` and `tagcloud` collections. You might back up the entire database only once a day, but want to back up these two collections once per hour. Fortunately, you can do that easily with mongobackup by using the `-c` option to specify the collection you wish to back up.

The mongodump utility does not clear its destination directories. This means that, for each collection you want to back up, you can call mongodump successively to add a given collection to your backup, as shown in the following example:

```
$mkdir ~/backuptemp
$cd ~/backuptemp
$mongodump -d blog -c posts
$mongodump -d blog -c tagcloud
...
    archive the dump folder ~/backuptemp away as a tar file
...
$ cd ~
$ rm -rf backuptemp
```

# Digging Deeper into Backups

At this point, you know how to perform the rudimentary tasks of backing up your data and subsequently restoring that data. Now you're ready to look at some of the powerful options that allow you to tailor MongoDB's backup and restore functionality to suit your particular needs.

The mongodump utility includes the following options:

```
$mongodump --help
options:
  --help                  produce help message
  -v [ --verbose ]        be more verbose (include multiple times for more
                          verbosity e.g. -vvvvv)
  -h [ --host ] arg       mongo host to connect to ("left,right" for pairs)
  --port arg              server port. Can also use --host hostname:port
  -d [ --db ] arg         database to use
  -c [ --collection ] arg collection to use (some commands)
  -u [ --username ] arg   username
  -p [ --password ] arg   password
  --ipv6                  enable IPv6 support (disabled by default)
  --dbpath arg            directly access mongod database files in the given
                          path, instead of connecting to a mongod  server -
                          needs to lock the data directory, so cannot be used
                          if a mongod is currently accessing the same path
  --directoryperdb        if dbpath specified, each db is in a separate
                          directory
  -o [ --out ] arg (=dump) output directory
  -q [ --query ] arg      json query
```

Most of the options listed here are self-explanatory, with the exception of last three, which are listed here:

- `--dbpath arg`: If you have a large amount of data to back up and fast drives, then it may be preferable to back up the database by copying the datafiles that the MongoDB server uses directly to the backup medium. This option allows you to back up directly from the server's datafiles, but it can only be used if the server is offline or otherwise *write frozen* (see the "Backing up Large Databases" section later in this chapter for more information).
- `--directoryperdb`: You use this command-line option in conjunction with the `--dbpath` option to specify that the MongoDB server that is being backed up was configured to place its datafiles for each database in a separate directory. By default, MongoDB places all of its datafiles in a single directory. You should use this option only if you have configured your server to operate in this mode.
- `-o [ --out ] arg`: You use this option to specify the directory where you want the database dumps to be placed. By default, the mongodump utility creates a folder called `/dump` in the current directory and writes the dumps into that. You can use the `-o/--out` option to choose an alternative path to place the output dumps.

# Restoring Individual Databases or Collections

You've just seen how the mongodump utility can back up a single database or collection; the mongorestore utility can do the same thing. You can use mongorestore to restore an item if the dump directory it is restoring from has the backup files for the required collection or database in it, you don't need to restore all the items present in the backup; if you wish, you can restore them individually.

Let's begin by looking at the options available in mongorestore:

```
$mongorestore --help
usage: mongorestore [options] [directory or filename to restore from]
options:
  --help                  produce help message
  -v [ --verbose ]        be more verbose (include multiple times for more
                          verbosity e.g. -vvvvv)
  -h [ --host ] arg       mongo host to connect to ("left,right" for pairs)
  --port arg              server port. Can also use --host hostname:port
  -d [ --db ] arg         database to use
  -c [ --collection ] arg collection to use (some commands)
  -u [ --username ] arg   username
  -p [ --password ] arg   password
  --ipv6                  enable IPv6 support (disabled by default)
  --dbpath arg            directly access mongod database files in the given
                          path, instead of connecting to a mongod  server -
                          needs to lock the data directory, so cannot be used
                          if a mongod is currently accessing the same path
  --directoryperdb        if dbpath specified, each db is in a separate
                          directory
  --objcheck              validate object before inserting
  --filter arg            filter to apply before inserting
  --drop                  drop each collection before import
  --indexesLast           wait to add indexes (faster if data isn't inserted in
                          index order)
```

You probably recognize most of these options from the discussion on mongodump; however, the following two options are worthy of special mention:

- `--drop`: This option instructs mongorestore to drop the existing collection before restoring it. This helps ensure that there are no duplicates. If this option is not used, then the restored data is appended (inserted) into the target collection. A planned future version of MongoDB intends to support an *upsert* mode of restoring collections, where the mongorestore utility will check to see whether a document of the same `_id` already exists in the collection. If the `_id` already exists, MongoDB will update it; if the `_id` doesn't already exist, MongoDB will insert it. This will remove the need to drop the target collection to guarantee data consistency.
- `--objcheck`: This option instructs mongorestore to validate the object before inserting it into the `destination` collection. For example, if there is corruption in the BSON data used to construct the object, then MongoDB will not restore it.

## Restoring a Single Database

You can use the mongorestore utility's `-d` option to restore a single database. As before, don't forget to use the `--drop` option if the database already exists in your MongoDB server:

```
$cd ~/testmongobackup
$mongorestore -d blog --drop
```

## Restoring a Single Collection

You use similar syntax to restore a single collection to a database; the difference is that you also specify a collection name with the `-c` option, as shown in the following example:

```
$cd ~/testmongobackup
$mongorestore -d blog -c posts --drop
```

# Automating Backups

For small installations or developer setups, the simple act of running the mongodump utility and saving the results is a perfectly adequate method of performing ad-hoc backups. For example, a common practice on a Mac OS X workstation is to let Time Machine (the Mac backup utility) store the backups.

For any kind of production setup, you will want to back up the server automatically. This is because regular backups can help you prevent or recover from trouble if you encounter any problems. This holds true not only with your installation (e.g., corrupted databases), but also if your users inadvertently damage or destroy data.

Let's look at some simple scripts that you can use to automate your backups.

## Using a Local Datastore

A simple backup script that creates archives in a specified directory will suffice if you have a large backup drive attached to your system or you can mount an external filesystem through NFS or SMB. The following backup script is easy to set up; simply edit the variables at the top of the script to match those of your local system:

```
#!/bin/bash
###########################################
# Edit these to define source and destinations

MONGO_DBS=""
BACKUP_TMP=~/tmp
BACKUP_DEST=~/backups
MONGODUMP_BIN=/usr/bin/mongodump
TAR_BIN=/usr/bin/tar

###########################################

BACKUPFILE_DATE=`date +%Y%m%d-%H%M`


# _do_store_archive <Database> <Dump_dir> <Dest_Dir> <Dest_file>

function _do_store_archive {
        mkdir -p $3
        cd $2
        tar -cvzf $3/$4 dump
}

# _do_backup <Database name>

function _do_backup {
        UNIQ_DIR="$BACKUP_TMP/$1"`date "+%s"`
        mkdir -p $UNIQ_DIR/dump
        echo "dumping Mongo Database $1"
        if [ "all" = "$1" ]; then
                $MONGODUMP_BIN -o $UNIQ_DIR/dump
        else
                $MONGODUMP_BIN -d $1 -o $UNIQ_DIR/dump
        fi
        KEY="database-$BACKUPFILE_DATE.tgz"
        echo "Archiving Mongo database to $BACKUP_DEST/$1/$KEY"
        DEST_DIR=$BACKUP_DEST/$1

        _do_store_archive  $1 $UNIQ_DIR $DEST_DIR $KEY

        rm -rf $UNIQ_DIR
}

# check to see if individual databases have been specified, otherwise backup the whole server
#  to "all"

if [ "" = "$MONGO_DBS"  ]; then
        MONGO_DB="all"
        _do_backup $MONGO_DB
else
```

```
        for MONGO_DB in $MONGO_DBS; do
                _do_backup $MONGO_DB
        done
fi
```

Table 9–1 lists the variables you have to change to make this simple backup script work with your system.

***Table 9–1.** The Variables Used in the Local Datastore Backup Script*

| Variable | Description |
|---|---|
| `MONGO_DBS` | Leave this variable empty ("") to back up all databases on the local server. Or you can place a list of databases into it to back up selective databases ("db1 db2 db3"). |
| `BACKUP_TMP` | Set this variable to a temporary directory suitable for holding the dump files for the backup. After the archive has been created, the temporary data used in this directory is deleted.<br>Be sure to choose a suitable directory that is relevant to using your script. For example, if you are using the script to create backups in your local account, then use `~/tmp`; if you are using it as a system cronjob that runs under a system account, then use `/tmp`. On an Amazon EC2 instance, you should probably use `/mnt/tmp`, so that the folder is not created on the system root partition, which is quite small. |
| `BACKUP_DEST` | This variable holds the destination folder for the backups, and individual folders will be created below this folder. Again, place this directory at a point relevant to how you use your backup script. |
| `MONGODUMP_BIN` | Because your backup script may be running under an account that does not have a full set of paths set up, it's wise to use this variable to specify the full path to this binary. You can determine the appropriate path on your system by typing "which mongodump" into a terminal window. |
| `TAR_BIN` | You use this variable to set the full path for the tar binary; use "which tar" in a terminal window to determine this path. |

You can now use this script to back up your databases; doing so will create a set of archival backups in the specified `BACKUP_DEST directory`. The files created follow this naming format:

```
[Database Name]/database-YYYYMMDD-HHMM.tgz
```

For example, the following snippet shows the backup names for this chapter's test database:

```
Backups:$ tree
.
|-- blog
|   |-- database-20100611-1144.tgz
|   `-- database-20100611-1145.tgz
`-- all
    |-- database-20100611-1210.tgz
    |-- database-20100611-1221.tgz
    |-- database-20100611-1222.tgz
    |-- database-20100611-1224.tgz
    `-- database-20100611-1233.tgz
```

### Installing the Script

If you want to run this script daily, just put it into /etc/cron.daily and restart the cron service to make it active. This approach will work on ubuntu, fedora, centos, and redhat. If you want less frequent backups, then just move the script to /etc/cron.weekly or /etc/cron.monthly. For more frequent backups, you can use /etc/cron.hourly.

## Using a Remote (Cloud-Based) Datastore

The script described in the previous section has a separate function for creating and storing the archive. This makes it relatively easy to modify the script so it uses an external datastore to store the backup archive. Table 9–2 provides a couple of examples, but many more other mechanisms are possible.

***Table 9–2.*** *Remote (Cloud-Based) Backup Storage Options*

| Method | Description |
|---|---|
| rsync/ftp/tftp or scp to another server | You can use rsync to move the archive to a backup storage machine. |
| s3 storage | s3 storage is a good place to put your backups if you run your system on EC2 because storage costs are low and Amazon makes redundant copies. |

We will examine the s3 method of storing your backup; however, the same principles apply to any of the other mechanisms.

This example uses the s3cmd utility available from http://s3tools.org. On Ubuntu, you can install this script using the sudo apt-get install s3cmd command; on Mac OSX, this script is available from the macport collection. On fedora, centos, and redhat, you can acquire the yum package from http://s3tools.net, and then install it using yum.

Once you have installed the package, run s3cmd -configure to set your Amazon s3 credentials. Note that you only need to supply two keys: AWS_ACCESS_KEY and AWS_SECRET_ACCESS_KEY. The s3cmd utility will create a config file that contains the information you need in this file: ~/.s3cfg.

Here are the changes that you need to make for your backup script to work with S3:

```
# _do_store_archive <Database> <Dump_dir> <Dest_Dir> <Dest_file>

BACKUP_S3_CONFIG=~/.s3cfg
```

```
BACKUP_S3_BUCKET=somecompany.somebucket
S3CMD_BIN=/usr/bin/s3cmd

function _do_store_archive {
        UNIQ_FILE="aws"`date "+%s"`
        cd $2
        tar -cvzf $BACKUP_TMP/$UNIQ_FILE dump
        $S3CMD_BIN --config $BACKUP_S3_CONFIG put $BACKUP_TMP/$UNIQ_FILE \
        s3://$BACKUP_S3_BUCKET/$1/$4
        rm -f $BACKUP_TMP/$UNIQ_FILE
}
```

Table 9–3 lists some variables that you need to configure to make this adapted script work.

***Table 9–3.*** *Configuring the Variables of Your Adapted Backup Script*

| Variable | Description |
|---|---|
| BACKUP_S3_CONFIG | The path to the s3cmd configuration file that was created when you ran `s3cmd -configure` to save the details of your s3 account. |
| BACKUP_S3_BUCKET | The name of the bucket that you want the script to store backups into. |
| S3CMD_BIN | The path to the s3cmd, executable program, again use “which s3cmd” to find it on your system. |

# Backing up Large Databases

Creating effective backup solutions can become a problem when working with large database systems. Often the time taken to make a copy of the database is significant and may even require hours to complete. During that time, you have to maintain the database in a consistent state, so the backup does not contain files that were copied at different points in time. The holy grail of a database backup system is a *point-in-time* snapshot, which can be done very quickly. The faster the snapshot can be done, the smaller the window of time where the database server must be *frozen.*

## Using a Slave Server for Backups

One technique used to perform large backups is to make the backup from a replication *slave server* that can be frozen while the backup is taken. This slave server is then restarted to catch up with the application after the backup is complete.

MongoDB makes it very simple to set up a slave server and have it track the *master server.* It's also relatively easy to halt and then restart the replication process (see Chapter 10 for more details on how to set up this type of configuration).

## Creating Snapshots with a Journaling Filesystem

Many modern volume managers have the ability to create snapshots of the state of the drive at any particular point-in-time. While setting up one of these systems is beyond the scope of this book, we can show you how to place the MongoDB server in a state where all of its data is in a consistent state on the disk. We also show you how to block writes so that further changes are not written to the disk, but are instead buffered in memory.

A snapshot is like a bookmark that allows you to read the drive exactly as it was when the snapshot was taken. A system's volume or filesystem manager makes sure that any blocks of data on the disk that are changed after the snapshot is taken are not written back to the same place on the drive; this preserves all the data on the disk to be read. Generally, the procedure for using a snapshot goes something like this:

1. Create a snapshot.
2. Copy data from the snapshot or restore the snapshot to another volume, depending on your volume manager.
3. Release the snapshot; doing so releases all preserved disk blocks that are no longer needed back into the free space chain on the drive.
4. Back up the data from the copied data while the server is still running.

The great thing about the method just described is that reads against the data can continue unhindered while the snapshot is taken.

Some volume managers that have this capability include:

- Linux and the LVM volume management system
- Sun ZFS
- Amazon EBS volumes
- Windows Server using shadow copies

Most of the preceding volume managers have the ability to perform a snapshot in a very short period of time—often just a few seconds—even on very large amounts of data. The volume managers don't actually copy the data out at this point; instead, they effectively insert a bookmark onto the drive, so that you can read the drive in the state it existed at the point in time the snapshot was taken.

Once the backup system has read the drive from the snapshot, then the old blocks that have been subsequently changed can be released back to the drive's free space chain (or whatever mechanism the filesystem uses to mark free space).

To make this an effective method of creating a backup, we have to get MongoDB to flush all outstanding disk writes to the disk so we can take a snapshot. The function that forces MongoDB to do this is called *fsync*; the function that blocks further writes is called a *lock*. MongoDB has the ability to perform both operations at the same time, so that, after the fsync, no further writes are done to the disk until the lock is released. This makes the image of the database on the disk *consistent*, and ensures it stays *consistent* until we have completed the snapshot.

You use the following commands to make MongoDB enter this state:

```
$mongo
>use admin
>db.runCommand({fsync:1,lock:1})
{
    "info" : "now locked against writes",
    "ok" : 1
}
```

You use these commands to check the current state of the lock:

```
$mongo
>use admin
```

```
>db.currentOp()
{
    "inprog" : [
    ],
    "fsyncLock" : 1
}
```

The "fsyncLock": 1 status indicates that MongoDB's fsync process, which is responsible for writing changes to the disk, is currently blocked from performing writes.

At this point, you can issue whatever commands are required to make your volume manager create the snapshot of the folders where MongoDB has its datafiles stored. Once the snapshot is completed, you can use the following commands to release the lock:

```
$mongo
>use admin
>db.$cmd.sys.unlock.findOne();
{ "ok" : 1, "info" : "unlock requested" }
```

Note that there may be a small delay before the lock is released; however, you can use the `db.currentOp()` function to check the result.

When the lock is finally cleared, `db.currentOp()` will return:

```
$mongo
>use admin
>db.currentOp()
{ "inprog" : [] }
```

The `{ "inprog" : [] }` line means that the lock has been released and that MongoDB can start writing to the disk again.

Now that you have the snapshot bookmark inserted, you can use the utilities associated with your volume manager to copy the contents of the snapshot to a suitable place so you can store your backup. Don't forget to release the snapshot once your backup is complete.

You can visit the following links for more information on snapshots:

- http://tldp.org/HOWTO/LVM-HOWTO/snapshots_backup.html
- http://docs.huihoo.com/opensolaris/solaris-zfs-administration-guide/html/ch06.html
- http://support.rightscale.com/09-Clouds/AWS/02-Amazon_EC2/EBS/Create_an_EBS_Snapshot

## Disk Layout to Use with Volume Managers

Some volume managers can take a snapshot of subdirectories on a partition, but most can't, so it is a good idea to mount the volume you are planning to store your MongoDB data on in a suitable place on your filesystem (e.g., /mnt/mongodb) and use the server configuration options to place the data directories, the configuration file, and any other MongoDB-related files (e.g., logfiles) solely on that mount.

This means that, when you take a snapshot of the volume, you capture the complete state of the server, including its configuration. It may even be a good idea to place the binaries of the server distribution directly on that volume, so that your backup contains a completely coordinated set of components.

# Importing Data into MongoDB

Sometimes, you need to load lots of bulk data into MongoDB for use as reference data. Such data might include zipcode tables, IP geolocation tables, parts catalogs, and so on.

MongoDB includes a bulk "loader" mongoimport, designed to import data directly into a particular collection on the server.

The mongoimport utility can load data from three different file formats:

1. *CSV*: In this file format, each line represents a document, and the fields are separated by a comma.
2. *TSV*: This file format is similar to CSV; however, it uses a tab character as the delimiter. This format is popular because it does not require the escaping of any text characters other than those for new lines.
3. *JSON*: This format contains one block of JSON per line that represents a document. Unlike the other formats, JSON can support documents with variable schemas.

The use of this utility is fairly intuitive. For input, it takes a file in one of the three preceding formats, a string or a file with a set of column header names (these form the element names in a MongoDB document), and several options that are used to control how the data is interpreted. The following example shows how to use the mongoimport utility:

```
$mongoimport --help
options:
  --help                  produce help message
  -v [ --verbose ]        be more verbose (include multiple times for more
                          verbosity e.g. -vvvvv)
  -h [ --host ] arg       mongo host to connect to ("left,right" for pairs)
  --port arg              server port. Can also use --host hostname:port
  -d [ --db ] arg         database to use
  -c [ --collection ] arg collection to use (some commands)
  -u [ --username ] arg   username
  -p [ --password ] arg   password
  --ipv6                  enable IPv6 support (disabled by default)
  --dbpath arg            directly access mongod database files in the given
                          path, instead of connecting to a mongod  server -
                          needs to lock the data directory, so cannot be used
                          if a mongod is currently accessing the same path
  --directoryperdb        if dbpath specified, each db is in a separate
                          directory
  -f [ --fields ] arg     comma separated list of field names e.g. -f name,age
  --fieldFile arg         file with fields names - 1 per line
  --ignoreBlanks          if given, empty fields in csv and tsv will be ignored
  --type arg              type of file to import.  default: json (json,csv,tsv)
  --file arg              file to import from; if not specified stdin is used
  --drop                  drop collection first
  --headerline            CSV,TSV only - use first line as headers
  --upsert                insert or update objects that already exist
  --upsertFields arg      comma-separated fields for the query part of the
                          upsert. You should make sure this is indexed
  --stopOnError           stop importing at first error rather than continuing
  --jsonArray             load a json array, not one item per line. Currently
                          limited to 4MB.
```

The following options deserve a little bit more explanation:

- `--headerline`: Uses the first line of the file as the list of field names. Note that this applies only to CSV and TSV formats.
- `--ignoreblanks`: Does *not* import empty fields. If a field is empty, then a corresponding element will not be created in the document for that row; if you don't invoke this option, then an empty element with the column name is created.
- `--drop`: Drops a collection and then recreates it with data only from this import; otherwise, the data is appended to the collection.

You also have to specify the database name and the collection name when you use mongoimport to import data with the -d and -c options, as in the following example:

```
$mongoimport -d blog -c tagcloud --type csv --headerline < csvimportfile.csv
```

# Exporting Data from MongoDB

The mongoexport utility is similar to mongoimport, but mongoexport, as its name implies, creates export files from an existing MongoDB collection instead. The following example shows how to use the mongoexport utility:

```
$mongoexport --help
options:
  --help                  produce help message
  -v [ --verbose ]        be more verbose (include multiple times for more
                          verbosity e.g. -vvvvv)
  -h [ --host ] arg       mongo host to connect to ("left,right" for pairs)
  --port arg              server port. Can also use --host hostname:port
  -d [ --db ] arg         database to use
  -c [ --collection ] arg collection to use (some commands)
  -u [ --username ] arg   username
  -p [ --password ] arg   password
  --ipv6                  enable IPv6 support (disabled by default)
  --dbpath arg            directly access mongod database files in the given
                          path, instead of connecting to a mongod  server -
                          needs to lock the data directory, so cannot be used
                          if a mongod is currently accessing the same path
  --directoryperdb        if dbpath specified, each db is in a separate
                          directory
  -f [ --fields ] arg     comma separated list of field names e.g. -f name,age
  --fieldFile arg         file with fields names - 1 per line
  -q [ --query ] arg      query filter, as a JSON string
  --csv                   export to csv instead of json
  -o [ --out ] arg        output file; if not specified, stdout is used
  --jsonArray             output to a json array rather than one object per
                          line
```

Notable options from the mongoexport utility include the following:

- -q: Specifies the query used to locate the records to output. This query can be any JSON query string that you might use with the db.collection.find() function to select a subset of records. If you don't specify this option or you set it to {}, then the mongoexport utility will output all records.
- -f: Lists the database element names to be exported.

The following example illustrates how to use the options for the mongoexport utility:

```
$mongoexport -d blog -c posts -q {} -f _id,Title,Message,Author --csv >blogposts.csv
connected to: 127.0.0.1
exported 1 records
```

# Securing Your Data

In some cases, your applications may be dealing with sensitive data, user records in social networks, or payment details in eCommerce applications. In many cases, there are rules that mandate that you have to ensure restricted access to sensitive data in your database systems.

MongoDB supports a simple authentication system that allows you to control who has access to each database, and what level of access they are granted.

## Restricting Access to a MongoDB Server

Most of the commands that change the configuration of or make major alterations to the structure of data on a MongoDB server are restricted to running only inside the special admin database that is created automatically during each new MongoDB installation.

Before you can issue these commands, you have to switch to the admin database with the use admin command.

Upcoming sections will note any command that is admin only, so you will always know you need to be in the admin database before you can use it. This chapter assumes that you can select the database and authenticate against it, if necessary.

By default, MongoDB does not use any authentication methods. Anybody with access to the network connection can connect and issue commands to the server.

However, you can add *users* to any database, and MongoDB can be configured to require both connection and console authentication to access the relevant database. This is the recommended mechanism for restricting access to admin functions.

# Protecting Your Server with Authentication

MongoDB supports a simple authentication model that allows the administrator to restrict access to databases on a per user basis.

MongoDB supports individual access control records on each database that are stored in a special system.users collection. For normal users to have access to two databases (e.g., db1 and db2), their credentials and rights must be added to both databases.

If you create individual logins and access rights for the same user on different databases, then there is no synchronization between those records. In other words, if you change a user password on one database, that does not change the password on any other database.

There is one exception to this rule: any users added to the special admin database will have the same access rights on all databases; you do not need to assign rights to such users individually.

---

■ **Note** Before you enable authentication on your server, make sure you have added your admin users to the admin database; if you enable authentication before adding the admin users, you will not be able to perform any actions on your database.

---

## Adding an Admin User

Adding the `admin` user is as simple as changing to the `admin` database and using the `addUser()` command:

```
$mongo
> use admin
>db.addUser("admin", "adminpassword")
```

You only need to add a single `admin` user at this point; once that user is defined, you can use it to add other `admin` users to the `admin` database or normal users to any other database.

## Enabling Authentication

Now you need to alter your server's configuration to enable authentication. Do so by stopping your server and adding `--auth` to the startup parameters.

If you installed MongoDB with a packaged installer (e.g., yum or aptitude), then typically you can edit `/etc/mongodb.conf` to enable `auth=true`. Next, you can use the following command to restart the server and enable authentication:

```
$sudo service mongodb restart
```

## Authenticating in the mongo Console

Before you can run restricted commands in the `admin` database, you will need to be authenticated as an `admin` user, as in the following example:

```
$mongo
> use admin
switched to db admin
>show collections
Sun Jun 13 11:05:04 JS Error: uncaught exception:
          error: { "$err" : "unauthorized for db [admin] lock type: -1 " }
>db.auth("admin", "adminpassword");
```

At this point, the mongo console will print either a `1` (a successful authentication) or a `0` (a failed authentication):

```
1
>show collections
system.indexes
system.users
```

If your authentication was successful, then you will be able to perform any of the restricted operations available in the admin database, as well as any read/write actions required in any other database.

If your authentication was unsuccessful, then you need to check whether your user/password is correct and whether the admin user has been correctly added to the admin database. Reset your server so it has no authentication, and then use the following command to list the contents of the system.users collection in the admin database:

```
$mongo
>use admin
> db.system.users.find()
{ "_id" : ObjectId("4c1449ef5f9f8fe6ae7b057b"), "user" : "admin",
        "readOnly" : false, "pwd" : "c91e3736e2dae03682a25805b6f81d99" }
```

---

■ **Note** If you are using an admin credential to access databases other than admin, then you must first authenticate against the admin database. Otherwise, you will not be able to access any other databases in the system.

---

The mongo console shows the contents of the user collection, enabling you to see what the userid is, while the password is shown as an MD5 hash of the original password you supplied:

```
$ mongo
> use blog
switched to db blog
> show collections
Sun Jun 13 12:02:36 JS Error: uncaught exception:
      error: { "$err" : "unauthorized for db [blog] lock type: -1 " }
> db.auth("admin","adminpassword")
0
> use admin
switched to db admin
> db.auth("admin","adminpassword")
1
> use blog
switched to db blog
> show collections
system.indexes
system.users
authors
posts
tagcloud
```

## Changing a User's Credentials

It's easy to change a user's access rights or password. You do this by executing addUser() function again, which causes MongoDB to update the existing user record. Technically, you can use any normal data manipulation command to change a user's record; however, only the addUser() function can create the password field.

Regardless, you can see how addUser() works by listing its contents:

```
$mongo
>use admin
> db.addUser
function (username, pass, readOnly) {
    readOnly = readOnly || false;
    var c = this.getCollection("system.users");
    var u = c.findOne({user:username}) || {user:username};
    u.readOnly = readOnly;
    u.pwd = hex_md5(username + ":mongo:" + pass);
    print(tojson(u));
    c.save(u);
}
```

addUser() is just a function defined in JavaScript. Knowing how the password is constructed is useful if you want to create a webform that allows you to add users to the database or you want to import users into the system en masse from another credential source.

Most mongo console functions can be listed in this fashion, enabling you to inspect the details of how they work.

## Adding a Read-Only User

The addUser() function includes an additional parameter that allows you to create a user that has only read-only permissions. The MongoDB client will throw an exception if a process authenticated as the newly created user attempts to do anything that would result in a change to the contents of the database. The following example gives a user access to the database for status monitoring or reporting purposes:

```
$mongo
>use admin
switched to db admin
> db.auth("admin","adminpassword")
1
>use blog
switched to db blog
>db.addUser(“shadycharacter”,”shadypassword”, true)
```

## Deleting a User

To remove a user from a database, simply use the normal remove() function for a collection. The following example removes the user just added; note that you have to authenticate against the admin database before you can remove the user:

```
$mongo
>use admin
switched to db admin
> db.auth("admin","adminpassword")
1
>use blog
switched to db blog
>db.system.users.remove({username:”shadycharacter”})
```

## Using Authenticated Connections in a PHP Application

In Chapter 2, you saw how to create a connection with PHP to a MongoDB server. Once you have enabled authentication on your server, PHP applications will also have to supply credentials before they can execute commands against the server. The following simple example shows how to open an authenticated connection to a database:

```
<?php

// Establish the database connection
$connection = new Mongo();
$db = $connection->selectDB("admin");
$result = $db->authenticate("admin", "adminpassword");
if(!$result['ok']){
    // Your Error handling here
    die("Authentication Error: {$result['errmsg']}");
}

// Your code here

// Close the database connection
$connection->close();

?>
```

# Managing Servers

As an administrator, you must ensure the smooth and reliable running of your MongoDB servers.

You will have to tune the servers to achieve maximum performance or reconfigure them to better match the environment you are operating in. To that end, you need to familiarize yourself with a number of procedures that enable you to manage and control your servers.

## Starting a Server

Most modern linux distributions now include a set of `/etc/init.d` scripts that are used to manage services. If you installed your MongoDB server using one of the distribution packages from the 10gen site (see Chapter 2 for more information on these packages), the `init.d` scripts for managing your server will already be installed.

You can use the service command on ubuntu, fedora, centos, and redhat to start, stop, and restart your server, as shown in the following example:

```
$sudo service mongodb start
mongodb start/running, process 3474
$sudo service mongodb stop
mongodb stop/waiting

$sudo service mongodb restart
mongodb start/running, process 3474
```

If you don't have an initialization script available, you can start the MongoDB server manually by opening a terminal window then typing the following:

```
$sudo mongod -f /etc/mongodb.conf
Sun Jun 13 13:33:52 Mongo DB : starting : pid = 3517 port = 27017
        dbpath = /var/lib/mongodb master = 0 slave = 0  64-bit
Sun Jun 13 13:33:52 db version v1.4.3, pdfile version 4.5
Sun Jun 13 13:33:52 git version: 47ffbdfd53f46edeb6ff54bbb734783db7abc8ca
Sun Jun 13 13:33:52 sys info: Linux domU-12-31-39-06-79-A1 2.6.21.7-2.ec2.v1.2.fc8xen
        #1 SMP Fri Nov 20 17:48:28 EST 2009 x86_64 BOOST_LIB_VERSION=1_41
Sun Jun 13 13:33:52 waiting for connections on port 27017
Sun Jun 13 13:33:52 web admin interface listening on port 28017
```

The server will show all connections being made, as well as other information you can use to monitor how the server is working.

To terminate the server in manual mode, just type ^C; this causes the server to shut down cleanly.

If you don't supply a configuration file, then MongoDB will start up with a default database path of /data/db and bind to localhost (127.0.0.1) using the default ports of 27017 and 28017, as in the following example:

```
$ sudo mkdir -p /data/db
$ sudo mongod
mongod --help for help and startup options
...
Sun Jun 13 13:38:00 waiting for connections on port 27017
Sun Jun 13 13:38:00 web admin interface listening on port 28017

^C typed here

Sun Jun 13 13:40:26 got kill or ctrl c signal 2 (Interrupt), will terminate after current cmd
ends
...
Sun Jun 13 13:40:26  dbexit: really exiting now
```

## Reconfiguring a Server

MongoDB supplies two main methods for configuring the server. First, you can use command-line options in conjunction with the mongod server daemon. Second, you can do so by loading a configuration file.

Most of the prepackaged MongoDB installers use the latter method, using a file that is normally stored in /etc/mongodb.conf on *nix systems.

You can change the configuration of your server by editing this file and restarting your server. The contents of this file look like this:

```
# mongodb.conf
dbpath=/var/lib/mongodb
logpath=/var/log/mongodb/mongodb.log
logappend=true
auth = false
#enable the rest interface
rest =true
```

You enable an option by removing the # code from the front of the option and setting its value as you require it.

Placing any of the following option values in the configuration file is the same as specifying --<optionname> <optionvalue> on the command line when starting up MongoDB:

- dbpath: Indicates where MongoDB will store your data; you should make sure it is on a fast storage volume that is large enough to support your database size.
- logpath: Indicates the file that MongoDB will store its logs in. The normal place to put this is /var/logs/mongodb/mongodb.log; you need to use logrotate to rotate this logfile and prevent it from filling up your server's drive.
- logappend: Setting this option to false causes the logfile to be cleared each time MongoDB is started up. Setting this option to true causes all log entries to be appended to the end of any existing logfile.
- auth: Enables or disables the authentication mode on MongoDB server; see the notes in this chapter for more information on authentication.
- rest: Enables or disables the rest interface to MongoDB. You must enable this interface if you want to use the links from the web-based status display to show additional information.

# Getting the Server's Version

You can use the version() command to get the build and version information for a server. This information is useful for determining whether upgrades are required or when reporting an issue to 10gen's support mail list. The following snippet shows how to use this command:

```
$mongo
> use admin
switched to db admin
> db.version()
version: 1.6.2
```

# Getting the Server's Status

MongoDB provides a simple method for determining the status of a server. The following example shows the information returned, including such things as server uptime, the maximum number of connections, and so on:

```
$mongo
> use admin
switched to db admin
> db.serverStatus()
{
    "version" : "1.6.2",
    "uptime" : 15685,
    "uptimeEstimate" : 0,
    "localTime" : "Thu Aug 12 2010 15:36:57 GMT+0800 (PHT)",
    "globalLock" : {
        "totalTime" : 15684704779,
        "lockTime" : 1731139,
```

```
        "ratio" : 0.00011037115612898206,
        "currentQueue" : {
            "total" : 0,
            "readers" : 0,
            "writers" : 0
        }
    },
    "mem" : {
        "bits" : 64,
        "resident" : 7,
        "virtual" : 2479,
        "supported" : true,
        "mapped" : 80
    },
    "connections" : {
        "current" : 1,
        "available" : 203
    },
    "extra_info" : {
        "note" : "fields vary by platform"
    },
    "indexCounters" : {
        "btree" : {
            "accesses" : 1,
            "hits" : 1,
            "misses" : 0,
            "resets" : 0,
            "missRatio" : 0
        }
    },
    "backgroundFlushing" : {
        "flushes" : 261,
        "total_ms" : 2517,
        "average_ms" : 9.64367816091954,
        "last_ms" : 1,
        "last_finished" : "Thu Aug 12 2010 15:36:33 GMT+0800 (PHT)"
    },
    "opcounters" : {
        "insert" : 2032,
        "query" : 48,
        "update" : 1,
        "delete" : 0,
        "getmore" : 0,
        "command" : 94
    },
    "asserts" : {
        "regular" : 0,
        "warning" : 0,
        "msg" : 0,
        "user" : 1,
        "rollovers" : 0
    },
    "ok" : 1
}
```

You can find the two most important sections of the information returned by this function in the "opcounters" and "asserts" sections.

The "opcounters" section shows the number of operations of each type that have been performed against the database server. You should have a good idea about what constitutes a normal balance for these counters for your particular application. If these counters start to move out of the normal ratio, then it may be an early warning that your application has a problem.

For example, the preceding profile has an extremely high ratio of inserts to reads. This could be normal for a logging application; however, for a blogging application, it could indicate that either a spambot was hitting your "comments" section or a URL pattern that caused writes to the database was being repeatedly crawled by a search engine spider. In this case, it would be time to either put a captcha on your comments form or to block the particular URL pattern in your `robots.tx file`.

The "asserts" section shows the number of server and client exceptions or warnings that have been thrown. If such exceptions or warnings start to rise rapidly, then it's time to take a good look through your server's logfiles to see whether a problem is developing. A high number of asserts may also indicate there is a problem with the data in the database, and you should consider using MongoDB's validation functions to check whether your data is intact.

## Shutting Down a Server

If you have installed your MongoDB server from a package, then you can use the operating system's service management scripts to shut down the server. For example, ubuntu, fedora, centos, and redhat let you shut down the server by issuing the following command:

```
$sudo service mongod stop
```

You can also shut down the server from the mongo console:

```
$mongo
>use admin
>db.shutdownServer()
```

You can use the posix process management commands to terminate a server, or you can use the SIG_TERM(-15) signal to shut down the server.

If—and only if—the server fails to respond to the two methods described above, then you can use the following command:

```
$sudo killall -15 mongod
```

---

■ **Warning** You must *not* use the SIG_KILL(-9) signal to terminate a server because this could result in a corrupted database, and you will probably have to repair the server.

---

It might be that you have a particularly active server with a lot of write activity, and you have reconfigured the server so it has a large sync delay. If that's the case, then the server may not respond immediately to a termination request because it is writing out all the in-memory changes to the disk. A little patience goes a long way here.

# Using MongoDB Logfiles

By default, MongoDB writes its entire log output to `stdout`; however, you can use the `logpath` option described previously to redirect the log output to a file instead.

You can use the contents of the logfile to spot problems such as excessive connections from individual machines and asserts (exceptions) that may indicate problems with your data.

# Validating and Repairing Your Data

It is possible that your data will be left in a damaged or incomplete state if your server unexpectedly reboots or your MongoDB server crashes for any reason.

Here are some indications that your data has been compromised:

- Your database server refuses to start, stating that the datafiles are corrupted.
- You start seeing *asserts* in your server log files or a high assert count when using the `db.serverStatus()` command.
- You get strange or unexpected results from queries.
- The records counts on collections don't match up with your expectations.

Any of the preceding signs can indicate corruption or inconsistency in your data.

Fortunately, MongoDB ships with tools to assist you in repairing or recovering your database server. Nevertheless, you might still suffer the loss of some data, so please remember the golden rule of making sure you have either a good backup of your data or a replication slave.

## Repairing a Server

Before you can initiate the server repair process, you must first shut down the server (assuming it is not already offline). This is one of the best arguments for using replica pairs: you don't have to stop your service if you have to take a machine offline to repair it.

To initiate the repair process, just use the manual server startup process (as described previously in this chapter). However, this time you need to add the "--repair" option to the end of the command, as in the following example:

```
$sudo mongod -f /etc/mongodb.conf --repair
Sun Jun 13 14:18:45 Mongo DB : starting : pid = 3697 port = 27017 dbpath = /var/lib/mongodb
                    master = 0 slave = 0  64-bit
Sun Jun 13 14:18:45 ****
Sun Jun 13 14:18:45 ****
Sun Jun 13 14:18:45 need to upgrade database admin with pdfile version 4.5, new version: 4.5
Sun Jun 13 14:18:45             starting upgrade
Sun Jun 13 14:18:45             admin repairDatabase admin
Sun Jun 13 14:18:45 allocating new datafile /var/lib/mongodb/$tmp_repairDatabase_0/admin.ns,
                    filling with zeroes...
Sun Jun 13 14:18:45 done allocating datafile /var/lib/mongodb/$tmp_repairDatabase_0/admin.ns,
                    size: 16MB, took 0.006 secs
Sun Jun 13 14:18:45 allocating new datafile /var/lib/mongodb/$tmp_repairDatabase_0/admin.0,
                   filling with zeroes...
Sun Jun 13 14:18:45 done allocating datafile /var/lib/mongodb/$tmp_repairDatabase_0/admin.0,
                   size: 64MB, took 0.026 secs
```

```
Sun Jun 13 14:18:45 allocating new datafile /var/lib/mongodb/$tmp_repairDatabase_0/admin.1,
                filling with zeroes...
Sun Jun 13 14:18:45 building new index on { _id: 1 } for admin.system.users
Sun Jun 13 14:18:45 Buildindex admin.system.users idxNo:0
                 { name: "_id_", ns: "admin.system.users", key: { _id: 1 } }
Sun Jun 13 14:18:45 done for 0 records 0secs
Sun Jun 13 14:18:45 done allocating datafile /var/lib/mongodb/$tmp_repairDatabase_0/admin.1,
                size: 128MB, took 0.052 secs
Sun Jun 13 14:18:45 finished checking dbs
Sun Jun 13 14:18:45  dbexit:
Sun Jun 13 14:18:45          shutdown: going to close listening sockets...
Sun Jun 13 14:18:45          shutdown: going to flush oplog...
Sun Jun 13 14:18:45          shutdown: going to close sockets...
Sun Jun 13 14:18:45          shutdown: waiting for fs preallocator...
Sun Jun 13 14:18:45          shutdown: closing all files...
Sun Jun 13 14:18:45          closeAllFiles() finished
Sun Jun 13 14:18:45          shutdown: removing fs lock...
Sun Jun 13 14:18:45          dbexit: really exiting now
```

In the preceding example, the `repair()` function detected that the `admin` database was probably created under an older version of MongoDB and that it required an upgrade of its storage format to match the currently running server.

---

■ **Note** It is normal for the server to exit after running mongod utility with the `--repair` option; to bring it back online, just start it up again without specifying the `--repair` option.

---

Once the repair process finishes, you should be able to start up the server as normal, and then restore any missing data from your backups.

If you're trying to repair a large database, you may find that your drive runs out of disk space because MongoDB may need to make a temporary copy of the database files on the same drive as the data (see the `.../$tmp_repairDatabase_0/..` directory in the preceding example).

To overcome this potential issue, the MongoDB repair utility supports an additional command-line parameter called `--repairpath`. You can use this parameter to specify a drive with enough space to hold the temporary files it creates during the rebuild process, as in the following example:

```
$sudo mongod -f /etc/mongodb.conf --repair --repairpath /mnt/bigdrive/tempdir
```

## Validating a Single Collection

Occasionally, you may suspect there is a problem with the data on a running server. In this case, you can use a handful of tools that ship with MongoDB to help you determine whether the server in question is corrupted or damaged.

You can use the `validate` option to validate the contents of a collection in a database. The next example shows how to run the `validate` option against a collection with one million records in it:

```
$mongo
> use blog
switched to db blog
```

```
>db.posts.ensureIndex({Author:1})
> db.posts.validate()
{
    "ns" : "blog.posts",
    "result" : "
                validate
                  firstExtent:0:24b00 ns:blog.posts
                  lastExtent:0:24b00 ns:blog.posts
                  # extents:1
                  datasize?:160 nrecords?:1 lastExtentSize:9984
                  padding:1
                  first extent:
                    loc:0:24b00 xnext:null xprev:null
                    nsdiag:blog.posts
                    size:9984 firstRecord:0:24bb0 lastRecord:0:24bb0
                  1 objects found, nobj:1
                      176 bytes data w/headers
                  160 bytes data wout/headers
                  deletedList: 0000000001000000000
                  deleted: n: 1 size: 9632
                  nIndexes:2
                    blog.posts.$_id_ keys:1
                    blog.posts.$Author_1 keys:1
                ",
    "ok" : 1,
    "valid" : true,
    "lastExtentSize" : 9984
}
```

The preceding example takes about 30 seconds to complete. By default, the validate option checks both the datafiles and the indexes, and it provides some statistics about the collection when it completes. The option will tell you if there are any problems with either the datafile or the indexes.

You can also use the validate option if you have a very large database and you want only to validate the indexes. Unfortunately, there is no shell helper command for this in the current version (1.6.1). That said, you can easily accomplish this using the runCommand option:

```
$mongo
>use TestMongo
>db.runCommand({validate:"testIndex", scandata:false})
```

In this case, the server does not scan the datafiles; instead, it merely reports the information stored about the collection.

## Repairing Collection Validation Faults

If running validation on your collections turns up an error, then you have several options for repairing the data. Again, it's impossible to overstress the importance of having good backups.

## Repairing a Collection's Indexes

If the validation process shows that the indexes are damaged, then you use the `reIndex()` function to reindex the affected collection. In the example that follows, you use the `reIndex()` function to reindex the blog's `posts` collection to which you added the `author` index previously:

```
$mongo
>use blog
> db.posts.reIndex()
{
    "nIndexesWas" : 2,
    "msg" : "indexes dropped for collection",
    "ok" : 1,
    "nIndexes" : 2,
    "indexes" : [
        {
            "name" : "_id_",
            "ns" : "blog.posts",
            "key" : {
                "_id" : 1
            }
        },
        {
            "_id" : ObjectId("4c63a5d56ffe6e590cfe9b58"),
            "ns" : "blog.posts",
            "key" : {
                "Author" : 1
            },
            "name" : "Author_1"
        }
    ],
    "ok" : 1
}
```

The MongoDB server will drop all the current indexes on the collection and rebuild them; however, if you use the database repair option, it will also run the `reIndex()` function on all the collections in the database.

# Repairing a Collection's Datafiles

The best way to repair all of the datafiles in a database is to use either the server's `--repair` option or the `repairDatabase()` command in the shell. This latter repairs all the collection files in an individual database, and then reindexes all of the defined indexes. However, `repairDatabase()` is not a suitable function to run on a live server because it will block any requests to the data while the datafiles are being rebuilt. This results in unindexed queries while the indexes are being reindexed. The following snippet shows the syntax for using the repairDatabase() function:

```
$mongo
>use blog
>db.repairDatabase()
{ "ok" : 1 }
```

# Upgrading MongoDB

Occasionally, 10gen releases versions of MongoDB that require you to upgrade the format of the database files. The guys and gals at 10gen are aware of the impact (including the resulting downtime) caused by running an upgrade on a running production service; however, there are times when the need to support heavily demanded new features requires that an upgrade take place.

Upgrading a server is similar to the server repair process discussed earlier. The difference is that you use the `--upgrade` option instead of the `--repair` option to make that happen.

---

■ **Warning** It is *essential* that you make a complete backup of your data before attempting any upgrade process.

---

MongoDB's developers try to anticipate every possible problem that will present itself during an upgrade; nevertheless, you must take steps to protect yourself as well. Upgrades will typically rewrite every piece of data in your system in a new format, which means that even the slightest problem with the process can have disastrous consequences.

The following list walks you through the proper steps required to upgrade a database server:

1. Back up your data and make sure that the backup is viable. If possible, restore the backup to another server and check whether it's ok.
2. Stop or divert your application to another server.
3. Stop your MongoDB server.
4. Upgrade the code of your MongoDB server to the desired version.
5. Run the following command: `sudo mongod -f <your configfile> --upgrade`.
6. When the upgrade completes, restart your MongoDB server.
7. Use the shell to perform some initial sanity checks on the data.
8. If anything looks suspicious, use the validation tools to check the data.
9. Re-enable your application when you are satisfied that everything looks OK.
10. Test your application carefully before reopening the service or diverting traffic back to this server.

# Monitoring MongoDB

The MongoDB distribution contains a simple status-monitoring tool called mongostat. This tool is designed mainly to provide a simple overview of what is happening on your server (see Figure 9–1).

The stats produced by this tool are not extensive, but they do provide a good overview on what is going on in your MongoDB installation. For example, this display lets you see how frequently database operations are being performed, the rate at which the index is hit, and how much time your application spends blocked as it waits for locks on the database to be released.

The main columns of interest are the first six columns, which show the rate at which the mongod server is handling certain operations (e.g., insert or query). Other columns worth keeping an eye on when diagnosing problems with your installation include the following:

- `%idx miss`: Shows the percentage of queries that could not use an index. A high value here indicates that you may need to add some indexes to your system.
- `conn`: Shows you how many connections are open to your mongod instance. High numbers here indicate that there is a problem with your application releasing connections after operations.
- `% locked`: Shows the amount of time the server has had its collections locked. A high number here indicates that you are performing blocking operations that may be best left to a maintenance period.

```
$ mongostat
connected to: 127.0.0.1
insert/s query/s update/s delete/s getmore/s command/s mapped  vsize    res % locked % idx miss  conn     time
       0       3        4        0         0         1   1056   1749    527 0.000404          0    47 11:02:17
      12       0        0        0         0         3   1056   1789    527 0.000143          0    51 11:02:18
       0       0        0        0         0         1   1056   1789    527        0          0    51 11:02:19
       0       0        0        0         0         1   1056   1789    527        0          0    51 11:02:20
       0       0        0        0         0         1   1056   1789    527        0          0    51 11:02:21
       0       0        0        0         0         1   1056   1789    527        0          0    51 11:02:22
       0       0        0        0         0         1   1056   1789    527        0          0    51 11:02:23
       0       0        0        0         0         1   1056   1789    527        0          0    51 11:02:24
       0       0        0        0         0         1   1056   1789    527        0          0    51 11:02:25
       0       0        0        0         0         1   1056   1789    527        0          0    51 11:02:26
       0       0        0        0         0         1   1056   1789    527        0          0    51 11:02:27
       0       0        0        0         0         1   1056   1789    527        0          0    51 11:02:28
       0       0        0        0         0         1   1056   1789    527        0          0    51 11:02:29
       0       0        0        0         0         1   1056   1789    527        0          0    51 11:02:30
       0       0        0        0         0         1   1056   1789    527        0          0    51 11:02:31
       0       0        0        0         0         1   1056   1789    527        0          0    51 11:02:32
       0       3        4        0         0         1   1056   1789    527  0.00039          0    51 11:02:33
      12       0        0        0         0         3   1056   1829    527 0.000156          0    55 11:02:34
       0       0        0        0         0         1   1056   1829    527        0          0    55 11:02:35
       0       0        0        0         0         1   1056   1829    527        0          0    55 11:02:36
insert/s query/s update/s delete/s getmore/s command/s mapped  vsize    res % locked % idx miss  conn     time
```

***Figure 9–1.*** *Monitoring the status of MongoDB with the mongostat utility*

# Rolling Your Own Stat Monitoring Tool

Much of the information provided by mongostat is the same information that you can get from the `db.serverStatus()` call. It would not be a big task to create a service that uses this API to poll the server every few seconds, and then places the results into a MongoDB collection.

The application of a few indexes, some carefully crafted queries, and a graphing package would enable you to use such a simple realtime monitor to produce historical logs.

There are also many third-party *adapters* available for MongoDB that let you use common opensource or commercial monitoring systems, including tools such as Nagios, ganglia, and cacti. As mentioned previously, 10gen maintains a page on its website that shares the latest information about monitoring interfaces available for MongoDB (for more information on this topic see `www.mongodb.org/display/DOCS/Monitoring+and+Diagnostics`).

# Using the mongod Web Interface

Most of the statistical information discussed so far is also available through the mongod web interface. When you start up mongod, by default it will automatically create a web interface on a port number that is *1000* higher than the port number used to access the server. For example, mongod will create a web interface on port 28017 for the default server port of 27017. This port can be accessed through your web browser; if you are running a server on your local machine using the default port, then you need to use the address: `http://localhost:28017` to access the web interface (see Figure 9–2).

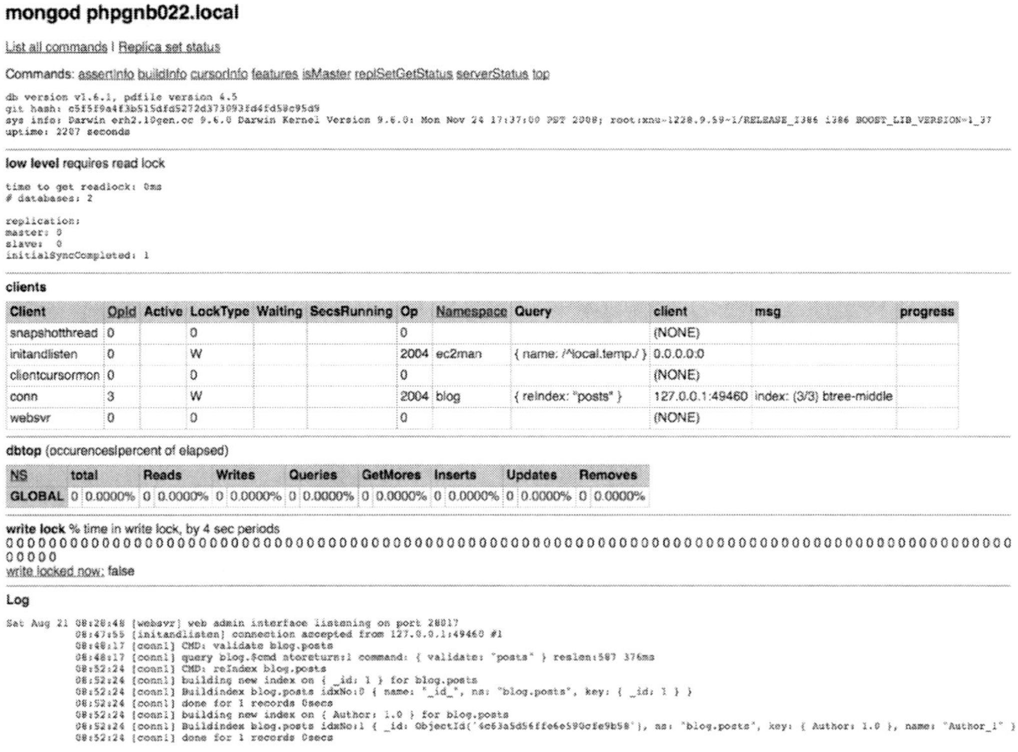


*Figure 9–2. Viewing statistics through a web browser*

# Summary

Keeping your MongoDB installation running smoothly typically requires very little effort. In this chapter, you have seen how you can use the tools provided with the MongoDB distribution to manage and maintain your system, as well as to stay on top of any problems that may develop.

However, it must be stressed that the most important lesson to take away from this chapter is this: as the administrator of a database system, your first responsibility is to ensure that a reliable backup and restoration scheme for your data is available.

CHAPTER 10

# Optimization

There is a tongue-in-cheek statement about MongoDB attributed to an unknown Twitter user: "If a MongoDB query runs for longer than 0ms, then something is wrong." This is typical of the kind of buzz that surrounded the product when it first burst onto the scene about a year ago.

The reality is that MongoDB is extraordinarily fast. But if you give it the wrong data structures, or you don't set up the database or collections with the right indexes, then MongoDB can slow down dramatically, like any data storage system.

MongoDB also contains some advanced features, such as grouping and map/reduce, that require some tuning to get them running with optimal efficiency.

The design of your data schemas can also have a big impact on performance; in this chapter, we will look at some techniques to shape your data into a form that makes maximum use of MongoDB's strengths and minimizes its weaknesses.

Before we look at improving the performance of the queries being run on the server or the ways of optimizing the structure of the data, we'll begin with a look at how MongoDB interacts with the hardware it runs on and the factors that affect performance.

## Optimizing Your Server Hardware for Performance

Often the quickest and cheapest optimization you can make to a database server is to right-size the hardware it runs on. If a database server has too little memory or uses slow drives, it can impact database performance significantly. And, while some of these constraints may be acceptable for a development environment where the server may be running on a developer's local workstation, they may not be acceptable for production applications, where some care must be used in calculating the correct hardware configuration to achieve the best performance.

### Understanding How MongoDB Uses Memory

MongoDB uses memory-mapped file I/O to access its underlying data storage. This method of file I/O has some characteristics that you should be aware of because they can affect both the type of operating system (OS) you run it under and the amount of memory you install.

The first notable characteristic of memory-mapped files is that, on 32-bit operating systems, the maximum file size that can be managed is 2 GB. This effectively limits the size of a MongoDB database on 32-bit operating systems. If you need to store more than 2 GB, then you should consider installing and running MongoDB on a 64-bit operating system where the limit is greater than 4 TB.

The second notable characteristic is that memory-mapped files use the operating system's virtual memory system to map the required parts of the database files into memory, as it needs them. This can result in the slightly alarming impression that MongoDB will use up your entire RAM. This is not really the case because MongoDB will share the virtual address space with other applications and the operating system, and it will release memory back to the operating system as it is needed. Using the free memory total as an indicator of excessive memory consumption is not a good practice because a good OS will ensure there is little or no free memory. This is because all of your expensive memory is pressed into good use through caching or buffering disk I/O. Free memory is wasted memory.

By providing a suitable amount of memory, MongoDB can keep more of its data mapped into memory, which reduces the need for expensive disk I/O.

In general, the more memory you give to MongoDB, the faster it will run. However, if you have a 2 GB database, then adding more than 2–3 GB of memory will not make much difference because the whole database will sit in RAM anyway.

## Choosing the Right Database Server Hardware

There is a general pressure to move to lower-power (energy) systems for hosting services. However, many of the lower-power servers use laptop or notebook components to achieve the lower power consumption. Unfortunately, lower-quality server hardware can use less expensive disk drives in particular. Such drives are not suited for heavy-duty server applications due to their disks' low rotation speed, which slows the rate at which data can be transferred to and from the drive. Also, make sure you use a reputable supplier, one that you trust to assemble a system that has been optimized for server operation.

If you plan to use replication or any kind of frequent backup system that would have to read across the network connections, then you should consider putting in an extra network card and forming a separate network so the servers can talk with each other. This reduces the amount of data being transmitted and received on the network interface used to connect the application to the server, which also has an effect on an application's performance.

# Evaluating Query Performance

MongoDB has two main tools for optimizing query performance: `explain()` and the MongoDB Profiler (the db profiler). The db profiler is a good tool for finding those queries that are not performing well and selecting candidate queries for further inspection, while `explain()` is good for investigating a single query, so you can determine how well it is performing.

Those of you familiar with MySQL will probably also be familiar with the use of the "slow query log" which helps you find queries that are consuming a lot of time; MongoDB uses the db profiler to provide this capability.

# MongoDB Profiler

The MongoDB profiler is a tool that records statistical information and execution plan details for every query that meets the trigger criteria. You can enable this tool separately on each database.

Once enabled, MongoDB inserts a document with information about the performance and execution details of each query submitted by your application into a special *capped* collection called `system.profile`. You can use this collection to inspect the details of each query logged using normal collection querying commands.

The `system.profile` collection is limited to a maximum of 128 KB of data, so that the profiler will not fill the disk with logging information. This limit should be enough to capture a few thousand profiles of even the most complex queries.

---

■ **Warning** When the profiler is enabled, it will impact the performance of your server, so it is not a good idea to leave it running on a production server unless you are performing an analysis for some observed issue. Don't be tempted to leave it running permanently to provide a window on recently executed queries.

---

# Enabling and Disabling the DB Profiler

It's a simple matter to turn on the MongoDB profiler:

```
$mongo
>use blog
>db.setProfilingLevel(2)
```

It is an equally simple matter to disable the profiler:

```
$mongo
>use blog
>db.setProfilingLevel(0)
```

MongoDB can also enable the profiler only for queries that exceed a specified execution time. The following example logs only queries that take more than half a second to execute:

```
$mongo
>use blog
>db.setProfilingLevel(1,500)
```

For profiling level 1, you can supply a maximum query execution time value in milliseconds (ms). If the query runs for longer than this amount of time, it is profiled and logged; otherwise, it is ignored. This provides the same functionality seen in MySQL's "slow query log."

## Finding Slow Queries

A typical record in the `system.profile` collection looks like this:

```
> db.system.profile.find()
{
     "ts" : "Mon Aug 23 2010 22:06:09 GMT+0800 (PHT)",
    "info" : "query blog.posts reslen:21342 nscanned:202  \nquery: { Tags: \"even\" }
nreturned:101
        bytes:21326",
        "millis" : 15
 }
```

Each record contains fields, and the following list outlines what they are and what they do:

- `ts`: Displays a timestamp in UTC that indicates when the query was executed.
- `info`: Shows statistical information about the query and its structure.
- `milis`: Records the number of milliseconds it took to execute the query.

Because the `system.profile` collection is just a normal collection, you can use MongoDB's query tools to home in quickly on problematic queries.

The next example finds all the queries that are taking longer than 10ms to execute. In this case, you can just query for cases where `millis >10` in the `system.profile` collection, and then sort the results by the execution time in descending order:

```
> db.system.profile.find({millis:{$gt:10}}).sort({millis:-1})
{ "ts" : "Mon Aug 23 2010 22:06:09 GMT+0800 (PHT)", "info" :
        "query blog.posts reslen:21342 nscanned:202  \nquery: { Tags: \"even\" }
        nreturned:101 bytes:21326", "millis" : 15 }
```

If you also know your problem occurred during a specific time range, then you can use the `ts` field to add query terms that restrict the range to the required slice.

## Analyzing a Specific Query with explain()

If you suspect a query is not performing as well as expected, then you can use the `explain()` modifier to break down how MongoDB is executing the query.

When you add the `explain()` modifier to a query, MongoDB executes the query, returning a document that describes how the query was handled, rather than a cursor to the results. The following query runs against a database of blog posts and indicates that the query had to scan 13325 records to form a cursor to return all the posts:

```
$mongo
>use blog
> db.posts.find().explain()
{
    "cursor" : "BasicCursor",
    "indexBounds" : [ ],
    "nscanned" : 13235,
    "nscannedObjects" : 13235,
    "n" : 13235,
    "millis" : 3,
    "allPlans" : [
        {
            "cursor" : "BasicCursor",
            "indexBounds" : [ ]
        }
    ]
}
```

You can see the fields returned by `explain()` listed in Table 10–1.

***Table 10–1.** Elements Returned by explain()*

| Element | Description |
| --- | --- |
| `Cursor` | Indicates the type of cursor created to enumerate the results. Typically, this is `BasicCursor`, a natural order reading cursor. |
| `indexBounds` | Indicates the min/max values used on an indexed lookup. |
| `nScanned` | Indicates the number of references scanned to find all the objects in the query. |

| Element | Description |
|---|---|
| nScannedObjects | Indicates the number of Physical objects that "nScanned" resolves to. |
| n | Indicates the number of items on the cursor (i.e., the number of items to be returned). |
| millis | Indicates the number of milliseconds it took to execute the query. |
| allPlans | Indicates the number of alternative methods the optimizer could use to execute this query. If there are multiple indexes available that would satisfy the query, then those plans would be shown here. This information is useful if you want to use the hint() modifier to move the query to a different plan than the one currently selected. |

## Using Profile and explain() to Optimize a Query

Now let's walk through a real-world optimization scenario and look at how we can use MongoDB's profile and explain() modifier tools to fix a problem with a real application.

The example discussed in this chapter is based on the blog database from Chapter 8. This database has a function to get the posts associated with a particular tag; this chapter will use the "even" tag. Let's assume that you have noticed this function runs slowly, so you want to determine whether there is a problem.

Let's begin by writing a little program to fill the aforementioned database with data so that we have something to run queries against, to demonstrate the optimiazaiton process.

```
<?php

// Get a connection to the database

$mongo = new Mongo();
$db=$mongo->blog;

// First let's get the first AuthorsID
// We are going to use this to fake a author

$author = $db->authors->findOne();

if(!$author){
        die("There are no authors in the database");
}

for( $i = 1; $i < 10000; $i++){
        $blogpost=array();
        $blogpost['author'] = $author['_id'];
        $blogpost['Title']  = "Completely fake blogpost number {$i}";
        $blogpost['Message'] = "Some fake text to create a database of blog posts";
        $blogpost['Tags'] = array();
        if($i%2){
```

```
                // Odd numbered blogs
                $blogpost['Tags'] = array("blog", "post", "odd", "tag{$i}");
        } else {
                // Even numbered blogs
                $blogpost['Tags'] = array("blog", "post", "even", "tag{$i}");
        }
        $db->posts->insert($blogpost);
}
?>
```

The preceding program finds the first author in the blog database's authors collection, and then pretends that the author has been extraordinarily productive. It creates 10,000 fake blog postings in the author's name, all in the blink of an eye. The posts are not very interesting to read; nevertheless, they are alternatively assigned "odd" and "even" tags. These tags will serve to demonstrate how to optimize a simple query.

The next step is to save the program as `fastblogger.php` and then run it using the command-line PHP tool:

```
$php fastblogger.php
```

Next, you need to enable the database profiler, which you will use to determine whether you can improve the example's queries:

```
$ mongo
> use blog
switched to db blog
> show collections
authors
posts
...
system.profile
tagcloud
...
users
> db.setProfilingLevel(2)
{ "was" : 0, "ok" : 1 }
```

Now wait a few moments for the command to take effect, open the required collections, and then perform its other tasks. Next, you want to simulate having the blog website access all of the blog posts with the even tag. Do so by executing a query that the site can use to implement this function:

```
$Mongo
use blog
$db.posts.find({Tags:"even"})
...
```

If you query the `profiler` collection for results that exceed 5ms, then you should see something like this:

```
>db.system.profile.find({millis:{$gt:5}}).sort({millis:-1})
{"ts" : "Mon Aug 23 2010 22:06:09 GMT+0800 (PHT)",
        "info" : "query blog.posts reslen:21342 nscanned:202  \nquery:
                { Tags: \"even\" }  nreturned:101 bytes:21326", "millis" : 15 }
...
```

The results returned in the preceding example show that some queries are taking longer than 0ms (remember the quote at the beginning of the chapter).

Next, you want to reconstruct the query for the first (and worst performing) query, so you can see what is being returned. The preceding output indicates that the poor performing query is querying `blog.posts` and that the query term is `{Tags:"even"}`. Finally, you can see that this query is taking a whopping 15ms to execute.

The reconstructed query looks like this:

```
>db.posts.find({Tags:"even"})
{ "_id" : ObjectId("4c727cbd91a01b2a14010000"), "author" :
ObjectId("4c637ec8b8642fea02000000"), "Title" : "Completly fake blogpost number 2", "Message"
: "Some fake text to create a database of blog posts", "Tags" : [ "blog", "post", "even",
"tag2" ] }
{ "_id" : ObjectId("4c727cbd91a01b2a14030000"), "author" :
ObjectId("4c637ec8b8642fea02000000"), "Title" : "Completly fake blogpost number 4", "Message"
: "Some fake text to create a database of blog posts", "Tags" : [ "blog", "post", "even",
"tag4" ] }
{ "_id" : ObjectId("4c727cbd91a01b2a14050000"), "author" :
ObjectId("4c637ec8b8642fea02000000"), "Title" : "Completly fake blogpost number 6", "Message"
: "Some fake text to create a database of blog posts", "Tags" : [ "blog", "post", "even",
"tag6" ] }
...
```

The preceding output should come as no surprise; this query was created for the expressed purpose of demonstrating how to find and fix a slow query.

The goal is to figure how to make the query run faster, so use the `explain()` command to determine how MongoDB is performing this query:

```
> db.posts.find({Tags:"even"}).explain()
{
    "cursor" : "BasicCursor",
    "nscanned" : 9999,
    "nscannedObjects" : 9999,
    "n" : 4999,
    "millis" : 14,
    "indexBounds" : {

    }
}
```

You can see from the preceding output that the query is not using any indexes. The `explain()` command shows that the query is using a "`BasicCursor`", which means the query is just performing a simple scan of the collection's records. Specifically, it's scanning all of the records in the database one by one to find the tags (all 9999 of them); this process takes 14ms. This may not sound like a very long time, but, if you were to use this query on a popular page of your website, then it would be causing additional load to the disk I/O, as well as a tremendous amount of stress on the web server. Consequently, this query would cause the connection to the web browser to remain open for longer while the page is being created.

---

■ **Note** If you see a detailed query explanation that shows a significantly larger number of scanned records (`nscanned`) than it returns (`n`), then that query is probably a candidate for indexing.

---

The next step is to determine whether adding an index on the "Tags" field improves the query's performance:

```
> db.posts.ensureIndex({Tags:1})
```

Now run the explain() command again to see the effect of adding the index:

```
> db.posts.find({Tags:"even"}).explain()
{
    "cursor" : "BtreeCursor Tags_1",
    "nscanned" : 4999,
    "nscannedObjects" : 4999,
    "n" : 4999,
    "millis" : 4,
    "indexBounds" : {
        "Tags" : [
            [
                "even",
                "even"
            ]
        ]
    }
}
>
```

The performance of the query has improved significantly. You can see that the query is now using a BtreeCursor driven by the Tags_1 index. The number of scanned records has been reduced from 9999 records to the same 4999 records you expect the query to return, while the execution time has dropped to 4ms.

---

**Note** The most common index type used by MongoDB is the btree (binary-tree type). A BtreeCursor is a MongoDB data cursor that uses the binary tree index to navigate from document to document. Btree indexes are very common in database systems because they provide fast inserts and deletes, yet also provide a reasonable performance when used to walk or sort data.

---

# Managing Indexes

You've now seen how much of an impact the introduction of carefully selected indexes can have.

As you learned in Chapter 3, MongoDB's indexes are used for both queries (find, findOne) and sorts. If you intend to use a lot of sorts on your collection, then you should add indexes that correspond to your sort specifications. If you use sort() on a collection where there are no indexes for the fields in the sort specification, then you may get an error message if you exceed the maximum size of the internal sort buffer. So it is a good idea to create indexes for sorts. In the following sections, we'll touch again on the basics, but also add some details that relate to how to manage and manipulate the indexes in your system. We will also cover how such indexes relate to some of the samples.

Each time you add an index to a collection, MongoDB must maintain it and update it every time you perform any write operation (e.g., updates, inserts, or deletes). If you have too many indexes on a collection, it can cause a negative impact on write performance.

Indexes are best used on collections where the majority of access is read access. For write-heavy collections such as those used in logging systems, introducing an index would reduce the peak documents per second that could be streamed into the collection.

---

■ **Warning** At this time, you can have a maximum of 40 indexes per collection.

---

# Listing Indexes

MongoDB maintains a special collection called `system.indexes` inside each database. This collection keeps track of all the indexes that have been created on all the collections in the databases, including which fields or elements they refer to.

The `system.indexes` collection is just like any normal collection. This means you can list its contents, run queries against it, and otherwise perform the usual tasks you can accomplish with a typical collection.

The following example lists the indexes in your simple database:

```
$mongo
>use blog
>db.system.indexes.find()
{ "name" : "_id_", "ns" : "blog.posts", "key" : { "_id" : 1 } }
{ "name" : "_id_", "ns" : "blog.authors", "key" : { "_id" : 1 } }
```

The blog database does not have any user-defined indexes, but you can see the two indexes created automatically for the `_id` field on your two collections: `posts` and `authors`. You don't have to do anything to create or delete these *identity indexes*; MongoDB creates and drops them whenever a collection is created or removed.

When you define an index on an element, MongoDB will construct an internal btree index, which it will use to locate documents efficiently. If no suitable index can be found, then MongoDB will scan all the documents in the collection to find the records that will satisfy the query.

# Creating a Simple Index

MongoDB provides the `ensureIndex()` function for adding new indexes to a collection. This function begins by checking whether an index has already been created with the same specification. If it has, then `ensureIndex()` just returns that index. This means you can call `ensureIndex()` as many times as you like, but it won't result in a lot of extra indexes being created for your collection.

The following example defines a simple index:

```
$mongo
>use blog
>db.posts.ensureIndex({Tags:1})
```

This preceding example creates a simple ascending btree index on the `Tags` field. Creating a descending index instead would require only small change:

```
>db.posts.ensureIndex({Tags:-1})
```

To index a field in an embedded document, you can use the normal dot notation addressing scheme; that is, if you have a `count` field that is inside a `comments` subdocument, then you can use this syntax to index it:

```
>db.posts.ensureIndex({"comments.count":1})
```

If you specify a document field, which is an array type, then the index will include all the elements of the array as separate index terms. This is known as a multi-key index, and each document is linked to multiple values in the index.

MongoDB has a special operator for performing queries where you wish to select only documents that have all of the terms you supply. In the blog database example, you have a posts collection with an element called Tags. This element has all the tags associated with the posting inside it. The following query finds all articles that have both the sailor and moon tags:

```
>db.posts.find({Tags:{$all: ['sailor', 'moon']}})
```

Without a multi-key index on the Tags field, the query engine would have to scan each document in the collection to see whether either term existed and, if so, to check whether both terms were present.

# Creating a Compound Index

It may be tempting to simply create a separate index for each field mentioned in any of your queries. While this may speed up queries without having to apply too much thought, it would unfortunately have a significant impact on adding and removing data from your database, as these indexes need to be updated each time.

Compound indexes provide a good way to keep down the number of indexes you have on a collection, allowing you to combine multiple fields into a single index, so you should try to use compound indexes wherever possible.

There are two main types of compound indexes: subdocument indexes and manually defined compound indexes.

MongoDB has some rules that allow it to use compound indexes for queries that do not use all of the component keys. Understanding these rules enables you to construct a set of compound indexes that cover all of the queries you wish to perform against the collection, without having to individually index each element (thereby avoiding the attendant impact on insert/update performance mentioned earlier).

One area where compound indexes may not be useful is when using the index in a sort. Sorting is not good at using the compound index unless the list of terms and sort directions exactly matches the index structure. In this case, individual simple indexes on each of the term fields may be a better choice.

## Creating Subdocument Compound Indexes

You can create a compound index using an entire subdocument; in this case, MongoDB will create a compound index where each element in the embedded document becomes part of the index. For example, assume you have an author subdocument with name and email elements inside it. The following snippet creates a compound index with two key terms in it: author.name and author.email:

```
>db.posts.ensureIndex({Author:1})
```

The preceding serves as a nice shortcut for creating compound indexes. However, you lose the ability to set the order of the keys in the index in this example because you can't set the direction of each.

## Constructing a Compound Index Manually

When you use a subdocument as an index key, the order of the elements used to build the multi-key index matches the order in which they appear in the subdocument's internal BSON representation. In many cases, this does not give you sufficient control over the process of creating the index.

To get around this while guaranteeing that the query uses an index constructed in the desired fashion, you need to make sure you use the same subdocument structure to create the index that you used when forming the query, as in the following example:

```
>db.articles.find({author:{name: 'joe', email: 'joe@blogger.com'}))
```

You can also create a compound index explicitly by naming all the fields that you wish to combine in the index, and then specifying the order to combine them in. The following example illustrates how to construct a compound index manually:

```
>db.posts.ensureIndex({"author.name":1, "author.email":1})
```

# Specifying Index Options

You can specify several interesting options when creating an index, such as creating unique indexes or enabling background indexing (you'll learn more about these options in the upcoming sections). You specify these options as additional parameters to the `ensureIndex()` function, as in the following example:

```
>db.posts.ensureIndex({author:1}, {option1:true, option2:true, ... })
```

## Creating an Index in the Background with {background:true}

When you instruct MongoDB to create an index by using the `ensureIndex()` function for the first time, the server must read all the data in the collection and create the specified index. By default, this is done in the foreground and all operations on the specified collection block until the index operation completes.

MongoDB also includes a feature that allows indexes to be created in the background. Operations by other connections on that collection are not blocked while that index is being built. No queries will use the index until it has been built, but the server will allow read and write operations to continue. Once the index operation has been completed, all queries that require the index will immediately start using it.

---

■ **Note** The index will be built in the background. However, the connection that initiates the request will block, if you issue the command from the MongoDB shell. A command issued on this connection won't return until the indexing operation is complete. At first sight, this appears to contradict the idea that it is a *background* index. However, if you have another MongoDB shell open at the same time, you will find that queries and updates on that collection run unhindered while the index build is in progress. It is only the initiating connection that is blocked. This differs from the non-background behavior you see with a simple `ensureIndex()` command, where operations on the second MongoDB shell would also be blocked.

---

## Killing the Indexing Process

You can also kill the current indexing process if you think it has hung or is otherwise taking too long. You can do this by invoking the `killOp()` function:

```
> db.killOp(<operation id>)
```

---

**Note** When invoking the `killOp()` command, the partial index will also be removed again. This prevents broken or irrelevant data from building up in the database.

---

## Creating an Index with a Unique Key {unique:true}

When you specify the `unique` option, MongoDB creates an index where all the keys must be different. This means that MongoDB will return an error if you try to insert a document where the index key matches the key of an existing document. This is useful for a field where you want to ensure that no two people can have the same identity (e.g., `userid`).

However, if you want to add a unique index to an existing collection that is already populated with data, then you must make sure that you have *deduped* the key(s). In this case, your attempt to create the index will fail if any two keys are not unique.

The `unique` option works for simple and compound indexes, but not for multi-key value indexes, where they wouldn't make much sense.

If a document is inserted with a field missing that is specified as a unique key, then MongoDB will automatically insert the field, but will set its value to `null`. This means that you can only insert one document with a missing key field into such a collection; any additional `null` values would mean the key is not unique, as required.

## Dropping Duplicates Automatically with {dropdups:true}

If you want to create a unique index for a field where you know that duplicate keys exist, then you can specify the `dropdups` option. This option instructs MongoDB to remove documents that would cause the index creation to fail. In this case, MongoDB will retain the first document it finds in its natural ordering of the collection, but then drop any other documents that would result in an index-constraint violation.

You need to be very careful when using this option because it *will* result in documents being deleted from your collection. You should be extremely aware of the data in your collection before using this option; otherwise, you might get unexpected (not to mention unwanted) behavior. It is an extremely good idea to run a group query against a collection for which you intend to make a key unique; this will enable you to determine the number of documents that would be regarded as duplicates *before* you executed this option.

## Dropping an Index

You can elect to drop all indexes or just one specific index from a collection. Use the following function to remove all indexes from a collection:

```
>db.posts.dropIndexes()
```

To remove a single index from a collection, you use syntax that mirrors the syntax used to create the index with `ensureIndex()`:

```
>db.posts.dropIndex({"author.name":1, "author.email":1});
```

## Re-Indexing a Collection

If you suspect that the indexes in a collection are damaged—for example, if you're getting inconsistent results to your queries—then you can force a re-indexing of the affected collection.

This will force MongoDB to drop and re-create all the indexes on the specified collection (see Chapter 9 for more information on how to detect and solve problems with your indexes), as in the following example:

```
> db.posts.reIndex()
{
    "nIndexesWas" : 2,
    "msg" : "indexes dropped for collection",
    "ok" : 1,
    "nIndexes" : 2,
    "indexes" : [
        {
            "name" : "_id_",
            "ns" : "blog.posts",
            "key" : {
                "_id" : 1
            }
        },
        {
            "_id" : ObjectId("4c7282c6d36e34765e2e6741"),
            "ns" : "blog.posts",
            "key" : {
                "Tags" : 1
            },
            "name" : "Tags_1"
        }
    ]
    ,
    "ok" : 1
}
```

The preceding output lists all the indexes the command has rebuilt, including the keys. Also, the `nIndexWas:` field shows how many indexes existed before running the command, while the `nIndex:` field gives the total number of indexes after the command has completed. If the two values are not the same, the implication is that there was a problem re-creating some of the indexes in the collection.

# How MongoDB Selects Which Indexes It Will Use

When a database system needs to run a query, it has to assemble a *query plan*, which is a list of steps it must run to perform the query. Each query may have multiple query plans that could produce the same result equally well. However, each plan may have elements in it that are more *expensive* to execute than others. For example, a scan of all the records in a collection is an expensive operation, and any plan that incorporates such an approach could be slow. These plans can also include alternative lists of indexes to use for query and sort operations.

Road directions serve as a good illustration of this concept. If you want to get to the diagonally opposite side of a block from one corner, then "take a left, then take a right" and "take a right, then take a left" are equally valid plans for getting to the opposite corner. However, if one of the routes has two stop signs and the other has none, then the former approach is a more expensive plan, while the latter approach is the best plan to use. Collection scans would qualify as potential stop signs when executing your queries.

MongoDB ships with a component called the query analyzer. This component takes a query and the collection the query targets. The component then produces a set of plans for MongoDB to execute. The `explain()` function described earlier in this chapter lists both the plan used and the set of alternative plans produced for a given query.

MongoDB also ships with a query optimizer component. The job of this component is to select which execution plan is best suited to run a particular query. In most relational database systems, a query optimizer uses statistics about the distribution of keys in a table, the number of records, the available indexes, the effectiveness of previous choices, and an assortment of weighting factors to calculate the cost of each approach. It then selects the least expensive plan to use.

The query optimizer in MongoDB is simultaneously dumber and smarter than the typical RDBMS query analyzer. For example, it does not use a cost-based method of selecting an execution plan; instead, it runs all of them in parallel and uses the one that returns the results fastest, terminating all the others after the winner crosses the finish line. Thus, the query analyzer in MongoDB uses a simple mechanism (dumb) to ensure that it always gets the fastest result (smart).

# Using Hint() to Force Using a Specific Index

The query optimizer in MongoDB selects the best index from the set of available indexes for a collection. It uses the methods just outlined to try to match the best index or set of indexes to a given query. However, there may be cases where the query optimizer does not make the correct choice, in which case it may be necessary to give the component a helping hand.

You can provide a *hint* to the query optimizer in such cases, nudging the component into making a better choice. For example, if you have used `explain()` to show which indexes are being used by your query, and you think you would like it to use a different index for a given query, then you can force the query optimizer to do so.

Let's look at an example. Assume that you have an index on a subdocument called `author` with `name` and `email` fields inside it. Also assume that you have the following defined index:

```
>db.posts.ensureIndex({Author:1})
```

You can use the following hint to force the query optimizer to use the preceding defined index:

```
>db.posts.find({author:{name:'joe', email: 'joe@10gen.com'}}).hint({Author:1})
```

If for some reason you want to force a query to use no indexes, that is, if you want to use collection document scanning as the means of selecting records, then you can use the following hint to do this:

```
>db.posts.find({author:{name: 'joe', email: 'joe@10gen.com'}}).hint({$natural:1})
```

# Optimizing the Storage of Small Objects

Indexes are the key to speeding up data queries. But another factor that can affect the performance of your application is the size of the data it accesses. Unlike database systems with fixed schemas, MongoDB stores all the schema data for each record inside the record itself. Thus, for large records with large data contents per field, the ratio of schema data to record data is low; however, for small records with small data values, this ratio can grow surprisingly large.

Consider a common problem in one of the application types that MongoDB is well suited for: logging. MongoDB's extraordinary write rate makes streaming events as small documents into a collection very efficient. However, if you want to optimize further the speed at which you can perform this functionality, you can do a couple of things.

First, you can consider *batching* your inserts. MongoDB ships with a multiple document `insert()` call. You can use this call to place several events into a collection at the same time. This results in fewer round-trips through the database interface API.

Second (and more importantly), you can reduce the size of your field names. If you have smaller field names, then MongoDB can pack more event records into memory before it has to flush them out to disk. This makes the whole system more efficient.

For example, assume you have a collection that is used to log three fields: a time stamp, a counter, and a four-character string used to indicate the source of the data. The total storage size of your data is shown in Table 10–2.

***Table 10–2.*** *The Logging Example Collection Storage Size*

| Field | Size |
|---|---|
| Timestamp | 8 bytes |
| Integer | 4 bytes |
| string | 4 bytes |
| Total | 16 bytes |

If you use `ts`, `n`, and `src` for the field names, then the total size of the field names is 6 bytes. This is a relatively small value compared to the data size. But now assume you decided to name the fields `WhenTheEventHappened`, `NumberOfEvents`, and `SourceOfEvents`. In this case, the total size of the field names is 48 bytes, or three times the size of the data itself. If you wrote 1 TB of data into a collection, then you would be storing 750 GB of field names, but only 250 GB of actual data.

This does more than waste disk space. It also affects all other aspects of the system's performance, including the index size, data transfer time, and (probably more importantly) the use of precious system RAM to cache the data files.

Another recommendation for logging applications is that you need to avoid adding indexes on your collections when writing records; as explained earlier, indexes take time and resources to maintain. Instead, you should add the index immediately before you start analyzing the data.

Also, you should consider using a schema that splits the event stream into multiple collections. For example, you might write each day's events into a separate collection. Smaller collections take less time to index and analyze.

# Summary

In this chapter, we looked at some tools for tracking down slow performance in MongoDB queries, as well as potential solutions for speeding up the slow queries that surface as a result. We also looked at some of the ways for optimizing data storage. For example, we looked at ways to ensure that we are making full use of the resources available to the MongoDB server.

The specific techniques described in this chapter enable you to optimize your data and tune the MongoDB system it is stored in. The best approach to take will vary from application to application, and it will be dependent on a lot of factors, including the application type, data access patterns, read/write ratios, and so on.

# CHAPTER 11

# Replication

Like many of its relational cousins, MongoDB supports the replication of a database's contents to another server in realtime or near realtime. MongoDB's replication features are simple to set up and use. They are also one of the key features in MongoDB that bolster the claim that the database is both a Web 2.0 and a cloud-based datastore.

There are many scenarios where you might want to use replication, so the replication support in MongoDB has to be sufficiently flexible that it can cope with all of them. 10gen, the company that publishes MongoDB, has gone to great lengths to make sure that its implementation of replication meets all of today's needs.

In this chapter, we will cover the following replication topologies that MongoDB supports:

- Single master/single slave replication
- Single master/multiple slave replication
- Multiple master/single slave replication
- Cascade replication
- Master/master replication
- Interleaved replication
- Replica pairs (legacy MongoDB clustering)
- Replica sets (advanced MongoDB clustering)

---

**Note** Replication is a feature that continues to evolve in MongoDB, and you can expect some changes to occur in how replication works as the product develops. This is particularly true with respect to the clustering of database servers. 10gen is investing considerable effort in ensuring that MongoDB meets and exceeds everybody's expectations for scalability and availability; replication support is one of the key features that 10gen is counting on to help it meet those expectations.

---

Before looking at the various replication setups in detail, let's review the goals the various setups are designed to achieve. We'll also look at the oplog and how it fits in with the communication between members of a replication topology. These two topics will provide the context for the rest of the chapter.

# Spelling Out MongoDB's Replication Goals

Among other things, replication can be used to achieve scalability, durability/reliability, and isolation. In the upcoming sections, we'll explore how you can use replication to achieve these goals along the way, while pointing out potential traps and mistakes you want to avoid.

## Improving Scalability

For web applications in particular, scalability is a critical design requirement, especially those that rely heavily on backend databases. Replication can help you create more scalable applications in two ways:

- *Improve performance*: Replication can help you improve an application's raw performance. This is particularly true for cases where you have a large web application with a predominantly read-based dataset, and you want to distribute queries to multiple database servers to increase parallelism.
- *Improve redundancy*: Replication can help you improve redundancy by enabling you to host an application in several data centers. In this approach, you ensure that there is a local copy of the data in each data center, so that the application can have high-speed access to it. Users can then be connected to the data center that is closest to them, minimizing latency.

---

■ **Note** MongoDB also supports another feature called sharding that is designed to assist you in creating more scalable applications with or without replication (see Chapter 12 for more information on using sharding and replication together in MongoDB).

---

## Improving Durability/Reliability

Replication is commonly used to help guard against hardware failure or database corruption. Some specific examples where people use replication in this manner include the following:

- *When you want to have a duplicate of your database that is no more than 30 minutes old.* You may want to protect yourself against flaws in your application or provide a simple mechanism to provide *trend* information by highlighting the differences between the results of queries against both datasets.
- *When you want to have an* aggregate *data server*: You may want to maintain copies of data from multiple master servers, to save the cost of having dedicated slaves for each.
- *When you have a large amount of data that changes rapidly*: You may want to run a replica as a backup in cases where normal backup schemes would take too long to make or restore the backup in the event of a system failure.

## Providing Isolation

There are some processes that, if run against the production database, would significantly impact that database's performance or availability. You can use replication to create synchronized copies that isolate processes from the production database, for example:

- *When you want to run reports or backups without impacting the performance of your production system*: Maintaining a read-only slave replica enables you to isolate queries from your reporting system and make sure that the end-of-month reports don't bring your site to its knees.
- *When you have a development or staging system that you want to provide access to live data*: Isolation enables you to provide this access without running the risk that a flaw or bug in a development version of your code will cause problems with your production system.

# Drilling Down on the Oplog

In simple terms, the oplog is a journal of all the changes that a master instance makes to its databases for the purpose of replaying those changes on a slave to ensure that the two databases are identical. The master server maintains the oplog, and the slaves query the master for new entries to apply to their own copies of the replicated databases.

The oplog creates a timestamp for each entry. This enables a slave to track how far it has read from the oplog during a previous read, and what entries it needs to transfer to catch up. If you stop a slave and restart it at a later time, it will use the master's oplog to retrieve all the changes it has missed while it has been offline.

Because it is not practical to have an infinitely large oplog, the oplog is limited or *capped* at a particular size.

You can think of the oplog as a window on the recent activity of your master instance; if that window is too small, then operations will be lost from the oplog before they can be applied to the slave. The `oplogSize` option allows you to set the size of your oplog in MB. For an average 64-bit system with average read/write patterns, the oplogSize should be set to at least five percent of the disk space available for data storage. If your system is write intensive, then you may need to increase this size to ensure that slaves can be offline for a reasonable amount of time without losing data.

For example, if you have a daily backup that is taken from the slave and it takes an hour to complete, then the size of the oplog will have to be set to allow the slave to stay offline for that hour plus an additional amount of time to provide a safety margin.

---

**Note** If you are hosting multiple databases on the master server, but only replicating one database to the slave, then the master instance still places all update operations for *all* its databases into the oplog, even if the slave is not reading them all. You have to remember this when determining the optimum size of your oplog.

---

It's critical that you take into account the update rate on all the databases present on the master when calculating a suitable size for the oplog.

You can get some idea about a suitable size for your oplog by using the `printReplicationInfo()` command that runs on the master instance:

```
$mongo
>db.printReplicationInfo()
configured oplog size:      192MB
log length start to end:     12365secs (3.43hrs)
oplog first event time:      Tue Jul 06 2010 21:11:02 GMT+0800 (PHT)
oplog last event time:       Wed Jul 07 2010 00:37:07 GMT+0800 (PHT)
now:                                Wed Jul 07 2010 00:37:08 GMT+0800 (PHT)
```

This preceding command shows you the current size of your oplog, as well as the amount of time it will take to fill up at the current update rate. From this, you can estimate whether you need to increase or decrease the size of your oplog.

# Implementing Single Master/Single Slave Replication

Single master/single slave replication is the simplest form of the replication/clustering configurations that MongoDB provides. It consists of only a single master instance and a single slave instance.

This mode of replication does not provide any automatic failover capabilities, and the application is normally set to interact with the master database only. Should the master instance fail, then the application must be reconfigured to attach to the slave instance instead.

This operating mode is typically used to isolate potentially long-running operations such as creating a backup or generating a substantial report. This mode enables you to perform those activities without significantly impacting the performance of a running application, while still providing a degree of redundancy in the case of server failure.

The characteristics of this replication model are listed in Table 11–1.

***Table 11–1.*** *Characteristics of Single Master/Single Slave Replication System*

| Property | Description |
|---|---|
| Number of masters | Single, fixed, role does not change |
| Number of slaves | Single, fixed, role does not change |
| Failover Mode | Manual |

Figure 11–1 shows a typical master/slave replication setup.

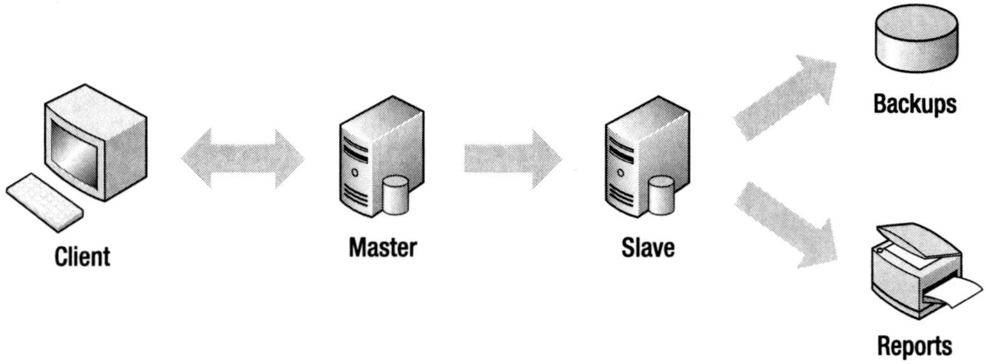


*Figure 11–1. Setting up single master/single slave replication*

# Setting Up a Master/Slave Replication Configuration

It's easy to set up two instances of MongoDB in a single master/single slave replication mode. You can do this either on separate machines in a production environment or as two instances on the same machine in a testing and development environment. If you run two instances on the same computer, then you will need to ensure that they are using separate *dbpaths* and network ports (see Table 11–2).

In this first example, you will learn how to set up two instances on the same server. However, the principles are the same for setting up master/slave replication on two different machines, but there is no need to ensure that there are different dbpaths and port numbers.

*Table 11–2. MongoDB Instances Used in a Single Master/Single Slave Example*

| Service | Daemon | Address | Dbpath |
|---|---|---|---|
| Master instance | mongod | `localhost:27017` | `/db/master/data` |
| Slave instance | mongod | `localhost:27018` | `/db/slave/data` |

You should begin by setting up the master server. You need to use `--master` option to let the mongod service know what its role will be in this replication setup; this option also instructs mongod to start recording any write, update, and delete commands into its oplog.

Open a new terminal window and type the following:

```
$sudo mkdir -p /db/master/data
$sudo mongod --master --dbpath /db/master/data
```

Be sure to leave the terminal window open as you test out the replication. This will enable you to see the console messages that MongoDB uses to tell you what is going on. If you close the terminal window, then MongoDB will terminate. The preceding snippet will start a copy of MongoDB running on the default port (27017); this instance will use the `/db/master/data` directory to store its databases and collections.

Next, you need to set up the slave server, open another terminal window and type:

```
$sudo mkdir -p /db/slave/data
$sudo mongod --slave --source localhost:27017 --dbpath /db/slave/data -port 27018
```

The --slave command-line option instructs this new instance that it is to take on the role of a slave. The --source option lets this instance know the address of the master it should synchronize its data from. The new instance will start and perform an initial synchronization of its databases with the master database, and then start tracking changes by polling the master's oplog.

At this point, you have two instances of MongoDB running: the master is running on the default port of 27017, while the slave is running on port 27018.

Now, let's check whether it's working. Begin by connecting to the master:

```
$ mongo
> show dbs
admin
local
> use local
switched to db local
> show collections
oplog.$main
slaves
system.indexes
>
```

This example shows that MongoDB has created a special database in the master called local; this database has two special collections called oplog.$main and slaves, the initial contents of the slaves collection for our example master/slave setup is shown below.

```
> db.slaves.find()
{ "_id" : ObjectId("4c332bbae1edee6634b251e5"), "host" : "localhost", "ns" :
"local.oplog.$main", "syncedTo" : { "t" : 1278422286000, "i" : 1 } }
>
```

---

▒ **Note** If you do not see a slaves collection, then check the version number of your MongoDB system; this collection was added as part of the general migration to Replication Sets in Version 1.6.x; versions prior to this may not show this collection.

---

The slaves collection holds a set of documents describing each slave that is connected to the master. The document contains the name of the second special collection, local.oplog.$main (the master's oplog), as well as a timestamp and a position indicator that shows the point in the oplog that the slave has read up to.

## Examining the Slave

Now let's take a moment to poke around in the slave and see what information it contains:

```
$mongo --port 27018
> show dbs
admin
```

```
local
> use local
switched to db local
> show collections
me
pair.sync
sources
system.indexes
```

Like the master, the slave has a *local* database that contains all the collections it uses to maintain its replication state. Let's take a couple minutes to examine some of these collections. The first collection of interest is the me collection, which is shown here:

```
> db.me.find();
{ "_id" : ObjectId("4c332bbae1edee6634b251e5") }
```

---

■ **Note** If you do not see a me collection, then check the version number of your MongoDB system. This collection was also added as part of the general migration to Replication Sets in Version 1.6; versions prior to this may not show this collection.

---

The me collection contains a single document with no fields except for ObjectId. Eagle-eyed readers will have noticed that this ID is identical to the ID shown in the corresponding slaves collection document that describes this slave on the master machine. This ID is the identity record for the slave, and it is used to find the slave's replication status on the master server:

```
> db.sources.find();
{ "_id" : ObjectId("4c332bbae1edee6634b251e4"), "host" : "localhost:27017",
        "source" : "main", "syncedTo" : { "t" : 1278423076000, "i" : 1 }, "localLogTs" : {
"t" : 0, "i" : 0 } }
```

The preceding example shows the sources collection maintained by the slave. This collection contains a set of documents that describes each of the masters the slave is connected to. Notice the synchedTo: element is the same as the corresponding slave document element of the same name in the master database's slaves collection. In our example, because there is only one master, there is only one document in the collection.

It is possible to specify the master that a slave is attached to by directly inserting the master's details into the sources collection, this is the method used to add multiple masters to a multiple master/slave configuration (you will learn more about such configurations later in this chapter).

Finally, there is the pair.sync collection that contains the status of the relationship between the two machines. This collection's initialsynccomplete element is set to 1, which indicates that the two machines have synchronized their initial contents. From now on, the slave will track changes on the master by periodically reading the master's oplog:

```
> db.pair.sync.find()
{ "_id" : ObjectId("4c332bbfe1edee6634b251e6"), "initialsynccomplete" : 1 }
```

You can prove the system is working by changing some data on the master, as shown in the following example:

```
$ mongo
> use testdb
switched to db testdb
> db.testcollection.insert({name:'tim',surname:'hawkins'})
> db.testcollection.find()
{ "_id" : ObjectId("4c33344c55ca4b3534b1d930"), "name" : "tim", "surname" : "hawkins" }
```

Now you can inspect the slave to see whether the change has been made there as well:

```
$ mongo --port 27018
> show dbs
admin
local
testdb
> use testdb
switched to db testdb
> show collections
system.indexes
testcollection
> db.testcollection.find()
{ "_id" : ObjectId("4c33344c55ca4b3534b1d930"), "name" : "tim", "surname" : "hawkins" }
```

In this case, your change has been replicated from the master to the slave, indicating that you've set up a master/slave replication successfully—gold stars all around!

As the preceding example illustrates, setting up simple replication is extremely easy on MongoDB. In its basic form, replication requires just a few commands to get it to work, which makes it considerably easier to implement in MongoDB than the relational database systems that MongoDB is often replacing.

# Implementing Single Master/Multiple Slave Replication

So far, you've learned how to set up a single master/single slave configuration; however, MongoDB also supports multiple slaves on a single master, and this configuration is just as easy to implement as the configuration you just learned about.

To add another slave, repeat the process you used to add the first slave to the master, as in the following example:

```
$sudo mkdir -p /db/slave2/data
$sudo mongod --slave --source localhost:27017 --dbpath /db/slave2/data -port 27019
```

This preceding snippet will add a second slave machine to the master/slave topology you configured previously, making the second slave available on `localhost:27019`.

Again, you can attach to the new slave and confirm that your `testdb/testcollection` has been replicated to the new slave.

# Configuring a Master/Slave Replication System

The simple replication set up shown previously will suffice for a large number of needs. However, MongoDB also includes a number of initialization options that allow you to tune the replication behavior to meet your needs more precisely (see Table 11-3). Before exploring some of the more complex replication topologies, let's take a minute to examine some of the available configuration parameters, which are common to most setups.

Like all mongod options, these options can be issued on the mongod startup command line or placed in a configuration file that is used when the server is initialized.

*Table 11–3. Command-Line Options that Affect Master/Slave Replication*

| Option | Description |
| --- | --- |
| `--only` arg | (Optional) Slave: By default, the replication system will replicate all databases on the master to the slave. If you want only one database to be replicated, then use the `-only` option to specify the single database you want replicated; all other databases on the master server will be ignored. |
| `--slavedelay` arg | (Optional) Slave: In any replication system, there is always a certain amount of delay between an update operation occurring on the master and its effect propagating down to the slave. In most cases, you would strive to minimize this delay, so that the slave reflects as accurate a replica of the master as possible at any point in time.<br><br>However, there are some cases where you will want to increase the size of this delay. For example, you might want to create a delayed backup that can be used if the data in the master becomes corrupted on a realtime system. By setting this option to a delay time in seconds, you can ensure the slave is always at minimum, the specified number of seconds behind the master. |
| `--fastsync` | (Optional) Slave: In the preceding example in this chapter, you started with an empty database, so the time to perform the initial synchronization of the slave to the master was extremely small. If you try adding an empty slave to a master that has a lot of data already in its databases, then it can take a long time to initially synchronize the two machines.<br><br>Often, it is much faster to copy the datafiles from the master server's dbpath to the slave server's dbpath using your operating system's filesystem copy commands. If you use this method to perform the initial synchronization of the two servers, then adding `--fastsync` to the slave server's startup routine will force it to add some required extra information to the copied database files. This option enables the slave to accept these files as its initial sync. |
| `--oplogSize` arg | (Optional) Master: You have already seen that the oplog is used to record changes to the contents of the master database. The size of the oplog determines how long a slave can stay offline before it is no longer capable of resyncing its data without copying the entire master dataset again. |

# Resynchronizing a Master/Slave Replication System

If you have taken a slave offline for longer than the time window the master server's oplog can support, then you will find that the slave will fail to restart replication. Instead, it will need to be resynchronized (*resynced*) with the master.

The following sections explain the three main methods you can use to resync a slave with its master.

## Issuing a Manual Resync Command to the Slave

The easiest way to force a resync is to use the mongo console tool to connect to the slave and request a resync. In the preceding case, the slave is running on port 27018 of your local machine. This following command forces the slave to resynchronize with the master server:

```
$mongo localhost:27018
>use admin
>db.runCommand({resync: 1})
```

## Resyncing by Deleting the Slaves Datafiles

Let's assume that you stop the slave server and delete its datafiles from the dbpath. When you restart the slave server (be careful to ensure it is started with the same startup parameters), it will detect this condition and resynchronize its dataset with its master automatically.

## Resyncing a Slave with the --fastsync Option

Both of the resynchronization methods described thus far work fine for small databases. However, it can take a considerable amount of time if you use those approaches to resynchronize a multi-gigabyte database. For large databases, it may be better to use a method introduced earlier, where you used the `--fastsync` option after moving a copy of the master's datafiles to the slave's dbpath. You can perform a manual resync by copying the datafiles stored in the dbpath from the master to the slave, and then restarting the slaves.

To do this without shutting down the master, you must *freeze* the master for writes by connecting to your master and issuing the following commands:

```
$mongo
>use admin
>db.runCommand({fsync:1,lock:1})
{
    "info" : "now locked against writes",
    "ok" : 1
}
```

The preceding snippet causes the master to flush all outstanding writes to the disk and to block any updates from being performed; however, read queries will continue to be serviced without any blocks applied. Now stop the slaves that you wish to update. Next, copy the contents of the directories specified in the `--dbpath` option (e.g., `/db/master/data`) to the slave servers, placing the files in the directory specified by the slave's `--dbpath` option (e.g., `/db/slave/data`).

After you do this, you can run the following commands to release the lock on the master server:

```
$mongo
>use admin
>db.$cmd.sys.unlock.findOne();
{ "ok" : 1, "info" : "unlock requested" }
```

Next, restart the slave with the `--fastsync` command-line option; this will tell the slave to use the newly copied datafiles as its own version of the database. The slave will check back in with the master, and then propagate any writes that the master stored in the oplog when the slave was being restarted.

## Implementing Multiple Master/Single Slave Replication

In some circumstances, it may be advantageous to have a single slave track the contents of multiple master servers. For example, you might want to adopt such an approach if you are using master/slave replication for backup and reporting, but have multiple applications with different master database servers (one for each application), as shown in Figure 11–2.

You can reduce your costs by sharing a common slave between masters. This is especially effective if the slave is not heavily loaded all of the time, and the backups of each application can be staggered.

The characteristics of this model are listed in Table 11–4.

***Table 11–4.*** *Characteristics of Multiple Master/Single Slave Replication*

| Property | Description |
| --- | --- |
| Number of masters | Multiple, fixed, role does not change |
| Number of slaves | Single, fixed, role does not change |
| Failover Mode | Manual |

Figure 11–2 shows a typical multiple master/single slave replication setup.

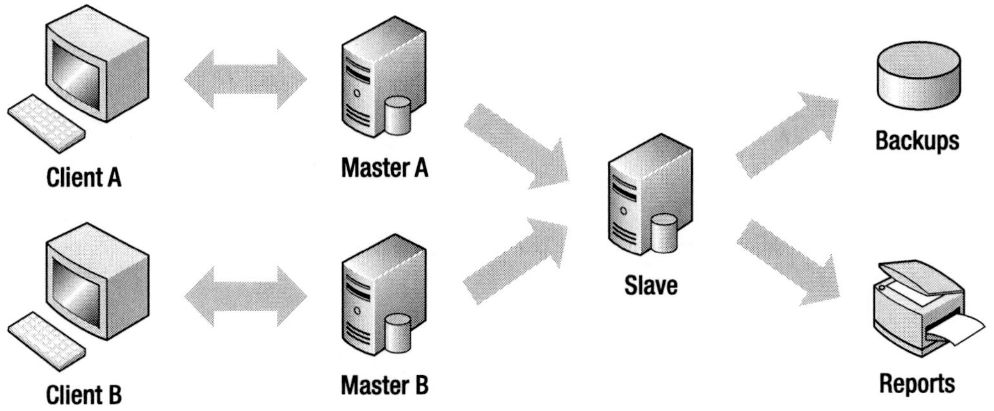


***Figure 11–2.*** *Setting up multiple master/single slave replication*

### Setting up a Multiple Master/Slave Replication Configuration

The essentials of setting up a multiple master/slave configuration are the same as for setting up a single master/slave configuration.

In the next example, you will set up a multiple master/slave configuration with the characteristics shown in Table 11–5.

*Table 11–5. MongoDB Instances Used in a Multiple Master/Single Slave Example*

| Service | Daemon | Address | Dbpath |
|---|---|---|---|
| Master 1: Holds database foo | mongod | localhost:27021 | /db/master1/data |
| Master 2: Holds database bar | mongod | localhost:27022 | /db/master2/data |
| Slave 1: Holds a replica of the databases foo and bar | mongod | localhost:27023 | /db/slave1/data |

As in the earlier example, your next step is to create a small example of this configuration running on a single machine (localhost). Begin by creating the first master (master1); as before, you type these commands into a fresh terminal window:

```
$sudo mkdir -p /db/master1/data
$sudo mongod --master --dbpath /db/master1/data --port 27021
```

Now open another terminal window to attach to this server and create a simple database named foo:

```
$mongo localhost:27021
>use foo
>db.foocollection.insert({foodata:'our first foo document'})
>quit()
$
```

At this point, you can set up the second master and its corresponding database by typing the following into another fresh terminal window:

```
$sudo mkdir -p /db/master2/data
$sudo mongod --master --dbpath /db/master2/data --port 27022
```

From your console window, enter the following code to launch the second instance of a MongoDB master database:

```
$mongo localhost:27022
>use bar
>db.barcollection.insert({bardata:'our first bar document'})
>quit()
$
```

At this point, you have two separate instances of MongoDB running in master mode, with each hosting a different database. The following code sets up the slave and attaches it to both masters:

```
$sudo mkdir -p /db/slave1/data
$sudo mongod --slave --dbpath /db/slave1/data -port 27023
```

This preceding snippet creates the slave. Notice that you haven't specified a source yet. This is because you will use the shell to add the two masters to the slave. In the window you are using for your MongoDB shell, enter this code to attach the slave to the two masters and start the initial sync of the databases for each master:

```
$mongo localhost:27023
>use local
> switched to db local
> db.sources.insert({host:'localhost:27021'})
> db.sources.insert({host:'localhost:27022'})
> db.sources.find()
{ "_id" : ObjectId("4c52347d6a26e5025bf5d6d5"), "host" : "localhost:27021", "source" : "main",
"syncedTo" : { "t" : 1280455835000, "i" : 1 }, "localLogTs" : { "t" : 0, "i" : 0 } }
{ "_id" : ObjectId("4c52348d6a26e5025bf5d6d6"), "host" : "localhost:27022", "source" : "main",
"syncedTo" : { "t" : 1280455825000, "i" : 1 }, "localLogTs" : { "t" : 0, "i" : 0 } }
```

After a short while, you should see the following when you look at your slave:

```
$ mongo localhost:27023
> show dbs
admin
bar
foo
local
> use foo
switched to db foo
> db.foocollection.find()
{ "_id" : ObjectId("4c52351575fdd94439dc9051"), "foodata" : "our first foo document" }
> use bar
switched to db bar
> db.barcollection.find()
{ "_id" : ObjectId("4c523551fce873451e9aa261"), "bardata" : "our first bar document" }
```

Don't be concerned if the replication of these tiny databases seems to take a long time. It takes a while because, as each slave source is initialized, it must create an empty database file to hold the contents of the initial sync. By default, this creates an empty 2 GB file on the disk. This is a one-time operation, and it will not happen again during normal operation. If you look at the log output in the slave's terminal window, you can see this process happening.

So far you have successfully configured a master-master/slave setup, and we can see from output that the slave has both databases replicated to it.

In the preceding example, you are replicating all of the databases from each master to the slave. Each master had only one database, and the names of those databases were unique; therefore, you encountered no problems with collisions on the slave. However, you can face potential issues if, for example, there is a common `temporary` database on each master that you don't want to replicate because it is only used for temporary operations. In this scenario, you can restrict the replication to a single database by adding the `only:` field to the specification of the source master when configuring the slave, as shown in the following example:

```
>db.sources.insert({ host:'localhost:27021', only:'foo' })
>db.sources.insert({ host:'localhost:27022', only:'bar' })
```

---

■ **Caution** You should not replicate the same database from two different masters; doing so is not supported, and it will lead to unpredictable results.

---

# Exploring Various Replication Scenarios

The master/slave and multiple master/slave topologies are the only "officially" supported approaches for simple mode replication; however, there are a number of variants that also work to varying degrees.

In the previous examples, you saw cases where a server ran in either master or slave mode. However, a MongoDB instance is capable of taking on both roles at the same time. You can place an instance into this schizophrenic mode by specifying both the master and the slave options when the instance starts up. The approach permits three additional topologies: cascade replication, master/master replication, and interleaved replication. You'll learn about each of these approaches in the following sections.

## Implementing Cascade Replication

A *cascade* replication model requires a minimum of three servers: one operates as a pure master, one operates as a slave/master, and one operates as a slave (see Figure 11–3). These servers are effectively *chained* or cascaded together. Thus, any changes applied to the first master will be passed to the intermediate slave/master, and then to the final slave, which is the last machine in the chain. Theoretically, you can apply this chaining to any number of levels; however, at some point the overall replication lag time will become excessive and render the downstream slaves unusable.

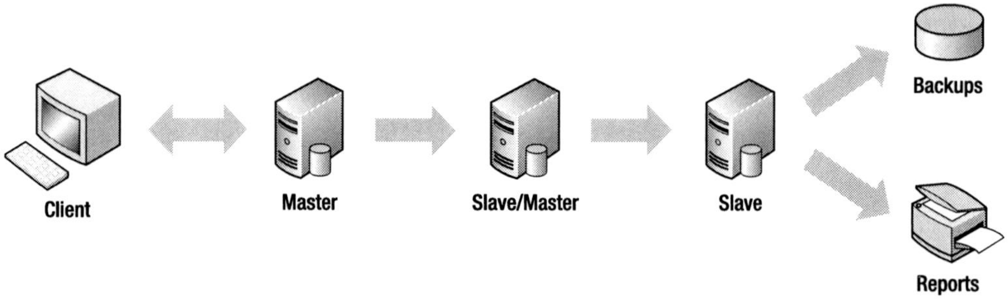


***Figure 11–3.*** *A cascade replication system*

This approach may provide an architectural benefit in cases where the final slave has a `--slavedelay` option applied to it during startup; this would offer the system integrator the opportunity to have both a near realtime slave *and* a time-delayed slave, so you get the best of both worlds.

## Implementing Master/Master Replication

The master/master replication topology is popular in relational database circles. This topology allows you to maintain a cluster where reads and writes can be made from Client A or Client B to either Master A or Master B, and the cluster will remain synchronized (see Figure 11–4).

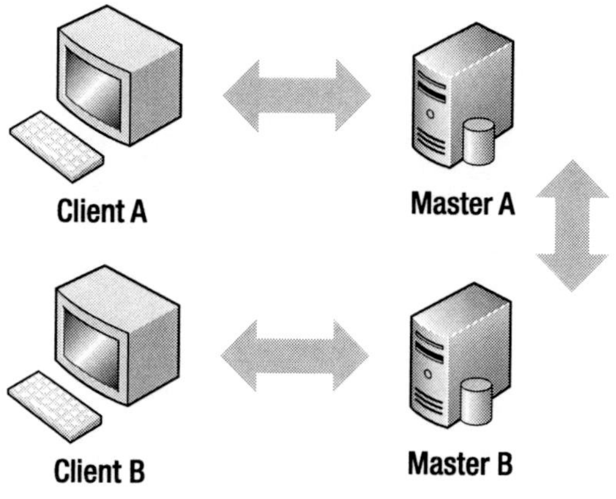


*Figure 11–4. Master/master replication*

However, you do need to be aware of a certain number of *edge cases* with MongoDB operating in master/master mode. For example, some database operations (e.g., `$inc` and `upsert`) may not operate correctly if there is appreciable lag between the two halves of the cluster, or if there are contention issues on documents.

The behavior of the cluster in these cases is not predictable. If your application does not use any of the potentially problematic operations, however, this may be a viable solution for you.

One point in favor of this topology is that, unlike when using MySQL and other relational database systems, the IDs for MongoDB documents are unique across an entire cluster. Relational database systems tend to use constructs such as auto-incrementing integers or sequences to create unique record IDs. If proper care and attention are not taken, then collisions can occur with insertions on different servers. MongoDB uses document ID values called `_id`. These values are safe from this problem because each ID generated on each server has as a component part of the Ethernet address of the server's network card; hence, MongoDB IDs are unique across both machines, and the server does not have to resolve collisions in master/master mode.

# Implementing Interleaved Replication

Interleaved replication is a simple variation on the master/slave replication approach. This approach is useful if you have multiple applications and multiple database servers. You can reduce the cost of your installations by allowing the master server for one application to act as the slave server for another, and vice versa. For example, if you have two applications, you can use two MongoDB servers that are configured as masters for one app and slaves for the other (see Figure 11–5).

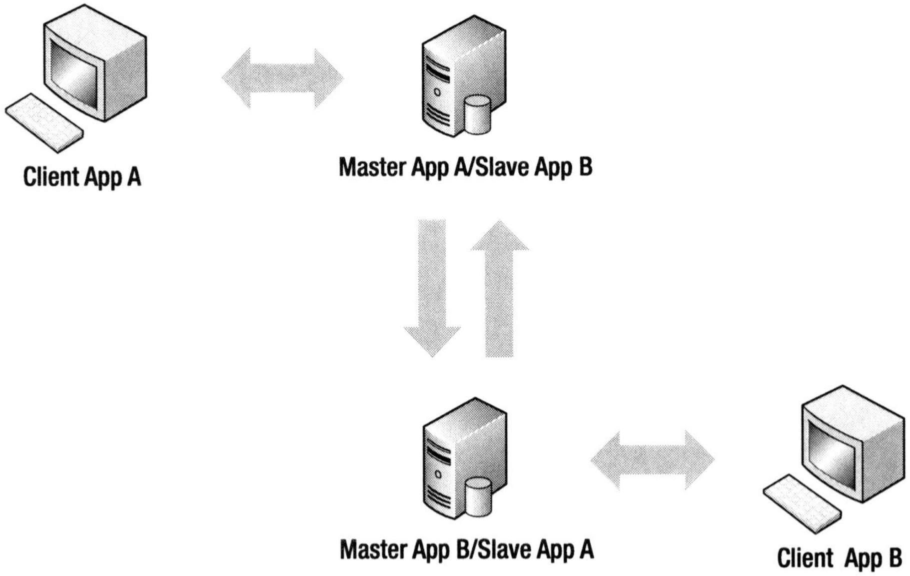


*Figure 11–5. Interleaved replication*

You can use the `--only` option to set which database is replicated on a master/slave pair. This enables you to determine which database each server is operating as a slave for.

# Using Replica Pairs

*Replica pairs* are a legacy MongoDB approach for implementing clusters of database servers. In this approach, each server in the pair is initially given master or slave status, which lets that server operate in a fashion similar to a simple master/slave configuration.

---

**Note** *Replica pairs* are available in MongoDB 1.4.x and earlier. Officially, these versions of MongoDB support only two servers per cluster. This mechanism will be deprecated in later versions of MongoDB in favor of *replica sets*, which provide a more flexible topology that allows more than two servers in a cluster.

---

The feature that differentiates replica pairs from the simple master/slave replication topologies is what happens if the machine that performs the role of master fails (or otherwise becomes unavailable). That failure could be a software fault in the master server or its operating system, a physical hardware failure of the server itself, or a network break between the server and the application.

To resolve this, machines are able to change their respective roles automatically. For example, a machine that had been operating as a slave can promote itself to the role of master when it finds it is no longer able to verify that the master is fully functional.

The interesting part occurs when the original master becomes available again (e.g., it reboots or a network cable is plugged back in). The original master can detect that it has been usurped in its role as master, assume the new role of slave, and then resynchronize itself with the new master. The two machines will remain in this reversed state until they are restarted and the original roles are reasserted, or another failure forces them to flip back.

The characteristics of this model are listed in Table 11–6.

***Table 11–6.*** *Characteristics of a Replica Pair*

| Property | Description |
|---|---|
| Number of masters | Single, dynamic, role will switch on failure |
| Number of slaves | Single, dynamic, role will switch on failure |
| Failover Mode | Automatic |

## Setting up a Replica Pair

Next, you will learn how to set up a replica pair using two separate instances of MongoDB running on the same machine. This procedure is similar to the process for setting up a master/slave configuration, but it uses a slightly different syntax to initialize the two halves of the pair.

Let's begin by setting up the first half of the replica pair. Open a new terminal window and type the following code:

```
$sudo mkdir -p /db/server1/data
$sudo mongod  --pairwith localhost:27018 --dbpath /db/server/data
```

The server will show a lot of fascinating but irrelevant messages about creating an oplog that is approximately 5% of available disk space, etc. Finally, the server will announce that it's ready to accept replication requests with the following notification:

```
Wed Jul  7 10:14:46 repl: from host:localhost:27018
Wed Jul  7 10:14:46 repl:  couldn't connect to server localhost:27018 localhost:27018
Wed Jul  7 10:14:46 repl: sleep 3sec before next pass
Wed Jul  7 10:14:49 repl: from host:localhost:27018
```

The server will repeat this phrase, showing that it is waiting for the other half of the replica pair to become available. You will see the following notification once the second machine starts up:

```
Wed Jul  7 10:19:04 connection accepted from localhost:35772 #1
Wed Jul  7 10:19:04 query local.oplog.$main ntoreturn:1 reslen:80 nscanned:1 { query: {},
orderby: { $natural: -1 } }  nreturned:1 138ms
Wed Jul  7 10:19:04 repl: from host:localhost:27018
Wed Jul  7 10:19:04 pair: setting master=0 was -1
Wed Jul  7 10:19:04 repl:   applied 1 operations
Wed Jul  7 10:19:04 repl:  end sync_pullOpLog syncedTo: Wed Jul  7 10:19:03 2010 4c33e417:1
Wed Jul  7 10:19:04 building new index on { _id: 1 } for local.pair.sync
Wed Jul  7 10:19:04 Buildindex local.pair.sync idxNo:0
       { name: "_id_", ns: "local.pair.sync", key: { _id: 1 } }
Wed Jul  7 10:19:04 done for 0 records 0.029secs
Wed Jul  7 10:19:15 repl: sleep 2sec before next pass
Wed Jul  7 10:19:17 repl: from host:localhost:27018
```

```
Wed Jul  7 10:19:17 repl:   applied 1 operations
Wed Jul  7 10:19:17 repl:  end sync_pullOpLog syncedTo: Wed Jul  7 10:19:17 2010 4c33e425:1
Wed Jul  7 10:19:17 repl: sleep 1sec before next pass
```

The preceding shows a copy of MongoDB running on the default port (27017); this instance uses the directory /db/server1/data to store its databases and collections.

Next, you need to set up the other half of the replica pair. Do this by opening up another terminal, and typing the following code:

```
$sudo mkdir -p /db/server2/data
$sudo mongod --pairwith localhost:27017 --dbpath /db/server2/data -port 27018
```

Again, you will see a lot of information about the slave machine starting up; eventually, you should see a notification like the following, which indicates that the slave has managed to connect to the master and start the replication process:

```
Wed Jul  7 10:19:04 connection accepted from localhost:52114 #1
Wed Jul  7 10:19:04 pair: setting master=1 was -1
Wed Jul  7 10:19:05 repl: from host:localhost
Wed Jul  7 10:19:05 building new index on { ns: 1, id: 1 } for local.temp.replIds
Wed Jul  7 10:19:05 Buildindex local.temp.replIds idxNo:0
        { name: "setIdx", ns: "local.temp.replIds", key: { ns: 1, id: 1 }, unique: true }
Wed Jul  7 10:19:05 done for 0 records 0.019secs
Wed Jul  7 10:19:05 building new index on { ns: 1, id: 1 } for local.temp.replModIds
Wed Jul  7 10:19:05 Buildindex local.temp.replModIds idxNo:0
       { name: "setIdx", ns: "local.temp.replModIds", key: { ns: 1, id: 1 }, unique: true }
Wed Jul  7 10:19:05 done for 0 records 0secs
Wed Jul  7 10:19:05 repl: sleep 2sec before next pass
Wed Jul  7 10:19:15 repl: from host:localhost
Wed Jul  7 10:19:15 repl:   applied 1 operations
Wed Jul  7 10:19:15 repl:  end sync_pullOpLog syncedTo: Wed Jul  7 10:19:14 2010 4c33e422:1
Wed Jul  7 10:19:15 repl: sleep 1sec before next pass
Wed Jul  7 10:19:16 repl: from host:localhost
```

If you don't see something like the preceding output, then you need to double-check your configuration.

If all is well, you will have two instances of MongoDB running as a replica pair with server1 on port 27017 and server2 on port 27018. You can perform the same tests that you did with the master/slave replication configuration; however, first you need to identify which server will be the master.

You need to find and connect to the master server. To determine which server is the master, you can check the replica status on both machines. The first server you started up is the instance on port 27017; the following output shows clearly this instance is not the master:

```
$ mongo
> db.$cmd.findOne({ismaster:1})
{
    "ismaster" : 0,
    "remote" : "localhost:27018",
    "info" : "direct negotiation",
    "ok" : 1
}
```

Connecting to the other server on port 27018 shows that this instance is the master, so the last server you started up has taken over the role of master server:

```
$mongo localhost:27018
> db.$cmd.findOne({ismaster:1})
{
    "ismaster" : 1,
    "remote" : "localhost",
    "info" : "CmdNegotiateMaster::run()",
    "ok" : 1
}
```

You can now run the same tests that you ran against the master/slave configuration to show that writes to the master server are replicated to the slave server.

## Coping with Failure

One of the key features of a replica pair is its ability to flip the roles of the two servers in response to a server failure. You can simulate a failure by shutting down the server that you started up on port 27018. You can do this by selecting the open terminal that you started the second server (server2) in, and then typing ^C to send a termination request to the server. Remember that this server has been operating as the master server. This should cause the server to shut down; if you are watching the terminal window of the first server, you should see a stream of messages like the following printed to the console:

```
Wed Jul  7 10:34:36 repl:  couldn't connect to server localhost:27018 localhost:27018
Wed Jul  7 10:34:36 pair: setting master=1 was 0
Wed Jul  7 10:34:36 repl: sleep 3sec before next pass
```

The preceding messages tell you that the first server (server1) has changed its role and is now operating as the master server of the pair. If you restart server2 again, you should see a message stream in the console output similar to the following once the server finishes starting up:

```
Wed Jul  7 10:56:09 connection accepted from localhost:48966 #1
Wed Jul  7 10:56:09 pair: setting master=0 was -1
Wed Jul  7 10:56:11 repl: from host:localhost
```

The preceding console output indicates that the newly restored server has started up and has assumed the role of the slave server. It adopted the slave role because it found an already active master server (server1). Your application will automatically stay attached to the active master, so bringing this server back online will have no effect on which server your application is using (see Figure 11–6). This is by design. A newly restored server will probably be busy immediately after being inserted back into the pair as it synchronizes itself with the current state of its peer. If the system were to restore itself to its pre-failover condition, then your application performance would be impacted by this synchronization activity.

This example illustrates how, in a replica pair, neither of the instances is naturally considered to be the master or the slave; which role a given server assumes will change based on the needs of the moment.

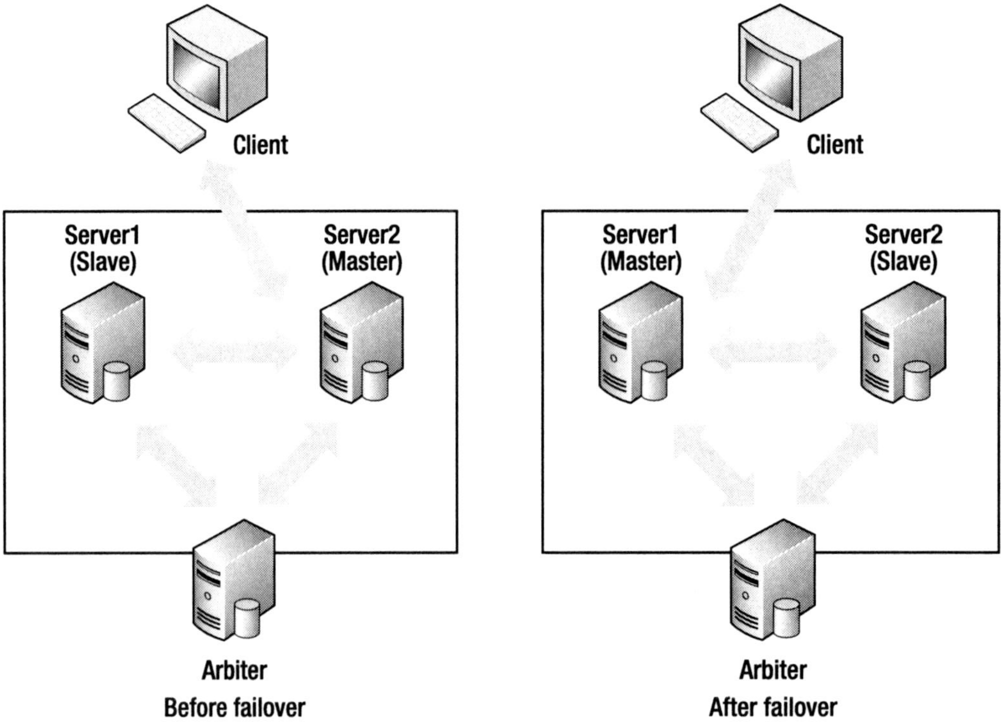


*Figure 11–6. The effect of a failover in a replica pair*

## Connecting Your Application to a Replica Pair

Failing over your replica pair servers is only one problem you must solve when creating a high availability cluster. To make this approach useful, your application must be able to switch seamlessly between the two when the flip occurs. Your application also needs to know which of the two servers is the active master server at all times, so it can direct all of its updates to that instance.

All of the MongoDB language drivers include the ability to make connections to a replica pair, as well as the ability to flip connections back and forth to the correct server. The following snippet shows how to set up a replica pair connection using PHP; the principles are the same in all of the other supported languages:

```
<?php
$m = new Mongo("mongodb://localhost:27017,localhost:27018");
?>
```

A connection that you establish in this fashion, with the URLs of both replica pair members, will track the status of the pair and ensure that commands and updates are sent to the correct server.

## Resolving Server Disputes with an Arbiter

A replica pair normally consists of only two servers, the two halves of the pair. However, some circumstances may require that you add a third server to the mix to resolve disputes between the two servers about which one should be the master and which should be the slave.

Assume that you have a large installation, or one that is physically distributed over a wide area, where each half of the pair is hosted in a different location, maybe one on the east coast and the other on the west coast. It is possible for the network path between the two servers to become disrupted or broken, so that the machines can no longer see each other. In this case, each server will assume that the other has failed, and both will attempt to assume the role of master.

If your application can still see both machines, then it will be presented with the confusing situation where both halves of the replica pair claim to be the master server. In this case, you can place a third server at the same location at which your application is hosted. This server will have the same ability to see the two servers that your app does, and will arbitrate these disputes to ensure that order is preserved. This type of machine is called an *arbiter*. A good place to install arbiters may be on the application's web servers, as they will have the same viewpoint of the two halves of the replica pair that your application has. It is just a small mongod instance running on the same servers, and it will consume virtually no memory, disk space, or processing capacity, and will only be needed when a negotiation occurs. No special configuration of the arbiter is required.

Configuring an arbiter is as simple as using mongod's `--arbiter` option:

```
--arbiter <ip or hostname>
```

Placing this option in the startup command line or configuration file of each of the servers in your replica pair enables you to instruct them to defer to the arbiter machine to cast the deciding vote on which machine should play which role. The arbiter server does not need to be running a full dataset, nor is it involved in any part of the replication process, other than to act as an unbiased observer to help iron out disputes between the two replica pair servers.

Figure 11–7 illustrates a scenario where replication has been enacted across a private link between two machines and this connection which has been disrupted, or *partitioned* in network speak. The arbiter server can still see both servers and maintains order.

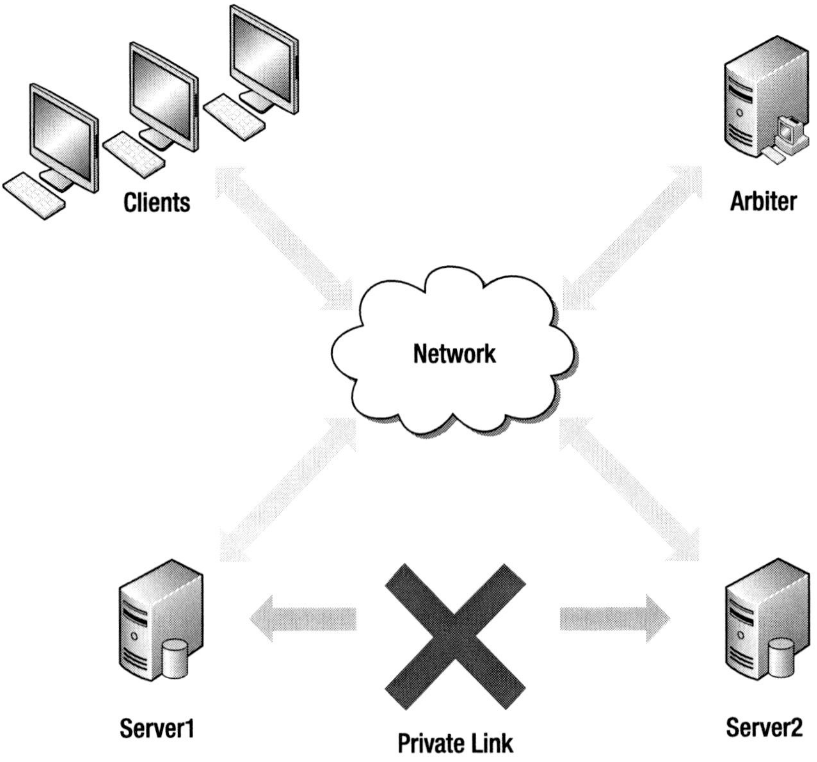


*Figure 11–7. Using an arbiter*

# Implementing Advanced Clustering with Replica Sets

*Replica sets* are a far more sophisticated and flexible version of the replica pair concept. Whereas replica pairs are limited to only two participants in the cluster, replica sets can have any number of participants.

---

■ **Note** Replica sets will be available in MongoDB 1.6.x and later. This feature will replace replica pairs as the primary clustering technology in MongoDB. Replica sets extend considerably the range of topologies that MongoDB can support, as well as the number of servers that can be aggregated together.

---

In this section, you will learn how to set up a simple replica set configuration. You will also learn how to add and remove members from the cluster. Like replica pairs, replica sets feature the concept of a single master server. In replica sets, this master server is called the *primary*, while the multiple slave servers are called *secondary* servers (see Figure 11–8).

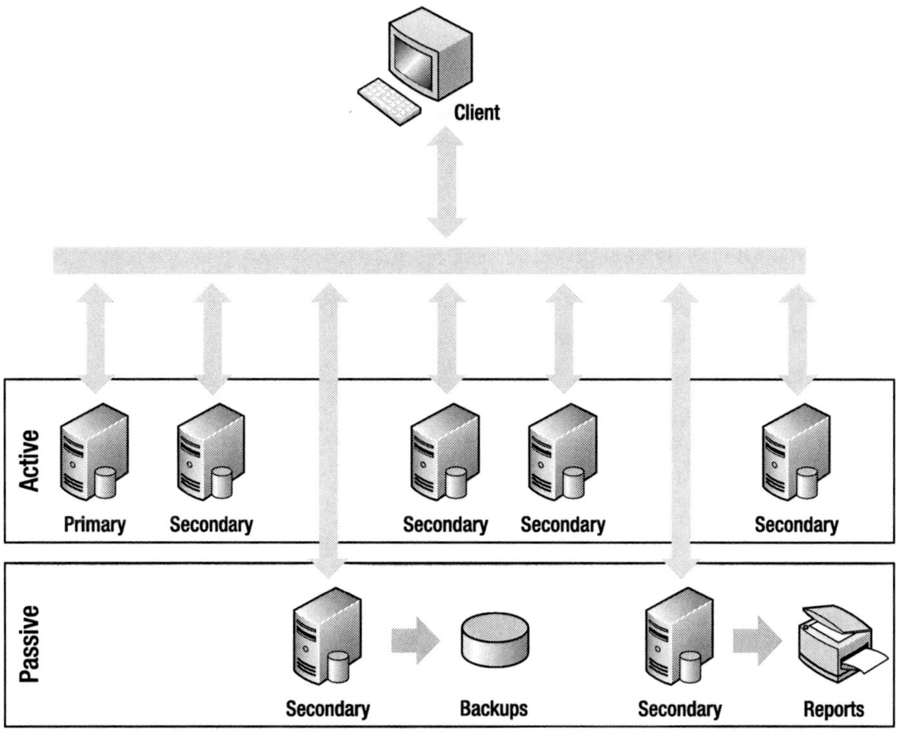


*Figure 11–8. A cluster implemented with a replica set*

The characteristics of this model are detailed in Table 11–7.

*Table 11–7. The Characteristics of a Replica Set*

| Property | Description |
| --- | --- |
| Number of masters | Single, dynamic, role will switch on failure |
| Number of slaves | Multiple, dynamic, role will switch on failure, supports mixed fixed and dynamic slaves |
| Failover Mode | Automatic |

Replica sets also feature the concept of *active* and *passive* members. Passive secondary servers don't participate in elections for a new primary when the current primary becomes unavailable; instead, they serve the same purpose as fixed slaves, and they can be used as reporting or backup datasets.

Member servers of replica sets do not need to be designated as set members on startup. Instead, configuration is done through server-level commands that are sent through the normal server interface.

This makes it easier to create configuration management tools that allow dynamic configuration and management of clusters of machines.

Note that the vocabulary for describing servers changes with replica sets; instead of master/slave servers, you now have primary/secondary servers, and the secondary servers can have either active or passive status. This change of vocabulary was necessary to reflect the more dynamic nature of replica sets; however, you will still find some vestiges of the master/slave vocabulary creeping back in with references to `isMaster()` tests, and *master* status.

In the upcoming sections, you will learn how to accomplish the following:

1. Create a replica set.
2. Create a working example of a replica set.
3. Add a server to a replica set.
4. Inspect and perform operations on a replica set.
5. Configure individual members of a replica set.
6. Connect to a replica set from your application.
7. Use the web interface to inspect the status of your replica set.

# Creating a Replica Set

The best way to learn how to create a replica set is by looking at an example. In the example that follows, you will create a replica set called testset. This set will have three members (two active and one passive). Table 11–8 lists the members of this set.

***Table 11–8.** Configuring the Replica Set*

| Service | Daemon | Address | Dbpath |
|---|---|---|---|
| Active Member 1 | mongod | `[hostname]:27021` | `/db/active1/data` |
| Active Member 2 | mongod | `[hostname]:27022` | `/db/active2/data` |
| Passive Member 1 | mongod | `[hostname]:27023` | `/db/passive1/data` |

Unfortunately, the replica set system won't allow you to use localhost or port 127.0.0.1, as you have in this chapter's previous examples. This locking out of local addresses is intended to stop people from misconfiguring clusters that run on multiple machines. All machines in a replica set cluster must be accessible to each other for the replication to work properly, and using a local address could result in inaccessible hosts, unless all components are running on the same host.

To get around this problem, you have to use the hostname of your machine; you can find this by using the `hostname` command, as in the following example:

```
$hostname
testlaptop.local
```

## Getting a Replica Set Member Up and Running

In the examples that follow, substitute the term "[hostname]" with whatever value is returned by running the hostname command on your own system.

The first step is to get the first active member up and running. To do so, open a terminal window and type the following:

```
$sudo mkdir -p /db/active1/data
$sudo mongod --dbpath /db/active1/data --port 27021
      --replSet testset/[hostname]:27022 --rest
```

The --replSet option tells the instance the name of the replica set it is joining, as well as the name of at least one other member of the set. This is the first member of the replica set, so you can give it the address of any other member, even if that member has not been started up yet. Only one member address is required, but you can also provide the names of other members by separating their addresses with commas, as shown in the following example:

```
$sudo mongod --dbpath /db/active1/data --port 27021
      --replSet
        testset/[hostname]:27022,[hostname]:27023  --rest
```

To keep things simple, this example will rely on only one address. The next step is to get the other members up and running. Do so by opening two more terminal windows, and then type the following into the first window to get the second member up and running:

```
$sudo mkdir -p /db/active2/data
$sudo mongod --dbpath /db/active2/data --port 27022
      --replSet testset/[hostname]:27021  --rest
```

Next, type this into the second window to get the final (passive) member up and running:

```
$sudo mkdir -p /db/passive1/data
$sudo mongod --dbpath /db/passive1/data --port 27023
      --replSet testset/[hostname]:27021  --rest
```

The --rest option in the preceding examples activates a rest interface on port+1000 (i.e., for port 27021, the rest interface is available on port 28021). This approach enables you to use the web interface to inspect the status of your replica set, as you'll see later in this chapter.

At this point, you have three server instances up and running and communicating with each other; however, you do not quite have your replica set running because you haven't yet initialized the replica set and instructed each member about its role and responsibilities.

To do that, you need to attach to one of the servers and initialize the replica set. The following code selects the first server to attach to:

```
$mongo [hostname]:27021
>use admin
```

Next, you need to set up a configuration data structure that lists all the servers and their respective roles:

```
> cfg = {
    _id: 'testset',
    members: [
        { _id: 0, host: '[hostname]:27021' },
        { _id: 1, host: '[hostname]:27022' },
        { _id: 2, host: '[hostname]:27023', priority: 0 }
        ]
    }
```

You've configured the structure of the replica set; notice the use of the "priority 0" in the configuration structure to specify that the passive member is not to be considered as a possible candidate for promotion to the primary role: next, you need to issue the command to initialize the replica set:

```
> rs.initiate(cfg)
{
    "info" : "Config now saved locally.  Should come online in about a minute.",
    "ok" : 1
}
```

Finally, you should check the status of the replica set to determine whether it has been set up correctly:

```
>rs.status()
{
    "set" : "testset",
    "date" : "Mon Jul 26 2010 01:57:06 GMT+0800 (PHT)",
    "myState" : 1,
    "members" : [
        {
            "name" : "[hostname]:27021",
            "self" : true,
            "errmsg" : ""
        },
        {
            "name" : "[hostname]:27023",
            "health" : 1,
            "uptime" : 1562,
            "lastHeartbeat" : "Mon Jul 26 2010 01:57:04 GMT+0800 (PHT)",
            "errmsg" : "initial sync done"
        },
        {
            "name" : "[hostname]:27022",
            "health" : 1,
            "uptime" : 1562,
            "lastHeartbeat" : "Mon Jul 26 2010 01:57:04 GMT+0800 (PHT)",
            "errmsg" : "initial sync done"
        }
    ],
    "ok" : 1
}
```

The output in the preceding example indicates that all is OK: you've successfully configured and set up your replica set. Remember that you should use the name of your own machine in place of `[hostname]` because neither "localhost" nor "127.0.0.1" will work.

## Adding a Server to a Replica Set

As your site grows in size, you may want to increase the number of MongoDB instances in your existing replica sets. Fortunately, this is easy to do. The next example will show you how to add a third active set member to replica set.

Begin by creating the MongoDB instance:

```
$sudo mkdir -p /db/active3/data
$sudo mongod --port 27024 --dbpath /db/active3/data --replSet testset/[hostname]:27021 --rest
```

Moving on, you need to add the new server to the replica set. This requires that you connect to the primary server instance with the mongo console, as in the following example:

```
$mongo [hostname]:27021
>use admin
>rs.add("[hostname]:27024")
{ "ok": 1}
```

# Managing Replica Sets

MongoDB provides a number of commands for managing the configuration and status of a replica set. Table 11–9 shows the available commands that you can use to create, manipulate, and inspect the state of a cluster in a replica set.

*Table 11–9. Commands for Manipulating and Inspecting Replica Sets*

| Command | Description |
|---|---|
| `rs.help()` | Returns the list of the commands in this table. |
| `rs.status()` | Returns information about the current state of the replica set. This command lists each member server, along with information about its status, including the last time it was contacted. This call can be used to provide a simple health check of the entire cluster. |
| `rs.initiate()` | Initializes a replica set using default parameters. This call is useful if you want to use the `rs.add(..)` command to add all the members individually, rather than supplying the entire configuration set all at once with a configuration description. |
| `rs.initiate(replSetcfg)` | Initializes a replica set using a configuration description. |
| `rs.add("host:port")` | Adds a member server to the replica set with a simple string that provides hostname and (optionally) a specific port. |
| `rs.add(membercfg)` | Adds a member server to the replica set using a configuration description. You must use this method if you want to specify specific attributes (e.g., a priority for the new member server). |
| `rs.addArbiter("host:port")` | Adds a new member server to operate as an arbiter. The member does not need to have been started with a `--replSet` option; any mongod instance running on any reachable machine can perform this task. Take care that this server is reachable by all members of the replica set. |
| `rs.stepDown()` | Makes the primary server relinquish its role and forces the election of a new primary server in the cluster when you run this command against the primary member of a replica set. Note that only active secondary servers are available as candidates for becoming the new primary server. |

| Command | Description |
| --- | --- |
| `rs.conf()` | Redisplays the configuration structure of the current replica set. This command is useful for obtaining a configuration structure for a replica set. This configuration structure can be modified and then supplied to `rs.initiate()` again to change the structure's configuration. This technique provides the only supported way to remove a member server from a replica set; there is currently no direct method available for doing that. |
| `db.isMaster()` | This function is not specific to replica sets; rather, it is a general replication support function that allows an application or driver to determine whether a particular connected instance is the master/primary server in a replication topology. |

The following sections will take a closer look at some of the more commonly used commands listed in Table 11–9, providing additional details about what they do and how you use them.

## Inspecting an Instance's Status with rs.status()

The `rs.status()` command is probably the most common command that you will use when working with replica sets. It allows you to inspect the status of the instance you are currently attached to, including its role in the replica set:

```
>rs.status()
{
    "set" : "testset",
    "date" : "Sat Jul 31 2010 12:17:46 GMT+0800 (PHT)",
    "myState" : 1,
    "members" : [
        {
            "name" : "[hostname]:27021",
            "self" : true,
            "errmsg" : ""
        },
        {
            "name" : "[hostname]:27023",
            "health" : 1,
            "uptime" : 78,
            "lastHeartbeat" : "Sat Jul 31 2010 12:17:44 GMT+0800 (PHT)",
            "errmsg" : "initial sync done"
        },
        {
            "name" : "[hostname]:27022",
            "health" : 1,
            "uptime" : 82,
            "lastHeartbeat" : "Sat Jul 31 2010 12:17:44 GMT+0800 (PHT)",
            "errmsg" : "initial sync done"
        }
    ],
    "ok" : 1
}
```

The myState field shown in the preceding example has the values shown in Table 11–10. These values indicate the status of any member you run the rs.status() command against.

*Table 11–10. Values for the myState Field*

| myState | Description |
|---|---|
| 0 | Member is starting up and is in phase 1. |
| 1 | Member is operating as a primary (master) server. |
| 2 | Member is operating as a secondary server. |
| 3 | Member is recovering; the sysadmin has restarted the member server in recovery mode after a possible crash or other data issue. |
| 4 | Member has encountered a Fatal Error; the errMsg field in the members array for this server should show more details about the problem. |
| 5 | Member is starting up and has reached phase 2. |
| 6 | Member is in an unknown state; this could indicate a misconfigured replica set, where some servers are not reachable by all other members. |
| 7 | Member is operating as an arbiter. |
| 8 | Member is down or otherwise unreachable. The lastheartbeat timestamp in the member array associated with this server should provide the date/time that the server was last seen alive. |

In the preceding example, the rs.status() command is run against the primary server member. The information returned for this command shows that the primary server is operating with a myState value of 1; in other words, the "Member is operating as a primary (master)."

## Forcing a New Election with rs.stepDown()

You can use the rs.stepDown() command to force a primary server to stand down; the command also forces the election of a new primary server. This command is useful in the following situations:

- You would like to take the server hosting the primary instance offline, whether to investigate the server or to implement hardware upgrades or maintenance.
- You would like to run a diagnostic process against the data structures.
- You would like to simulate the effect of a primary failure and force your cluster to fail over, enabling you to test how your application responds to such an event.

The following example shows the output returned if you run the rs.stepDown() command against the testset replica set:

```
> rs.stepDown()
{ "ok" : 1 }
> rs.status()
{
    "set" : "testset",
    "date" : "Sat Jul 31 2010 12:57:14 GMT+0800 (PHT)",
    "myState" : 2,
    "members" : [
        {
            "name" : "[hostname]:27021",
            "self" : true,
            "errmsg" : ""
        },
        {
            "name" : "[hostname]:27023",
            "health" : 1,
            "uptime" : 2446,
            "lastHeartbeat" : "Sat Jul 31 2010 12:57:13 GMT+0800 (PHT)",
            "errmsg" : "initial sync done"
        },
        {
            "name" : "[hostname]:27022",
            "health" : 1,
            "uptime" : 2450,
            "lastHeartbeat" : "Sat Jul 31 2010 12:57:13 GMT+0800 (PHT)",
            "errmsg" : ""
        }
    ],
    "ok" : 1
}
```

In the preceding example, you run the `rs.stepDown()` command against the primary server. The output of the `rs.status()` command shows that the server now has a `myState` value of `2`: "Member is operating as secondary."

## Determining If a Member is the Primary Server

The `db.isMaster()` command isn't strictly a replica set command. Nevertheless, this command is extremely useful because it allows an application to test whether it is connected to a master/primary server:

```
>db.isMaster()
{
    "ismaster" : false,
    "secondary" : true,
    "msg" : "",
    "hosts" : [
        "[hostname]:27021",
        "[hostname]:27022"
    ],
    "passives" : [
        "[hostname]:27023"
    ],
```

```
    "primary" : "[hostname]",
    "ok" : 1
}
```

If you run isMaster() against your testset replica set cluster at this point, it shows that the server you have run it against is not a master/primary server ("ismaster" == false). If the server instance you run this command against is a member of a replica set, the command will also return a map of the known server instances in the set, including the roles of the individual servers in that set.

# Configuring the Options for Replica Set Members

The replica set functionality ships with a number of options you can use to control the behavior of a replica set's members. When you run the rs.initiate(replSetcfg) or rs.add(membercfg) options, you have to supply a configuration structure that describes the characteristics of a replica set's members:

```
{
  _id : <setname>,

  members: [
    {
      _id : <ordinal>,
      host : <hostname[:port]>,
      [, priority: <priority>]
      [, arbiterOnly : true]
      [, votes : <n>]
    }
    , ...
  ],

  settings: {
    [heartbeatSleep : <seconds>]
    [, heartbeatTimeout : <seconds>]
    [, heartbeatConnRetries : <n>]
    [, getLastErrorDefaults: <lasterrdefaults>]
  }
}
```

For rs.initiate(), you should supply the full configuration structure, as shown in the preceding example. The topmost level of the configuration structure itself includes three levels: _id, members, and settings. The _id is the name of the replica set, as supplied with the --replSet command-line option when you create the replica set members. The members array consists of a set of structures that describe each member of the set; this is the member structure that you supply to the rs.add() command when adding an individual server to the set. Finally, the settings array contains options that apply to the entire replica set.

## Organization of the Members Structure

The members structure contains all the entries required to configure each of the member instances of the replica set; you can see all of these entries listed in Table 11–11.

*Table 11–11. Configuring Member Server Properties*

| Option | Description |
| --- | --- |
| members.$._id | (Mandatory) Integer: This element specifies the ordinal position of the member structure in the member array. Possible values for this element include integers greater than or equal to 0. This value enables you to address specific member structures, so you can perform add, remove, and overwrite operations. |
| members.$.host | (Mandatory) String: This element specifies the name of the server in the form host:port; note that the host portion *cannot* be localhost or 127.0.0.1. |
| members.$.priority | (Optional) Float: The element represents the *weight* assigned to the server when elections for a new primary server are conducted. If the primary server becomes unavailable, then a secondary server will be promoted based on this value. Any secondary server with a non-zero value is considered to be active and eligible to become a primary server. Thus, setting this value to zero forces the secondary to become passive. If multiple secondary servers share equal priority, then a vote will be taken, and an arbiter (if configured) may be called upon to resolve any deadlocks. The default value for this element is 1.0, unless you specify otherwise. |
| members.$.arbiterOnly | (Optional) Boolean: This member operates as an arbiter for electing new primary servers. It is not involved in any other function of the replica set, and it does not need to have been started with a --replSet command-line option. Any running mongod process in your system can perform this task. The default value of this element is false. |
| members.$.votes | (Optional) Integer: This element specifies the number of votes that this instance can cast to elect other instances as a primary server; the default value of this element is 1. |

## Exploring the Options Available in the Settings Structure

Table 11–12 lists the replica set properties available in the Settings structure. These settings are applied globally to the entire replica set; you use these properties to configure how replica set members communicate with each other.

*Table 11–12. Inter-server Communication Properties for the Settings Structure*

| Option | Description |
|---|---|
| settings.heartbeatSleep | (Optional) Integer: This element specifies how often the members of the replica set should announce themselves to each other, and its value is expressed in milliseconds. If not specified, this element has a default value of 2000 (2 seconds). |
| settings.heartbeatTimeout | (Optional) Integer: This element specifies the amount of time that the members of a replica set should wait after not hearing from a specific member before assuming it is unavailable. This value is expressed in milliseconds; if not specified, this element has a default value of 10000 (10 seconds). |
| Settings.heartbeatConnRetries | (Optional) Integer: The element specifies the number of attempts a member should make to reach another member before assuming it is down. If not specified, this element has a default value of 3. |

# Determining the Status of Replica Sets

Replica sets are only becoming available as a stable implementation in the very latest version of MongoDB (1.6.x) at the time of writing.

10gen (the company that produces MongoDB) is very proactive in rolling out enhancements, so it is a good idea to peruse the online documentation to see what has changed since this book's publication. For up-to-the-minute information on replica sets, visit this page on the MongoDB site:

www.mongodb.org/display/DOCS/Replica+Sets.

You should keep in mind the fact that, from version 1.6.x onwards, replica sets will become the preferred mechanism for setting up replicated clusters of machines, and the simpler "Replica Pairs" will become deprecated.

# Connecting to a Replica Set from Your Application

Connecting to a replica set from PHP is similar to connecting to a single MongoDB instance. The only difference is that it can provide either a single replica set instance address or a list of replica set members; the connection library will work out which server is the primary server and direct queries to that machine, even if the primary server is not one of the members that you provide. The following example shows how to connect to a replica set from a PHP application:

```
<?php

$m = new Mongo("mongodb://localhost:27021,
        localhost:27022", array("replicaSet" => true));
...
?>
```

## Viewing Replica Set Status with the Web Interface

MongoDB maintains a web-based console for viewing the status of your system. For our previous example, you can access this console by opening the URL `http://localhost:28021` with your web browser. The port number of the web interface is set by default to port *n*+1000, where *n* is the port number of your instance. So, assuming your primary instance is on port 27021, as in this chapter's example, its web interface can be found on port 28021. If you open this interface in your web browser, you will see a link to the status of the replica set at the top of the page (see Figure 11–9).

***Figure 11–9.** Viewing the status of the replica set in a browser*

Clicking the `Replica set status` link will take you to the `Replica Set` dashboard shown in Figure 11–10.

***Figure 11–10.** The replica set dashboard in the MongoDB web interface*

# Summary

MongoDB provides a rich set of tools for implementing a wide range of clustering and replication topologies. In this chapter, you learned about many of these tools, including some of the reasons and motivations for using them. You also learned how to set up a number of different replication topologies, from the simplest replication configuration all the way through to the latest, most advanced replica set capability introduced in the most recent version of MongoDB. Additionally, you learned how to inspect the status of replication systems using both the command-line tools and the built-in web interface.

Please take the time required to evaluate each of the topologies described in this chapter to make sure you choose the one best suited to your particular needs before attempting to use any of them in a production environment. It is incredibly easy to use MongoDB to create test beds on a single machine; therefore, you are strongly encouraged to experiment with each method to make sure that you fully understand the benefits and limitations of each approach, including how it will perform with your particular data and application.

CHAPTER 12

# Sharding

Whether you're building the next Facebook or just a simple database application, you will probably need to scale your app up at some point if it's successful. If you don't want to be continually replacing your hardware, then you will want to use a technique that allows you to add capacity incrementally to your system, as you need it. *Sharding* is a technique that allows you to spread your data across multiple machines, yet does so in a way that mimics an app hitting a single database.

Ideally suited for the new generation of cloud-based computing platforms, sharding as implemented by MongoDB is perfect for dynamic, load-sensitive automatic scaling, where you ramp up your capacity as you need it and turn it down when you don't.

This chapter will walk you through implementing sharding in MongoDB.

## Exploring the Need for Sharding

When the World Wide Web was just getting under way, the number of sites, users, and the amount of information available online was low. The Web consisted of a few thousand sites and a population of only tens or perhaps hundreds of thousands of users predominantly centered on the academic and research communities. In those early days, data tended to be simple: hand-maintained HTML documents connected together by hyperlinks. The original design objective of the protocols that make up the Web was to provide a means of creating navigable references to documents stored on different servers around the Internet.

Even current big brand names such as Yahoo had only a minuscule presence on the Web compared to its offerings today. The Yahoo directory that comprised the original product around which the company was formed was little more than a network of hand-edited links to popular sites. These links were maintained by a small but enthusiastic band of people called *the surfers*. Each page in the Yahoo directory was a simple HTML document stored in a tree of filesystem directories and maintained using a simple text editor.

But as the size of the net started to explode—and the number of sites and visitors started its near-vertical climb upwards—the sheer volume of resources available forced the early Web pioneers to move away from simple documents to more complex dynamic page generation from separate data stores.

Search engines started to spider the Web and pull together databases of links that today number in the hundreds of billions of links and tens of billions of stored pages.

These developments prompted the movement to datasets managed and maintained by evolving content management systems that were stored mainly in databases for easier access.

At the same time, new kinds of services evolved that stored more than just documents and link sets. For example, audio, video, events, and all kinds of other data started to make its way into these huge datastores. This is often described as the "industrialization of data"—and in many ways it shares parallels with the evolution of the industrial revolution centered on manufacturing during the 19th century.

Eventually, every successful company on the Web faces the problem of how to access the data stored in these mammoth databases. They find that there are only so many queries per second that can be handled with a single database server, and network interfaces and disk drives can only transfer so many megabytes per second to and from the web servers. Companies that provide web-based services can quickly find themselves exceeding the performance of a single server, network, or drive array. In such cases, they are compelled to divide and distribute their massive collections of data. The usual solution is to *partition* these mammoth chunks of data into smaller pieces that can be managed more reliably and quickly. At the same time, these companies need to maintain the ability to perform operations across the entire breadth of the data held in their large clusters of machines.

Replication, which you learned about in some detail in Chapter 11, can be an effective tool for overcoming some of these scaling issues, enabling you to create multiple copies of your data in multiple servers. This enables you to spread out your server load across more machines.

Before long, however, you run headlong into another problem, where the size of the individual tables or collections that make up your data set grow so large that they exceed the capacity of a single database system to manage them effectively. For example, Flickr announced that on October 12th 2009 it had received its 4 *billionth* photo, and the site is now well on its way to crossing the 10 billion photos mark.

Attempting to store the details of 10 billion photos in one table is not feasible, so Flickr looked at ways of distributing that set of records across a large number of database servers. The solution adopted by Flickr serves as one of the better-documented (and publicized) implementations of sharding in the real world.

# Partitioning Horizontal and Vertical Data

Data partitioning is the mechanism of splitting data across multiple independent datastores. Those datastores can be co-resident (on the same system) or remote (on separate systems). The motivation for co-resident partitioning is to reduce the size of individual indices and reduce the amount of I/O that is needed to update records. The motivation for remote partitioning is to increase the bandwidth of access to data, by having more network interfaces and disc data I/O channels available.

## Partitioning Data Vertically

In the traditional view of databases, data is stored in rows and columns. Vertical partitioning consists of breaking up a record on column boundaries and storing the parts in separate tables or collections. It can be argued that a relational database design that uses joined tables with a one-to-one relationship is a form of co-resident vertical data partitioning.

MongoDB, however, does not lend itself to this form of partitioning because the structure of its records (documents) does not fit the nice and tidy row and column model. Therefore, there are few opportunities to cleanly separate a row based on its column boundaries. MongoDB also promotes the use of *embedded* documents, and it does not directly support the ability to *join* associated collections together.

## Partitioning Data Horizontally

Horizontal partitioning is where all the action is when using MongoDB, and *sharding* is the common term for a popular form of horizontal partitioning. Sharding allows you to split a collection across multiple servers to improve performance in a collection that has a large number of documents in it.

A simple example of sharding occurs when a collection of user records is divided across a set of servers, so that all the records for people with last names that begin with the letters A–G are on one server, H–M are on another, and so on. The rule that splits the data is known as the *sharding key function*, or the *data hashing function*.

In simple terms, sharding allows you to treat the *cloud* of shards as through it were a single collection, and an application does not need to be aware that the data is distributed across multiple machines. Traditional sharding implementations require the application to be actively involved in determining which server a particular document is stored on, so it can route its requests properly. Traditionally, there is a library bound to the application, and this library is responsible for storing and querying data in sharded data sets.

MongoDB is virtually unique in its support for *auto-sharding*, where the database server manages the splitting of the data and the routing of requests to the required shard server. If a query requires data from multiple *shards*, then MongoDB will manage the process of merging the data obtained from each shard back into a single cursor.

This feature, more than any other, is what earns MongoDB its stripes as a *cloud* or web-oriented database.

# Analyzing a Simple Sharding Scenario

Let's assume you want to implement a simple sharding solution for a fictitious Gaelic social network. Figure 12–1 shows a simplified representation of how this application could be sharded.

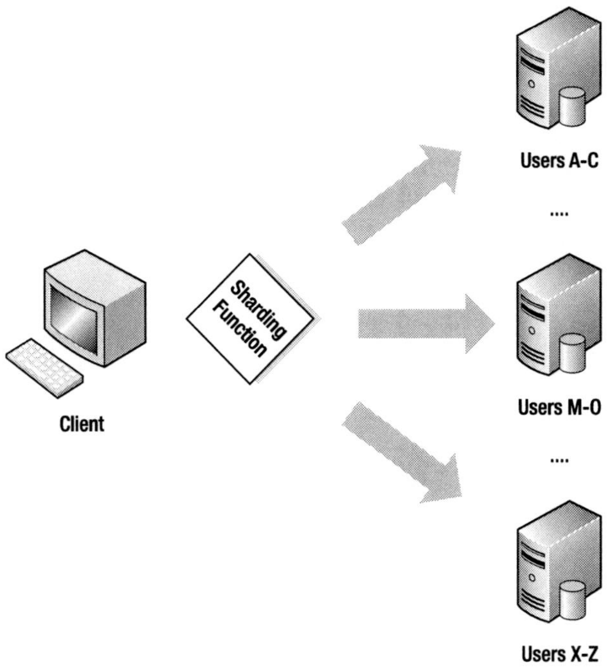


***Figure 12–1.*** *Simple sharding of a User collection*

There are a number of problems with this simplified view of our application. Let's look at the most obvious ones.

First, if your Gaelic network is targeted at the Irish and Scottish communities around the world, then the database will have a large number of names that start with *Mac* and *Mc* (e.g., MacDonald, McDougal, and so on) for the Scottish population and *O'* (e.g., O'Reilly, O'Conner, and so on) for the Irish population. Thus, using the simple sharding key function based on the first letter of the last name will place an undue number of user records on the shard that supports the letter range "M–O." Similarly, the shard that supports the letter range "X–Z" will perform very little work at all.

An important characteristic of a sharding system is that it must ensure that the data is spread evenly across the available set of shard servers. This prevents *hotspots* from developing that can affect the overall performance of the cluster. Let's call this *Requirement 1: The ability to distribute data evenly across all shards.*

Another thing to keep in mind: when you split your dataset across multiple servers, you effectively increase your dataset's vulnerability to hardware failure. That is, you increase the chance that a single server failure will affect the availability of your data as you add servers. Again, an important characteristic of a reliable sharding system is that—like a RAID system commonly used with disk drives—it stores each piece of data on more than one server, and it can tolerate individual shard servers becoming unavailable. Let's call this *Requirement 2: The ability to store shard data in a fault-tolerant fashion.*

Finally, you want to make sure that you can add or remove servers from the set of shards without having to back up and restore the data and *redistribute* it across a smaller or larger set of shards. Further, you need to be able to do this without causing any downtime on the cluster. Let's call this *Requirement 3: The ability to add or remove shards while the system is running.*

The upcoming sections will cover how to address these requirements.

# Implementing Sharding with MongoDB

MongoDB uses a *proxy* mechanism to support sharding (see Figure 12–2); the provided mongos daemon acts as a *controller* for multiple *mongod*-based shard servers. Your application attaches to the mongos daemon as though it were a single MongoDB database server; thereafter, your application sends all of its commands (e.g., updates, queries, and deletes) to that mongos daemon.

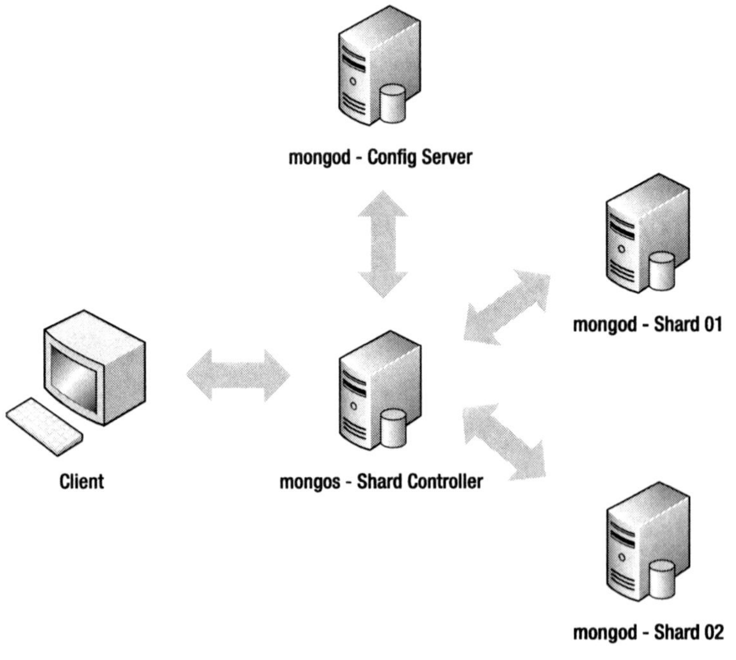


***Figure 12–2.*** *A simple sharding setup without redundancy*

The mongos daemon is responsible for managing which MongoDB server is sent the commands from your application, and this daemon will reissue queries that cross multiple shards to multiple servers and aggregate the results together.

MongoDB implements sharding at the collection level, not the database level. In many systems, only one or two collections may grow to the point where sharding is required. Thus, sharding should be used judiciously; you don't want to impose the overhead of managing the distribution of data for smaller collections if you don't need to.

Let's return to the fictitious Gaelic social network example. In this application, the `user` collection contains details about its users and their profiles. This collection is likely to grow to the point where it needs to be sharded. However, other collections such as `events`, `countries`, and `states` are unlikely to ever become so large that sharding would provide any benefit.

The sharding system uses a sharding key function to map data into *chunks*, which are blocks of storage containing documents (see Chapter 5 for more information on chunks). Each chunk stores documents with a particular continuous range of sharding key values; these values enable the mongos controller to quickly find a chunk that contains a document it needs to work on. MongoDB's sharding system then stores this chunk on an available shard store; the config servers keep track of which chunk is stored on which shard server. This is an important feature of the implementation because it allows you to add and remove shards from a cluster without having to back up and restore the data.

When you add a new shard to the cluster, the system will redistribute its chunks across the new set of servers in order to improve performance. Similarly, when you remove a shard, the sharding controller will *drain* the chunks out of the shard being taken offline and redistribute them to the remaining shard servers.

A sharding setup for MongoDB also needs a place to store the configuration of its shards, as well as a place to store information about each shard server in the cluster. To support this, a MongoDB server called a *config server* is required; this server instance is a normal mongod server running in a special role. As explained above, the config servers also act as directories that allow the location of each chunk to be determined

At first glance, it appears that implementing a solution that relies on sharding requires a lot of servers! However, similar to what you saw in Chapter 11's coverage of replication, you can co-host multiple instances of each of the different services required to create a sharding setup on a relatively small number of physical servers. Figure 12–3 shows a fully redundant sharding system that uses replica sets for the shard storage and the config servers, as well as a set of mongos daemons to manage the cluster. It also shows how those services can be condensed to run on just three physical servers.

Carefully placing the shard storage instances so that they are correctly distributed among the physical servers enables you to ensure that your system can tolerate the failure of one or more servers in your cluster. This mirrors the approach used by RAID disk controllers to distribute data across multiple drives in stripes, enabling RAID configurations to recover from a failed drive.

---

■ **Note** If you don't supply a sharding key, then MongoDB will automatically use the `_id` field to distribute documents among your database's shards; however, this field may not provide the optimal data value to use to shard your data.

---

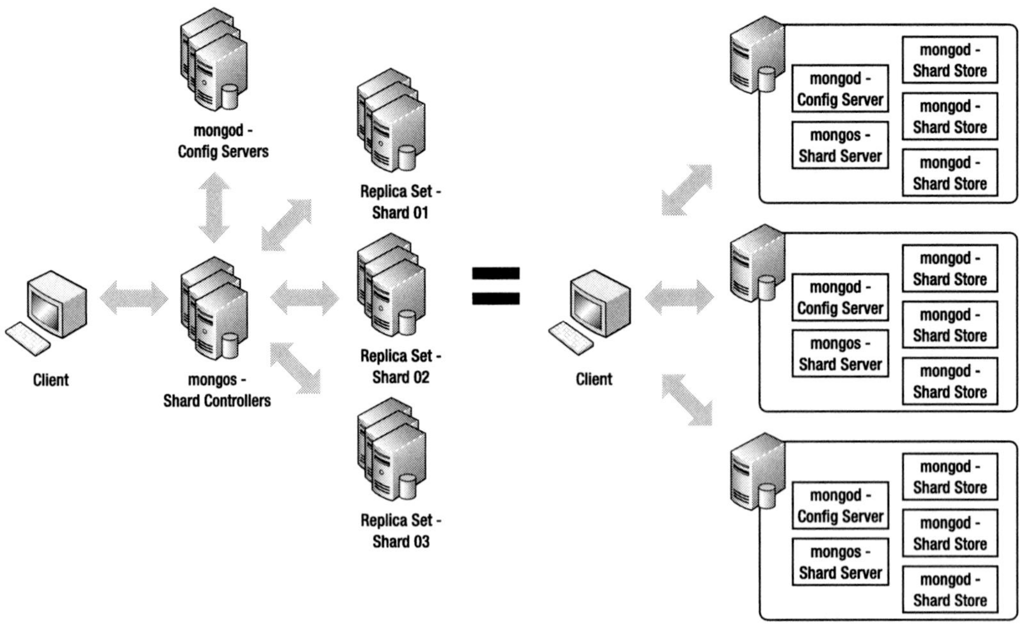


***Figure 12–3.*** *A redundant sharding configuration*

# Setting Up a Sharding Configuration

To use sharding effectively, it's important that you understand how it works. The next example will walk you through how to set up a test configuration on a single machine. You will configure this example like the simple sharding system shown in Figure 12–2, with one difference: this example will keep things simple by using only two shards. Finally, you will learn how to create a sharded collection and a simple PHP test program that demonstrates how to use this collection.

In this test configuration, you will use the services listed in Table 12–1.

***Table 12–1.*** *Server Instances in the Test Configuration*

| Service | Daemon | Port | Dbpath |
|---|---|---|---|
| Shard Controller | mongos | 27021 | N/A |
| Config Server | mongod | 27022 | `/db/config/data` |
| Shard0 | mongod | 27023 | `/db/shard1/data` |
| Shard1 | mongod | 27024 | `/db/shard2/data` |

Let's begin by setting up the configuration server. Do so by opening a new terminal window and typing the following code.

```
$sudo mkdir -p /db/config/data
$sudo mongod --port 27022 --dbpath /db/config/data --configsvr
```

Be sure to leave your terminal window open once you have the config server up and running. Next, you need to set up the shard controller (mongos). To do so, open a new terminal window and type the following:

```
$sudo mongos --configdb localhost:27022 --port 27021 --chunkSize 1
```

This brings up the shard controller, which should announce that it's listening on port 27021. If you look at the terminal window for the config server, you should see that the shard server has connected to its config server and registered itself with it.

In this example, you set the chunk size to its smallest possible size of 1 MB. This is not a practical value for real-world systems because it means that the chunk storage is smaller than the maximum size of a document (4 MB). However, this is just a demonstration, and the small chunk size allows you to create a lot of chunks to exercise the sharding setup without also having to load a lot of data. By default, chunkSize is set to 128 MB unless otherwise specified.

Finally, you're ready to bring up the two shard servers. To do so, you will need two fresh terminal windows, one for each server. Type the following into one window to bring up the first server:

```
$sudo mkdir -p /db/shard0/data
$sudo mongod --port 27023 --dbpath /db/shard0/data --shardsvr
```

And type the following into the second window to bring up the second server:

```
$sudo mkdir -p /db/shard1/data
$sudo mongod --port 27024 --dbpath /db/shard1/data --shardsvr
```

You have your servers up and running. Next, you need to tell the sharding system where the shard servers are located. To do this, you need to connect to your shard controller (mongos). It's important to remember that, even though mongos is not a full MongoDB instance, it appears to be a full instance to your application. Therefore, you can just use the mongo command shell to attach to the shard controller and add your two shards, as shown in the following example:

```
$ mongo localhost:27021
> use admin
switched to db admin
> db.runCommand( { addshard : "localhost:27023", allowLocal : true } )
{ "added" : "localhost:27023", "ok" : 1 }
> db.runCommand( { addshard : "localhost:27024", allowLocal : true } )
{ "added" : "localhost:27024", "ok" : 1 }
```

Your two shard servers are now activated; next, you need to check the shards using the listshards command:

```
> db.runCommand({listshards:1})
{
    "shards" : [
        {
            "_id" : "shard0",
            "host" : "localhost:27023"
        },
        {
```

```
            "_id" : "shard1",
            "host" : "localhost:27024"
        }
    ],
    "ok" : 1
}
```

You now have a working sharded server; next, you will create a new database called testdb, and then activate a collection called testcollection inside this database. You will shard this collection, so you will give this collection an entry called testkey that you will use as the sharding function:

```
> testdb = db.getSisterDB("testdb")
testdb
> db.runCommand({ enablesharding: "testdb"})
{ "ok" : 1 }
> db.runCommand({ shardcollection : "testdb.testcollection", key : {testkey : 1}})
{ "collectionsharded" : "testdb.testcollection", "ok" : 1 }
```

Thus far, you have created a sharded cluster with two shard storage servers. You have also created a database on it with a sharded collection. A server without any data in it is of no use to anybody, so it's time to get some data into this collection, so you can see how the shards are distributed.

To do this, you will use a small PHP program to load the sharded collection with some data. The data you will load consists of a single field called testkey. This field contains a random number and a second field with a fixed chunk of text inside it (the purpose of this second field is to make sure you can create a reasonable number of chunks to shard). This collection serves as the main data table for a fictitious website called TextAndARandomNumber.com. The following code creates a PHP program that inserts data into your sharded server:

```
<?php
// Open a database connection to the mongos daemon
$mongo = new Mongo("localhost:27021");
// Select the test database
$db = $mongo->selectDB('testdb');
// Select the TestIndex collection
$collection = $db->testcollection;

for($i=0; $i < 100000 ; $i++){
        $data=array();
        $data['testkey'] = rand(1,100000);
        $data['testtext'] = "Because of the nature of MongoDB, many of the more "
                        . "traditional functions that a DB Administrator "
                        . "would perform are not required.  Creating new databases, "
                        . "collections and new fields on the server are no longer
necessary, "
                        . "as MongoDB will create these elements on-the-fly as you access
them."
                        . "Therefore, for the vast majority of cases managing databases
and "
                        . "schemas is not required.";
        $collection->insert($data);
}
```

This small program will connect to the shard controller (mongos) and insert 100,000 records with random testkeys and some **testtext** to pad out the documents. As mentioned previously, this sample text causes these documents to occupy a sufficient number of chunks to make using the Sharding mechanism feasible.

The following command runs the test program:

```
$php testshard.php
```

Once the program has finished running, you can connect to the mongos instance with the command shell and verify that the data has been stored:

```
$mongo localhost:27021
>use testdb
>db.testcollection.count()
100000
```

At this point, you can see that your server has stored 100,000 records. Now you need to connect to each shard and see how many items have been stored in `testdb.testcollection` for each shard. The following code enables you to connect to the first shard and see how many records are stored in it from the `testcollection` collection:

```
$mongo localhost:27023
>use testdb
>db.testcollection.count()
48875
```

And this code enables you to connect to the second shard and see how many records are stored in it from the `testcollection` collection:

```
$mongo localhost:27024
>use testdb
>db.testcollection.count()
51125
```

---

■ **Note** You may see different values for the number of documents in each shard, depending on when exactly you look at the individual shards. The mongos instance may initially place all the chunks on one shard, but over time it will *rebalance* the shard set to evenly distribute data among all the shards by moving chunks around. Thus, the number of records stored in a given shard may change from moment to moment. This satisfies "Requirement 1: The ability to distribute data evenly across all shards."

---

## Adding a New Shard to the Cluster

Let's assume business is really jumping at `TextAndARandomNumber.com`. To keep up with the demand, you decide to add a new shard server to the cluster to spread out the load a little more.

Adding a new shard is easy; all it requires is that you repeat the steps described previously. Begin by creating the new shard storage server and place it on port 27025, so it does not clash with your existing servers:

```
$ sudo mkdir -p /db/shard2/data
$ sudo mongod --port 27025 --dbpath /db/shard2/data --shardsvr
```

Next, you need to add the new shard server to the cluster. You do this by logging into the sharding controller (mongos), and then using the admin addshard command:

```
$mongo localhost:27021
>use admin
admin
>db.runCommand( { addshard : "localhost:27025", allowLocal : true } )
```

At this point, you can run the listshards command to verify that the shard has been added to the cluster. Doing so reveals that a new shard server (shard2) is now present in the shards array:

```
>db.runCommand({listshards:1})
{
    "shards" : [
{
                "_id" : "shard0",
                "host" : "localhost:27023"
        },
        {
                "_id" : "shard1",
                "host" : "localhost:27024"
        },
        {
                "_id" : "shard2",
                "host" : "localhost:27025"
        }

    ],
    "ok" : 1
}
```

If you log in to the new shard storage server you have created on port 27025 and look at testcollection, you will see something interesting:

```
$mongo localhost:27025
> use testdb
switched to db testdb
> show collections
system.indexes
testcollection
> db.testcollection.count()
4657
> db.testcollection.count()
4758
> db.testcollection.count()
6268
```

This shows that the number of items in the testcollection on your new shard2 storage server is slowly going up. What you are seeing is proof that the sharding system is rebalancing the data across the expanded cluster. Over time, the sharding system will migrate chunks from the shard0 and shard1 storage servers to create an even distribution of data across the three servers that make up the cluster. This process is automatic, and it will happen even if there is no new data being inserted into the testcollection collection. In this case, the mongos shard controller is moving chunks to the new server, and then registering them with the config server.

This is one of the factors to consider when choosing a chunk size. If your chunkSize value is very large, then you will get a less even distribution of data across your shards; conversely, the smaller your chunkSize value, the more even the distribution of your data will be.

# Removing a Shard from the Cluster

It was great while it lasted, but now assume that TextAndARandomNumber.com was a flash in the pan and its sizzle fizzled. After a few weeks of frenzied activity, the site's traffic started to fall off, so you had to start to look for ways to cut your running costs—in other words, that new shard server had to go!

In the next example, you will remove the shard server you added previously. To initiate this process, log in to the shard controller (mongos) and issue the removeShard command:

```
$ mongo localhost:27021
> use admin
switched to db admin
> db.runCommand({removeShard : "localhost:27025"})
{
    "msg" : "draining started successfully",
    "state" : "started",
    "shard" : "shard2",
    "ok" : 1
}
```

The removeShard command responds with a message indicating that the removal process has started. It also indicates that the shard controller (mongos) has begun relocating the chunks on the target shard server to the other shard servers in the cluster. This process is known as *draining* the shard.

You can check the progress of the draining process by reissuing the removeShard command. The response will tell you how many chunks and databases still need to be drained from the shard:

```
> db.runCommand({removeShard : "localhost:27025"})
{
    "msg" : "draining ongoing",
    "state" : "ongoing",
    "remaining" : {
        "chunks" : NumberLong( 12 ),
        "dbs" : NumberLong( 0 )
    },
    "ok" : 1
}
```

Finally, the removeShard process will terminate, and you will get a message indicating that the removal process is complete:

```
> db.runCommand({removeShard : "localhost:27025"})
{
    "msg" : "removeshard completed successfully",
    "state" : "completed",
    "shard" : "shard2",
    "ok" : 1
}
```

To verify that the removeShard command was successful, you can run listshards to confirm that the desired shard server has been removed from the cluster. For example, the following output shows that the shard2 server that you created previously is no longer listed in the shards array:

```
>db.runCommand({listshards:1})
{
    "shards" : [
        {
            "_id" : "shard0",
            "host" : "localhost:27023"
        },
        {
            "_id" : "shard1",
            "host" : "localhost:27024"
        }
    ],
    "ok" : 1
}
```

At this point, you can terminate the Shard2 mongod process and delete its storage files because its data has been migrated back to the other servers.

---

**Note** The ability to add and remove shards to your cluster without having to take it offline is a critical component of MongoDB's ability to support highly scalable, highly available, large-capacity datastores. This satisfies the final requirement: "Requirement 3: The ability to add or remove shards while the system is running."

---

# Determining How You're Connected

Your application can be connected either to a standard non-sharded database (mongod) or to a shard controller (mongos). MongoDB makes both of these processes; for all but a few use cases, the database and shard controller look and behave exactly the same way. However, sometimes it may be important to determine what type of system you are connected to.

MongoDB provides the `isdbgrid` command, which you can use to interrogate the connected data system to determine whether it is sharded. The following snippet shows how to use this command, as well as what its output looks like:

```
$mongo
>use testdb
>db.runCommand({ isdbgrid : 1});
{ "isdbgrid" : 1, "hostname" : "localhost", "ok" : 1 }
```

The response includes the `isdbgrid:1` field, which tells you that the database you are connected to is enabled for sharding. A response of `isdbgrid:0` would indicate that you are connected to a non-sharded database.

# Listing the Status of a Sharded Cluster

MongoDB also includes a simple command for dumping the status of a sharding cluster: `printShardingStatus()`.

This command can give you a lot of insight into the internals of the sharding system. The following snippet shows how to invoke the printShardingStatus() command, but strips out some of the output returned to make it easier to read:

```
 $mongo localhost:27021
>use admin
>db.printShardingStatus();
--- Sharding Status ---
  sharding version: { "_id" : 1, "version" : 3 }
  shards:
      { "_id" : "shard0", "host" : "localhost:27023" }
      { "_id" : "shard1", "host" : "localhost:27024" }
  databases:
    { "_id" : "admin", "partitioned" : false, "primary" : "config" }
    { "_id" : "testdb", "partitioned" : true, "primary" : "shard0",
      "sharded" : { "testdb.testcollection" : { "key" : { "testkey" : 1 }, "unique" : false }
} }
        testdb.testcollection chunks:
            { "testkey" : { $minKey : 1 } } -->> { "testkey" : 47 } on : shard1 { "t" : 2000,
"i" : 2 }
            { "testkey" : 47 } -->> { "testkey" : 1702 } on : shard1 { "t" : 66000, "i" : 0 }
            { "testkey" : 1702 } -->> { "testkey" : 3356 } on : shard1 { "t" : 66000, "i" : 1
}
            { "testkey" : 3356 } -->> { "testkey" : 5020 } on : shard1 { "t" : 66000, "i" : 2
}
            { "testkey" : 5020 } -->> { "testkey" : 6679 } on : shard1 { "t" : 66000, "i" : 3
}
            { "testkey" : 6679 } -->> { "testkey" : 8137 } on : shard1 { "t" : 66000, "i" : 4
}
            { "testkey" : 8137 } -->> { "testkey" : 9637 } on : shard1 { "t" : 66000, "i" : 5
}

...

            { "testkey" : 64878 } -->> { "testkey" : 66399 } on : shard0 { "t" : 66000, "i" :
152 }
            { "testkey" : 66399 } -->> { "testkey" : 67934 } on : shard0 { "t" : 66000, "i" :
148 }
            { "testkey" : 67934 } -->> { "testkey" : 69410 } on : shard0 { "t" : 66000, "i" :
43 }
            { "testkey" : 69410 } -->> { "testkey" : 70962 } on : shard0 { "t" : 66000, "i" :
44 }
            { "testkey" : 70962 } -->> { "testkey" : 72470 } on : shard0 { "t" : 66000, "i" :
45 }
            { "testkey" : 72470 } -->> { "testkey" : 73991 } on : shard0 { "t" : 66000, "i" :
46 }
            { "testkey" : 73991 } -->> { "testkey" : 75478 } on : shard0 { "t" : 66000, "i" :
47 }
            { "testkey" : 75478 } -->> { "testkey" : 77063 } on : shard0 { "t" : 66000, "i" :
48 }
            { "testkey" : 77063 } -->> { "testkey" : 78654 } on : shard0 { "t" : 66000, "i" :
49 }

...
```

```
            { "testkey" : 96954 } -->> { "testkey" : 98468 } on : shard0 { "t" : 66000, "i" :
62 }
            { "testkey" : 98468 } -->> { "testkey" : 99979 } on : shard0 { "t" : 66000, "i" :
145 }
            { "testkey" : 99979 } -->> { "testkey" : { $maxKey : 1 } } on : shard0 { "t" :
6000, "i" : 4 }

>
```

This output lists the shard servers, the configuration of each sharded database/collection, and each chunk in the sharded dataset. Because you used a small chunkSize value to simulate a larger sharding setup, this report lists a lot of chunks. An important piece of information that can be obtained from this listing is the range of *sharding keys* associated with each chunk. The preceding output also shows which shard server the specific chunks are stored on. You can use the output returned by this command as the basis for a tool to analyze the distribution of a shard server's keys and chunks. For example, you might use this data to determine whether there is any *clumping* of data in the dataset.

# Using Replica Sets to Implement Shards

The examples you have seen so far rely on a single mongod instance to implement each shard. In Chapter 11, you learned how to create replica sets, which are clusters of mongod instances working together to provide redundant and fail-safe storage.

When adding shards to the sharded cluster, you can provide the name of a replica set and the address of a member of that replica set, and that shard will be instanced on each of the replica set members. Mongos will track which instance is the primary server for the replica set; it will also make sure that all shard writes are made to that instance.

Combining sharding and replica sets enables you to create high-performance, highly reliable clusters that can tolerate multi-machine failure. It also enables you to maximize the performance and availability of cheap, commodity-class hardware.

---

■ **Note** The ability to use replica sets as a storage mechanism for shards satisfies "Requirement 2: The ability to store shard data in a fault-tolerant fashion."

---

# Sharding to Improve Performance

In the MongoDB versions available at the time of writing, several MongoDB operations are *single-threaded* only, such as background indexing and aggregate functions (e.g., grouping and map/reduce). The JavaScript engine (spidermonkey) used in MongoDB also imposes this restriction.

Modern CPUs support features such as multiple cores and hyperthreading. These features enable simultaneous code execution, so it is advantageous to break up long-running tasks into separate processes to take advantage of the multiple cores.

If you have a four core CPU, it may be advantageous to create a four-shard database configuration inside a single physical machine because all of the aforementioned operations will be passed to the individual shard storage server instances for execution. Doing this enables each core to handle a separate operation at the same time.

---

■ **Caution** If you are planning to run multiple shards on the same machine, then it is advisable to dedicate a separate drive to each shard. With many different threads trying to access different shards at the same time, it can over-stress a single drive, by forcing it to perform rapid read/write head movements between shards. By confining each shard on its own drive, you can minimize the movement of the heads and improve the overall performance considerably.

---

# Summary

Sharding enables you to scale your datastores to handle extremely large datasets. It also enables you to grow the cluster to match the growth in your system.

MongoDB provides a simple automatic sharding configuration that works well for most requirements. Even though this process is automated, you can still fine-tune its characteristics to support your specific needs.

Auto-sharding is one of the key features of MongoDB that set it apart from other data-storage technologies. We hope this book has helped you see the many ways that MongoDB is designed to cope better with the rigorous demands of modern web-based applications than is possible using more traditional database tools.

Topics you have learned about in this book include the following:

- How to install and configure MongoDB on a variety of platforms.
- How to access MongoDB from various development languages.
- How to connect with the community surrounding the product, including how to obtain help and advice.
- How to design and build applications that take advantage of MongoDB's unique strengths.
- How to optimize, administer, and troubleshoot MongoDB-based datastores.
- How to create scalable fault-tolerant installations that span multiple servers.

You are strongly encouraged to explore the many samples and examples provided in this book. Other PHP examples can be found in the PHP MongoDB driver documentation located at `www.php.net/manual/en/book.mongo.php`. MongoDB is an extremely approachable tool, and its ease of installation and operation encourage experimentation. So don't hold back: crank it up and start playing with it! And remarkably soon you too will begin to appreciate all the possibilities that this intriguing product opens up for your applications.

# Index

## Symbols



## A

## B



## C

## D

## E



## F

## J



## K



## L

## N



## O

## P

## Q

## R

## S

## T

## U



## V



## W



## X

CPSIA information can be obtained at www.ICGtesting.com
Printed in the USA
LVOW050257251111

256391LV00013B/5/P

9 781430 230519